CRITICAL ACCLA
MY SEARCH FOI

CW00530896

"Tirelessly researched. Told me a lot of t
case"

MARTIN BRUNT,
SKY NEWS **CRIME CORRESPONDENT**

"Jon is clearly about as steeped in the story as it's possible to be, and it's a
fascinating account of the inner workings of what sounds like an extremely
seedy place."

SUSIE DOWDALL,
DAILY MAIL

"Jon Clarke is a remarkably experienced journalist who has dug deeply
into the movements and life of German new-age traveler and fixated pref-
erential sex offender Christian Brueckner, who should have been a prime
suspect in 2007.
"This book breaks a lot of new ground on the case and is a real investigative trawl and deep dive into the world of organized child traffickers… and
he has interviews with all the key players from all over Europe.
"It is an investigative man-hunt and Jon's book is compelling. He has a
long heritage in the story and his crusade is journalistically sound and his
journalistic instincts are sharp."

DONAL MACINTYRE,
TV PRODUCER AND INVESTIGATOR

"Jon Clarke's book exposes the secret dark world behind the biggest mystery of the 21st century."

MIKE RIDLEY,
THE SUN

ABOUT THE AUTHOR

Jon Clarke has been a journalist for 25 years writing for national newspapers in the UK before moving to Spain and setting up *the Olive Press* media group with offices in Malaga, Gibraltar and Valencia. He is married with two children.

ACKNOWLEDGEMENTS

This book is dedicated to the art-form of real journalism. A craft that I hope will never be lost. Without gumshoe reporting – involving hours of tread, thousands of phone calls and emails and mostly slammed doors and dead-ends – the world would be a poorer place, missing valuable checks and balances.

In particular I would like to thank the many Fleet Street journalists, who have helped me along the way, plus a couple in Germany and Sandra Felgueiras at RTP in Portugal. There are many of you, but Abul Tahir and James Mellor at *the Mail on Sunday*, Arthur Martin and Interdeep Bains at the *Daily Mail*, Martin Fricker and Patrick Hill at the *Daily Mirror*, Sarah White and Paul Thompson at *The Sun*, plus Hubert Gude in Germany, have been legendary.

The help of Rob Hyde, freelancer and translator extraordinaire in Germany, was invaluable, as were his research skills and love of detail. Martin Brunt at Sky TV was always a good egg to bounce things off, as was *The Olive Press* digital editor Fiona Govan, who spent nearly half a year in Praia da Luz on the story for *the Telegraph*. Laurence Dollimore was a superb trusty sidekick, always full of ideas, on the road, while Dilip Kuner, *The Olive Press'* indefatigable news editor was a constant support. On the TV front, thanks go to Netflix and RTP in Portugal for trusting my skills and fearless investigative legend Donal MacIntyre for the frequent guidance.

Thanks must also go to my amazing British law specialist Adam Oliver in London, who has got me out of plenty of scrapes and carefully checked this book ... as well as my editor Kate Bohdanowicz and agent Robert Smith, both also based in the UK. Thanks Keith for your book design skills. Cheers too to Arthur van Amerongen for your recent help at the end on the Algarve.

Most of all though, there is no way this book could have been written without my incredible wife, who has depths of patience unknown to human-kind, as well as a canny way to look and analyse things. Your suggestions on where to go next and hunches were vital for this book. And finally for my kids, M and A.

Who knows, maybe one day you'll carry the investigative torch. Although I'm not holding my breath ... or encouraging it.

COPYRIGHT AND PUBLISHING DETAILS

My Search for Madeleine, By Jon Clarke
Published by OP Books, Clarke Media Limited, Gibraltar

Laid out and designed by Keith Franks

Clarke Media Limited is a registered company in Gibraltar that can be contacted at info@opbooks.eu

MY SEARCH
FOR
MADELEINE

ONE REPORTER'S 14-YEAR HUNT TO
SOLVE EUROPE'S MOST HARROWING
CRIME

Jon Clarke

Contents

PART ONE 2007-2019

Chapter 1

Open Borders

'I'm sure he snatched Maddie. He was a pervert and a very strange man,' so insisted Michael 'Micha' Tatschl to me in June 2020. 'I know he did it.'

Talking about his 'best friend' Christian Brueckner, with whom he'd lived in Portugal and spent eight months in prison, he went on: 'He was always on the dark web. I don't know exactly what he did, but I think it involved drugs and pornography. He was also always bragging about money and making money, particularly from burglaries. He was an excellent thief. He even talked about selling kids, maybe to Morocco ... and I think he probably sold Maddie to someone. Maybe a sex ring.'

I nearly dropped my *caña* and almonds, as did the two other witnesses to this mobile phone conversation. They looked at me with shock as we sat around a garden table in a leafy *finca* in the heart of rural Andalucia. For we were talking about the German drifter, who had just been made the prime suspect in the disappearance of Madeleine McCann. In what was easily the strangest interview of my long journalism career, I was talking to Tatschl in Austria, while sitting in the back garden of the home he had shared with his British ex-girlfriend Emma for a number of years in the town of Orgiva in the Alpujarras in southern Spain. Alongside Emma was her good friend Ben, another long-term British expat, who had also made his home in the stunning mountainous area, south of Granada.

The area has long been a haven for new age travellers in camper-vans, also known as 'van lifers'. There are three distinct van lifer settlements around Orgiva – including Beneficio (meaning appropriately 'Benefit') – and a character like Micha, with his pierced nipples and nose, and skull and crossbones tattoo on his neck, would happily fit into this footloose, transient community. So too would Brueckner.

Emma and Micha lived in one such settlement, Tablones, next door to the grandson of celebrated British novelist Robert Graves – himself something of an '*alternativo*'. Only 200m down the hill was a scruffy plot called, appropriately, the 'German field', where Brueckner had frequently parked up his vans on his many trips back and forth between Germany and Portugal.

Much to the shock of the three of us sitting there drinking cold Alhambra beer, Brueckner had been to stay on numerous occasions, often for weeks at a time. And, according to Micha, he had turned up in late May or early June 2007, with what he described as 'one of the most expensive camper-vans money could buy.' If true, the timing was incredible. For his visit to this isolated part of southern Spain with his pricey new van was just three or four weeks after Maddie had vanished in Praia da Luz, Portugal, some 585km to the west.

During that month in 2007, the whole world had been following the heart-wrenching story unfold … how Kate and Gerry McCann's 3-year-old daughter had apparently been snatched from her holiday apartment by an intruder, while the parents ate dinner at a restaurant nearby. It was every parent's nightmare, and if it could happen on an upmarket Mark Warner holiday, it could happen anywhere.

By the time Christian Brueckner had rolled in and parked the huge cream and brown Tiffin Allegro Bay RV on an area of waste ground near Tablones, the story had easily garnered 100 front pages and was fast becoming one of the biggest missing persons mysteries in history. Yet here was this dangerous German paedophile – with, as we now know, a prison record as long as his arm – brazenly driving into the Alpujarras in a 30-foot long motorhome, ostensibly looking to buy and sell marijuana and probably other drugs, as he frequently did on many occasions.

'We all wondered where he'd got this expensive new van,' continued Micha on the second of three calls I made to him in Austria.

'We assumed a big drug deal or something like that. Now I definitely suspect it was Maddie.'

I'll come to his reasoning later, and his evidence, which is damning and includes a video that Brueckner allegedly made of a rape of a pensioner that he insisted had to be cleared away from the home they shared for a number of years.

•••

Now a married father-of-one, living near Graz in Austria, Michael Tatschl has twice been interviewed at length by the German police over his connections to Brueckner and his movements around 2006 and 2007, in particular. He told me he had been grilled for two long days at his local police station by four police, two from Germany's federal Bundeskriminalamt (BKA) and two from Austria. I am certain that he had been one of two people to have tipped off the German Federal Criminal Police following a groundbreaking eight-part Netflix documentary, *The Disappearance of Madeleine McCann*, with which I was closely involved in 2019. Another former friend of Brueckner, German Helge Busching, had put his name forward in 2017. 'Micha certainly thinks he could be up for a reward,' Emma, an artist, told me later. 'He said it could apparently be shared with someone else.'

Few people knew Brueckner better than Tatschl, specifically around the time of the disappearance. Around a year before, in April 2006, Micha even spent prison time with Brueckner as the pair were caught stealing fuel from lorries on the Algarve. At their trial in December of that year, Brueckner admitted to the judge that he had convictions for sex offences back in Germany. In a bombshell confession, which his lawyer at the time now insists was unnecessary, he told the judge that he had committed various burglaries and sex crimes, (yes plural) as a teenager.

For some reason the specifics of these crimes were not probed. Certainly not properly logged. And that was not the first time his dangerous nature had come up in the two decades he spent on and off in Portugal. It had actually come to police attention at least once before in 1999, when he was extradited back to Germany to serve another child sex offence from 1994. This time against a 6-year-old girl in Bavaria, whom he molested, only stopping when she started screaming. He later dropped his trousers and exposed himself to a 9-year-old-girl, reported the German newspaper *Bild*.

Portuguese police certainly took the criminal seriously as they took a large set of photos of him while on remand in Faro waiting to be extradited. Full face, side on and even full length to get a good look at his physiology – they were the perfect snaps in case he needed to be apprehended again. And it turns out he did, many times.

He was prosecuted in 2004 for driving illegally on foreign German plates. He was processed for the 'crime of disobedience' as it is called in Portugal, but failed to pay the fine, forcing police in Lagos to track him down and make him cough up. They even came looking for him over the disappearance of Maddie, just weeks after she vanished, I have discovered, when they turned up in late May 2007 at Portimao Prison, some six months AFTER he had been discharged.

This was another case of them behaving like Keystone Cops, who didn't really know what to do with Herr Christian Brueckner, or how to keep tabs on his movements. If only they had, they might have taken a closer look at the sex offender when a young Irish woman was brutally raped in Lagos in 2004, or when a 72-year-old American was viciously assaulted in Praia da Luz in 2005, for which he was found guilty a staggering 12 years later.

These were particularly sadistic rapes because in both attacks the assailant had rigged up a video to film the crime. He spent time carefully focusing the lens before tying his victims up tighter and tighter, then beating them sadistically and forcing them to give him oral sex, while he wore a mask. Both women recalled their assailant's piercing blue eyes and his English spoken with a German accent.

A friend of Brueckner's, who was tasked with disposing of a video in which the elderly woman was raped, was shocked to discover that at the end of the film, the perpetrator sat on the bed and removed his mask. So, with Brueckner identified, he should have been brought in for questioning over a string of rapes around the Portimao area at the same time, including various sexual assaults on children, such as a 10-year-old German girl on a beach one month before Maddie went missing, not to mention nearly 50 burglaries in the sleepy resort of Praia da Luz, in 2005 and 2006, that tellingly stopped when he was in prison with his friend Micha between April 2006 and December that year.

So what happened when Maddie was allegedly snatched from the resort just five months after he had been let out of prison? Yes, you guessed it ... when a shortlist of 600 potential suspects was drawn up and handed to British police, Christian Brueckner was inexplicably NOT on it. Despite his track record of sex offences being made known locally to the courts and police at least twice, plus their apparent visit to Portimao Prison to find him, he was not considered a person of interest. Even five months later in November 2007, when his name was given as a suspect in the theft of 100,000 euros some 30 minutes away from Praia de Luz, police apparently didn't include him on the wanted list for Madeleine McCann, the girl whose name was, by then, known around the entire world.

While his name would later come up – and to be fair it had been handed to British police in 2011 – it was almost completely ignored by the local force tasked with solving the highest profile missing person case in their country's history.

...

Ultimately then, we must take a look at the force employed to catch one of the most wanted and most dangerous criminals in European history. Incompetent at best, we will study the levels they went to in order to track down the perpetrator – or perpetrators – who snatched Maddie, the seriousness they showed from the beginning and the skills they employed. In particular, we will look at their botched mistakes over fingerprinting, sealing off the McCanns' apartment and the failure to collect CCTV on time. And we must certainly shine a light on the leader of the initial investigation, Goncalo Amaral, who was removed after criticising British detectives and claiming they were only following leads the McCanns asked them to pursue.

We will also look at credible claims that Maddie's DNA might have been planted in a hire car the McCanns had hired three weeks AFTER she had vanished, and claims that crucial evidence was destroyed. Amaral – who later wrote a lucrative book claiming the McCanns killed their daughter and buried her during a 40-minute window – had himself been charged (and was later convicted) with corruption over the case of another missing girl exactly ONE day before Maddie went missing. And then we will consider his Policia Judiciaria (PJ) deputy, Paulo Pereira Cristovao, who recently went to prison for his involvement in a robbery and kidnapping ring near Lisbon.

Finally, I will look, for the first time, at two other retired police officers – both English expats – lurking like a bad smell in the background. One, a senior career detective who has spent years supporting the Portuguese police and trolling the McCanns for being guilty of the crime, as well as publishing thousands of words of lies about me potentially being involved, and exposing my family and children to danger.

And two, a former Scotland Yard inspector, who also defended the Portuguese investigation, while sensationally living right next door to a home where Brueckner and a potential female sidekick lived for a number of years along with a string of troubled German teenagers. I will name them both and explore in detail the village where Brueckner spent considerable time with his on/off girlfriend Nicole Fehlinger, who came from his hometown of Wurzburg, in Bavaria.

The nondescript village of Foral, where the hunt for clues in the case really began to widen, is one of the keys to the entire case. For it was here, some 45 minutes north east of Praia da Luz that I found a veritable nest of vipers; a place that was totally uninvestigated and where so many strange people resided and so many odd things happened.

With my colleague from *The Olive Press*, Laurence Dollimore who acted as my photographer, we were the first journalists to find the house, where Nicole and Brueckner cohabited for much of 2007 (and for some time after that) and where I suspect a child sex trafficking ring was centred. I will lay out my theory that Brueckner was at the centre of this ring transporting children around Europe and locally in Portugal through his connections to an agency that brought vulnerable teenagers to the country from Germany.

It was in Foral that the gun-toting crook was linked to an underage teenager who got pregnant and in the nearby town of Messines where he was caught (and yet again, inexplicably, not tried) for exposing himself to children.

Some readers might get the feeling that someone is protecting Herr Brueckner. After all, he was wandering around Europe at will, hanging around children and teens, and managing to offend repeatedly with surprisingly little consequence. And when we add in Portugal's truly shocking Casa Pia case – involving government ministers, doctors and judges – you will start to understand why I think Brueckner was being given a helping hand.

Chapter 2

Just Another Early Morning Job

It was an extraordinarily early start. Up and out of the house before 7am was rare for my new life in Spain. It was May 2007 and I was living in the stunning Serrania de Ronda mountains, near Malaga, having relocated from London, and Fleet Street, to set up as a stringer in southern Spain.

As I had just set up a regional newspaper, *The Olive Press*, I was used to taking trips around the country and its islands – usually involving celebrities on holiday, tourists falling out of windows or something connected to the costa del crime ... so to be sent off by the *Daily Mail* on a missing child story in Portugal wasn't too out of the ordinary.

What was different though, was the family involved. The professional, middle-class doctor couple Kate and Gerry McCann were not your typical Brits abroad-type victims – the least likely of British tourists to want to get involved with the press, particularly on holiday. But they were clearly in desperate need for help. Conjuring up a legion of journalists to help in their hunt for their missing daughter (the prettiest, most striking of little girls) seemed to be the best way forward.

I didn't know the poor minion who had called me from the *Daily Mail*'s London HQ half an hour earlier. I think he was new to the job, and, as is the way with *the Mail*, there were few pleasantries (when I worked there in the 1990s, its computer password for casual staff was 'Yes Sir').

'Can you get to the Algarve ASAP?' he said (for it was more an order than a request). 'Some girl's gone missing. A doctor's kid. The Foreign Office is already on it. Place called Ocean Club in Praia da Luz. Just get going, we'll call you with more en route.'

It was fairly standard stuff for a stringer abroad and I was on the road within about 15 minutes, with just enough time to grab a cup of tea, my always-packed overnight bag and give a quick kiss to my wife Francesca and soon to be 2-year-old daughter Maria.

It was a beautiful May morning and my British-registered Subaru Impreza loved the empty roads through the stunning Serrania de Ronda, where many a car advert had been filmed. We'd been living there for a couple of years and were about to finish renovating an eighteenth-century farmhouse.

One of Spain's most scenic drives, the winding A-374 skirts the rugged Grazalema Natural Park, past the emblematic white villages of Zahara de la Sierra and Algodonales before striking north towards Sevilla and the dry, flat Guadalquivir plane. It was a journey I knew well, so I was on auto-pilot, losing myself in the excellent early morning show on Spain's Radio 3.

It wasn't until I got to my usual roadside venta for a coffee and a tostada near Utrera, about an hour into the journey, that I began to dwell on the job at hand. By then my mobile had rung twice more, once from *The Sun* and once from the *Daily Mirror*, asking me to cover it for them as well. Putting me 'on an order' as it is called in Fleet Street, I knew it was going to be a fairly lucrative day by the time I'd added in expenses. I didn't have any more clues to the media storm that was beginning to blow in from a tiny, little-known seaside resort at the other end of the Iberian Peninsula's long southern coastline.

The story had first appeared as a news flash on *Sky News* at around 7.45am in the UK, but I figured it would be over by the time I got there: she would be found, like the vast majority of other kids that wander off during their holidays, either dead or alive, in a swimming pool or a ditch somewhere. As a father to a toddler, I understood how the parents must be feeling. Some years later, our own son, Albert, who would be born in 2008, wandered off during a holiday in Portugal deciding, at two years old, that he fancied picking plums in the grounds of the rental home. We lost him for a terrifying ten minutes.

As I drove, my mind turned to my daughter's second birthday that coming Sunday and my wife's that we had celebrate a few days before at a new restaurant that had recently opened in Ronda. I was excited about our pending move into the main part of the ancient farmhouse that we had nearly finished renovating after a year of builders and dust … and thankful, I guess, to have some decent work to pay for it all – in pounds from the UK.

So I was loaded up with positive thoughts of my future as I finally sped into the sleepy resort of Praia da Luz, some three-and-a-half hours later.

•••

It wasn't hard to locate the Ocean Club, which sits in the heart of 'Luz', as it is known locally. Almost dead centre in the seaside village, just up from its main supermarket, Baptista, and about 300m from its stunning beach, it's the sort of unremarkable, low-rise block of flats that typifies most southern European resorts.

I soon found out it was a Mark Warner resort, which made it all the more surprising, as for some reason I imagined it running far more modern, slicker and certainly more security-conscious centres. It was immediately apparent that security was not one of its strengths.

It was now between 9.45am and 10.15am local time (an hour earlier than Spain and sensibly in the same time zone as the UK) and I was the first British journalist on the scene. A small group of expats and tourists were already getting mobilised after a night of drama and anxiety.

The McCanns' apartment was on the corner of the block at the junction of Rua da Escola Primaria and Dr Agostinho da Silva. Easily spotted, it had a flimsy bit of police tape run up the side of it by a rickety gate, and another bit of tape around the front where the car park was.

After establishing the name of the missing toddler as Maddie or 'Maddy' from one of the expats hovering outside, I walked up the short flight of stairs to the apartment, number 5A, – completely unimpeded by police – to speak to the parents, as any decent journalist is programmed to do on arrival at a job like this.

I walked inside the open front door and bumped straight into the McCanns, who were heading off to the police station in nearby Lagos to make an official missing persons statement. They looked fraught and stressed, but were somehow still functioning, despite presumably not sleeping a wink. I smiled and said 'hello', introducing myself as a local hack, working for *the Mail*, just arrived from Malaga. I promised I'd help as best I could to find their daughter.

They seemed grateful and smiled ... well grimaced to be fair – saying 'thank you' and mumbling a few other pleasantries, before telling me their daughter's name and the rough time she had disappeared, which was between 9pm and 9.45pm. I don't remember much but I do remember them describing it as 'a nightmare' and saying they were 'sure' she had been snatched. I scribbled it down in my notepad.

It was clear they couldn't hang around and needed to go and get the local police force to actually give a damn, for it was apparent right from the start that they really didn't care very much. This was obvious from the shortage of officers on hand. There were two local bobbies on duty, but the side of the house was unguarded and life in the resort was going on as normal.

The police, meanwhile, refused to give me any help. Not a thing. No comments, no clues, nothing. I was shocked to see some sniffer dogs making an appearance later on that afternoon, some 18 hours after the child had gone missing.

•••

From the very first moment I arrived in Praia da Luz that May morning in 2007, my overbearing drive was to solve the mystery and find young Maddie. The rules of journalism revolve around the five ws: When, Where, Why, Who and hoW. Stick to these and you can't go wrong. I now knew when she had gone missing, more or less, so now I needed to try and work out where she had gone and why. I knew that the parents, friends and half the neighbourhood had been up all night searching the resort, but it didn't stop my inbuilt sense of optimism from thinking I could somehow make a difference.

I quickly teamed up with three local expat women, one with a daughter about Maddie's age, who had spiritedly made up some rather rough and ready A4 printouts to hand out and pin up on around the resort. They featured a photo of Maddie in pink pyjamas and some handwritten blurb about her age and where she was staying.

I grabbed a stack – probably around a dozen – and wandered down to the already busy Baptista supermarket just below the Ocean Club to chat to the staff, as it was a good place to stick up a poster. Naturally, the disappearance was the talk of the town. All the locals were discussing how on Earth she had gone missing. The general mood was shock and disbelief and the locals kept saying, as if in a mantra, that 'things like this' don't happen in Luz.

Over the course of the next seven or eight hours I put in a classic shift of what is known in the trade as 'gumshoe reporting' or 'putting in some tread'. I literally hacked my way around the resort and its nearby hills looking for any possible clues that might point me towards the missing toddler.

Starting at the Ocean Club, I had a chat to a receptionist, who insisted he was unable to tell me anything, and referred me to his manager, John Hill. He was quickly at the entrance and, to my mind, was immediately defensive – perhaps understandably – and certainly didn't want to tell me anything about the family, or much about the circumstances of the disappearance.

I then took a closer look at Apartment 5A, where by now someone had stuck up one of the missing posters. Firstly, I marvelled at the lack of CCTV camera near the entrance and noted with surprise just how flimsy the small back gate was (see photos in section later). Anyone could have wandered in while the parents were out. It would be a burglar's dream. The McCanns had definitely been handed the short straw – the raised ground corner apartment overlooking two streets – in the sharing out of the accommodation between them and their friends. But they hadn't thought that at the time. In fact Kate McCann recalls that they actually noted how nice it seemed and how light it was.

Even more shocking was how open the resort was. There was a back alley behind the block that the McCanns and their friends were staying in, all on the ground floor, bar one family on the first floor. Again, anyone could wander right into the complex and have a poke about the south facing terraces of the block. I did, even though there was a serious crime scene developing.

While no one was admitting it – even mentioning it – there had been a serious number of burglaries around the resort the previous year, with at least 40 reported over the early part of 2006, and many more during the previous two months. A further 25 were allegedly committed by one individual in just eight months in 2005, three in one intensive 24-hour period (more on which later). That's a lot of reported break-ins for a village of just 3,500 residents. It has also since emerged that up to three former Ocean Club employees are said to have been connected to burglaries, with one, Euclides Monteiro, laid off for theft.

And then I met Robert Murat.

No names in the disappearance of Madeleine McCann are as distinctive – or as controversial and memorable – as Robert Murat's

Along with the McCanns themselves, he is the only other person to have been made an arguido, or official suspect, in the case. And not without good reason, with so many inconsistencies surrounding his movements and behaviour. There were numerous pointers and plenty of suspicious activity around his work, friendships and timings in the run up to Maddie's abduction.

That's for later. Now, I want you to picture the scene and how exactly this 34 year old emerged as suspicious on my radar. After being largely blocked at the Ocean Club reception, I had walked up to the junction of the block, close to the front door of Apartment 5A, when, bang, he was there. Slightly scruffy and dishevelled, and with what looked like a lazy eye, he was earnest, excited and definitely over-friendly; he immediately asserted himself as being an important source in the ongoing search.

Standing under the shade of a line of willow-type trees planted just inside the wall of the car park of the Ocean Club, he was keen to regale me with his colourful account of the previous night and morning's plans. Once I had explained I was working for three British newspapers he gushed even more which, considering his position, he must have known was wrong.

As is so often the case on jobs around Portugal and Spain, the locals are easy to talk to and only too happy to help, which is frequently the opposite in the UK. But the way he was helping was a little unusual, perhaps forced. All said, he was incredibly helpful in getting some of the facts and timings established. I knew I would have to file something to the various news desks by mid-afternoon and they had already called a few times to get a steer on what was happening.

Over a ten-minute chat, Murat told me more about the family, and the friends the McCanns were with. He explained that Gerry and Kate were doctors – he a cardiologist and she a GP – from Leicestershire and were on holiday with three other families, including eight children. He explained that they had been having dinner at the tapas restaurant in the grounds just below their apartments, checking on the kids every so often. (Although leaving children alone isn't normal in Spain or Portugal, this is something my wife and I had done in Mallorca once when armed with a listening device, we headed to a restaurant 50m away from our hotel.)

Murat was clearly relishing his moment in the spotlight, and as I thanked him and left, I mulled over how, despite apparently having no formal training and no official registration with the police, the bilingual local had been casually drafted in as a translator for the family. It seemed odd, especially when most of the staff at the Ocean Club spoke fluent English and Portuguese. Why did the police, resort and family allow him to traipse around Apartment 5A leaving his fingerprints and DNA all over a potential crime scene? Was he appointed by the now-disgraced police officer Goncalo Amaral? It didn't make sense.

It was now around midday, and a dribble of local journalists were arriving. I chatted to an expat reporter from the local paper, *The Portugal News*, as well as Portuguese TV reporter Sandra Felgueiras, who was then on one of her first assignments for national news network RTP, the Portuguese equivalent of the BBC. Based in nearby Lagos, she had come down with a cameraman and had set up to broadcast from the road outside the Ocean Club. Young and keen, she seemed to know a few local characters, which has helped with her recent in-depth exposés that have begun to finally turn the Portuguese public away from the belief that the McCanns killed their own daughter. Saying that, Sandra herself was convinced of it, at one point, and even directly accused them in a famous live TV broadcast soon after their arrests. Later she would tell me it was due to a continual drip drip of off-the-record briefings from senior police in both the JP and *Guarda Nacional Republicana* (GNR).

I also met a TV reporter from *Sky News*, who happened to be on holiday in Praia da Luz, and had been dragged in to do an ad-hoc piece to camera, while in her holiday garb. There was also Dan Mason, who was working for Sky, although there are plenty of conspiracy theorists who claim he had been planted there a few days before by the British establishment or MI5, and that coincidentally, so was I (more of which later).

It was clear that the story was gathering pace and the TV networks back home were showing interest in this pretty blue-eyed English girl, who had vanished while on a Mark Warner holiday. That her parents were doctors, and it was a quiet news day certainly helped. It was the main 'breaking news' on Sky from 7.45am to well past 9am and it became something of a scramble for British newspapers to get their reporters out to the Algarve as none had correspondents, even stringers, down there. With few daily flights to the Algarve at this unseasonable time of early May, they were sent in via Germany, France and Spain, with some having to fly to Lisbon and take the three-hour drive south.

None of them made it until late afternoon so I carried on my investigations more or less unimpeded for the rest of the day. I headed off in all directions and even into the nearby countryside noting various curiosities and colour in my notepad, such as 'loads of run-down farms and fincas', the latter being a Spanish word for smallholding, usually with a small home or shack and a few hectares of land.

I now realise that I walked up the track, but I don't think as far as the home known as the 'Yellow House', which was where Christian Brueckner lived on and off for seven years. I also walked right to the top of the cliff that overlooks the wonderful Luz Beach and took a couple of photos, as well as inland a little from there on another track that would have eventually led to the home Brueckner is said to have rented from 1999 to 2006.

Among other pertinent information that I still feel to this day is bizarre, possibly even relevant to the case, was coming across a road crew – well actually two men – working in a deep trench in the road near the Ocean Club. While I now admit I cannot recall exactly which road it was (I was filmed on the Netflix documentary, insisting it was right outside, but I'm happy to admit that now I'm not sure), I definitely stopped to talk to the men, who were down in the trench, probably working on a gas main or sewer pipe. I have since been accused of deliberately lying over this by the conspiracy brigade, although I am baffled to know why it matters (apart from to discredit me, I guess), but I distinctly remember asking them if they knew about missing Maddie, and they clearly did not. I told them in a mixture of English and Spanish what had happened and showed them one of my posters.

I remember asking them if 'it wouldn't be better to stop working' in the trench, which must have been 100m long, and if it 'was possible' that she had fallen into it and her body had got buried? They shrugged their shoulders and ploughed on. I made a point of looking down the entire length of the trench, as I'm sure (and hope) others did the night before and later that day.

Knowing it would be a busy evening ahead I took half an hour to find a hotel and gather my thoughts to send over a detailed memo to the desks on the day so far. Among the information I filed was the arrival of the sniffer dogs at around 4pm. My time-stamped photograph shows a policeman lifting up the yellow police tape in order to let a dog pass.

At the time, I didn't know if they had been there the night before (in Kate McCann's book *Madeleine: Our Daughter's Disappearance and the Continuing Search for Her,* she insists they had two dogs brought in to track the surrounding area at around 2am the night Maddie went missing), but it struck me as tardy to bring them into the actual apartment.

Chapter 3

The McCanns Face The World

Not long after 6pm, the world's press started to descend. I say 'world's press' as over the next couple of months, I met reporters from up to ten different countries, including America and even Australia, investigating what was quickly known as 'the Maddie case'.

While her parents had insisted that they never called her 'Maddie', the shortening somehow stuck. Probably for the convenience of the red- top tabloids, as the name fitted into their formats. It was even spelt 'Maddy' on a few front pages, in particular in the *Daily Mirror*. I have always called her Maddie, because that was the name the local expats I met were calling her on that first fateful day, and I apologise to Kate and Gerry if they take any offence.

The assembling journalists slowly made their way to the Ocean Club and one by one I was summoned to brief reporters from the *Mail, Sun* and *Mirror,* who all had me on a shift. They each arrived tired from their tricky convoluted journeys, armed with a legion of questions and a lead or two of their own they wanted to explore. Unlike me they were dressed in suits, and they gave off an air of superiority, barking orders at me – as I was their stringer – from the get-go, which was very stressful and just a little bit annoying. I insisted we would be better off working together, pooling all the information available. After all, I argued, this was a missing child and it would be in all our interests if she was found as quickly as possible. Thankfully they agreed.

Martin Fricker from *the Mirror*, who had flown in, via Lisbon I think, with a photographer called Alban and driven all the way down in a hire car was relatively new on the paper and very enthusiastic, which I found motivating after a long day of finding relatively little. We tried fruitlessly to get a briefing from any of the local policemen, who were now milling around the Ocean Club and some posted rigidly outside.

We were met by brick walls. It soon became clear that the culture of police working with the media in the UK was different in Portugal. Law enforcement around the Maddie case mostly involved a shrug of the shoulders and a cynical smile, at least in those early days. But the truth is, as I learnt later, they didn't know much at all, and had strict instructions to say nothing to the press.

We did, however, know that there would be a press conference later that evening, although we weren't sure what it would comprise, nor who would be speaking. The build-up saw a number of Portuguese TV networks arrive, as well as the BBC, ITN and Sky. By the time it started to get dark at 8pm there must have been around 60 or 70 journalists and photographers huddled up in the car park outside Apartment 5A, plus dozens of locals and tourists.

The McCanns had been absent for most of the day, undertaking a series of police interviews in Portimao, where the local headquarters of the PJ were based. A 25-minute drive from Praia da Luz, they didn't arrive back until around 8.30pm and were shocked by the phalanx of clicking cameras and flashbulbs as they were led upstairs to a new apartment at 4A. They said nothing.

By now they had quite an entourage in tow. The British ambassador John Buck had joined consul John Henderson, who had been aiding them at the police station, while the British government also sent down the consul for Lisbon, as well as a press officer for additional help. It was clear this was turning into something of a dramatic case. There were lots of whispers and conjecture, but I can honestly say that not one reporter, at that stage, considered for a second that the family might in any way be involved.

It was approaching 10pm when the door of Apartment 4A finally opened and down the steps marched around half a dozen people, including the McCanns. After a few short words from manager John Hill, he allowed the parents to step forward and address the crowd, which at the time was an unheard-of practice in Portugal, where missing child cases were dealt with quietly (although not necessarily quickly) without any press intervention.

Kate and Gerry were clearly nervous, with Kate clutching the now famous Cuddle Cat their missing daughter had brought with her on holiday. Putting his left arm around Kate, while somehow holding a torch and reading from a script in his right hand, Gerry, who was shaking with emotion, addressed the assembled throng:

'Words cannot describe the anguish and despair that we are feeling as the parents of our beautiful daughter Madeleine. We request that anyone who may have information relating to Madeleine's disappearance, no matter how trivial, contact the Portuguese police and help us get her back safely.

'Please, if you have Madeleine, let her come home to her mummy, daddy, brother and sister. As everyone can understand how distressing the current situation is, we ask that our privacy is respected to allow us to continue assisting the police in their current investigation.'

With that he turned around and took Kate's hand to lead her back up the stairs. It was clear there would be no questions and we were left trying to grab a few quotes from the various diplomats and staff from the Ocean Club.

It was the performance of a lifetime and immensely moving, partly due to the evening darkness, the silence as they spoke and the fact they were living through every parent's worst fear. As I watched and listened, I thought of my wife and I having to deal with a similar situation with our own toddler daughter. It still brings me close to tears, all these years on.

After the journalists rushed to file their update back to the desks in London, we discussed the drama over a beer back at my hotel, the Belavista da Luz, where a few of them were also staying. We began to grasp the enormity of the story, the implications and the likelihood that it would only grow in stature the longer she didn't turn up. We agreed that if they hadn't been doctors and Maddie hadn't been blonde with blue eyes, these hacks would have been on an early flight home the next day.

•••

As journalists invariably do on 'foreigns', we discussed other stories we had covered. While a freelance based in Spain, I was accepted as one of theirs, having done my time on the *Daily Mail* as a news and showbiz reporter in London before spending three years working as an investigative reporter at *The Mail on Sunday*. I had been able to travel the world in these roles and picked up a few tricks (but less of the dark arts of others, I'm proud to say). I'd worked on the death of Princess Diana and discovered intriguing links between the convicted paedophile Jeffrey Epstein and Prince Andrew way back in 1999.

Since moving to Spain in September 2003, I'd reported on dozens of stories from Magaluf to Marbella and Tenerife to Tangiers. A stringer covering Spain will have to be prepared to cover a lot of kilometres. It is a big country, the second biggest in Europe after France, but also the most mountainous, meaning journeys frequently take half a day. It is a six-hour drive between the two main coastal strips of the Costa del Sol and Costa Blanca, where you would probably spend around half of your time.

Then expect the odd trip to Madrid and Barcelona, some five hours and ten hours respectively in a car from Malaga, and frequent flights to the Balearics and Canaries. By the time you've added in Portugal and regular calls to 'hop over' to Morocco covering this or that, you might drive more than 6,000km in a busy month. While good for expenses, it had certainly not been easy for my wife, to have me sent off on regular three or four day missions, particularly over a weekend when we had been planning something special. And it had become increasingly hard once our daughter Maria was born in 2005, with my wife short of help being away from family and friends in London and me hardly the most attentive husband and father at the best of times.

We had come to Spain to find a bolthole to develop our creative sides and get away from the stress of deadlines. My wife to immerse herself in painting – being a talented artist – and me to get away from the unpredictability of Fleet Street, its punishing hours and uncertain future. While I had covered some incredible tales and it was anything but boring, it had become a little like a conveyor belt to me, with today's news becoming yesterday's chip paper, reinforced by the famous adage that you were 'only as good as your next story'. I had a gnawing urge to do something with more substance, to write a book or screenplay or develop a documentary. I also wanted to develop my skills for renovation, having had a long-term passion for architecture.

We had however, made it implicitly clear to each other, and family and friends, that we were not intending to move abroad, merely take a sabbatical and find ourselves a holiday home, where we could develop other skills. The opportunity had arisen after an unexpected windfall while working on a feature about the movie, *Cold Mountain*, filmed in Romania and starring Jude Law and Nicole Kidman. I'd come across photographs of the leading actors 'getting intimate' at the wrap party. They dutifully made the front page of *The Sun*, paid for our trip to Spain and, by the time the story had been followed up by *Hello! Magazine* and the rest, had paid for a deposit on a stone farmhouse in Ronda.

We had initially set up in a rental home in the hills above Malaga, with Gabs painting a string of local characters, and me chancing my arm at a novel, *Huevos Fritos,* which proved a shocker, before landing a non-fiction book deal on an unsavoury expat called Tony King and better known as *'the Costa Killer'*.

We quickly settled into our new life in the stunning countryside of the Axarquia region, half an hour inland from Malaga city, enjoying its pace and rural customs. We enjoyed the outdoor life of hiking and cycling and visiting the historic cities of Sevilla, Cordoba and Granada, not to mention the massively underrated Malaga, and perhaps inevitably ended up opting to move to Ronda. We had no interest in the fleshpots and bling of the Costa del Sol, nor its ugly over-construction and plastic people.

By the end of 2004, we found ourselves so immersed in the local culture and countryside we simply forgot to move back home. When our daughter Maria came along in May 2005 things changed. It became harder to go away on long trips and I tried to cherrypick the more interesting, local ones, closer to home. It meant committing the cardinal rule of freelancing; turning down work. It meant less money but allowed me to cultivate relationships with the broadsheets, writing more about culture and history and, in particular, doing more travel writing.

But when an opportunity arose to cover a meaty case for a number of the tabloids it was too good a chance to miss.

Chapter 4

Suspicions Abound

I woke up on Saturday May 6 with, effectively, a new boss. While *the Mail* had asked me to stay on to 'monitor developments', *the Sunday Mirror* drafted me in to work with their reporter Lori Campbell, who was teaming up with *the Mirror*'s snapper Alban. She had arrived late on the Friday evening and texted me about meeting for an early breakfast at my hotel.

Attractive, assertive and keen to impress, she insisted we were taking our *pasteis de nata* with an English Breakfast tea by 8am.

Although a little groggy after the hacks' late-night post-mortem, I agreed to take her through what I had learned, starting at the Ocean Club, where she had already started grilling locals who were up and out early. I filled her in on my theories of what had happened, pointing out the shockingly poor security at the resort and how wide open the apartment had been … and then I brought up Murat.

I explained how I had met this strange-looking chap, who was hanging around outside Apartment 5A for much of the day. I told her he had introduced himself as 'Rob' and had shown a lot of interest in which newspapers I was working for and what I was reporting. I described him as being dishevelled and odd-looking, and remember telling her he seemed 'over-eager', which I am now prepared to accept may have been unfair, given he was a local expat, and would, understandably, want to try and solve the crime. After all, we had chatted about how young the missing girl was and that we both had young daughters, mine nearly two and his a year older, the same age as Maddie.

I told Lori how friendly he had been and that he was doing some translation work and had been inside the apartment. I said he had given me some useful background information about the family and details on the timings of Maddie's disappearance. She took it all in quietly, noting it down in her small reporter's notebook.

By late morning I could see that not much was coming out of Praia da Luz. The place was teeming with journalists and any tourists or locals coming in or out of the Ocean Club were getting mobbed by reporters desperate for a new line. I told Lori I might be better off utilised elsewhere. I suggested

I take a tour of the nearby countryside or perhaps a trip to Portimao to try and speak to someone with the PJ.

She agreed and I decided to make the short journey to Portimao, a place I had only visited on a brief holiday once before. Essentially a port town, once known for shipbuilding, it has become increasingly popular as a resort thanks to its excellent nearby beaches, in particular Rocha, which is backed by ochre cliffs, as well as the medieval Fort of Santa Catarina de Ribamar. It has a relaxed feel and a charming town centre with cobbled streets and a few decent shops.

But while it has a number of historic sights and a few grand buildings, the headquarters of Western Algarve's law enforcement, the Departamento de Investigacao Criminal de Portimao, to give its full name, is decidedly low key. Sitting just off the large, unremarkable May 1 Park, where there is conveniently an underground carpark, the four floor building on Rua do Pe da Cruz looks like any normal terraced house, with a small front door and the tiniest of plaques bearing the name 'Policia Judiciaria'. The only other giveaways are the flagpoles and the small video camera facing the door.

I arrived around 12.30pm to find my entrance blocked. I was told that the boss, Guilhermino Encarnacao, was otherwise engaged and the PJ's press officer Olegario da Souza (aka *Inspector Oleg No Clues*, as he came to be known) was busy 'formulating' some sort of response to numerous press enquiries that morning from Portugal and abroad. Thankfully there were no other journalists around and, on a further plus side, there were upwards of a dozen detectives milling around the square opposite, chatting, smoking cigarettes or speaking on their phones. Despite being plain clothed you could tell them a mile off by their demeanour, as well as their physiques, most being decidedly buff under their t-shirts and jeans. I realised this could be rich pickings and, after cadging a cigarette, gently started to probe a few of them.

The majority were simply not interested in talking to me, or they didn't speak English (and while I spoke Spanish, my Portuguese was poor, although I could read it OK: to this day I don't think the newsdesks in the UK have any idea that Portuguese is really as different to Spanish as Latin is to Greek). However, all of them were friendly, despite surely guessing I was a journalist, albeit wearing jeans and a t-shirt like them.

Finally one of them asked where I had come from. On telling him across the border in Ronda, his face lit up as he said his sister-in-law was from nearby Sevilla and he had visited the previous year. We got talking about the golden city, the crucible of the new world from where Columbus had originally set off.

Finally we got down to Maddie … and it turned out the majority of them had been drafted in from Faro and a few further afield from Lisbon. These were the crack troops of the PJ, now enlisted in the missing girl inquiry under senior detective Goncalo Amaral. My new pal Rui, as I'll call him, was raring to get going. He said they had plenty of leads, but for some reason were hanging around waiting to be deployed.

He said they were convinced that Maddie had been snatched by a local paedophile and they had been monitoring half a dozen in the area for the previous few months. He added that while they didn't have a sex offenders' register, they knew where they all lived and 'had already been round to check on two or three local paedophiles who lived between Praia da Luz and Lagos', which were less than 4km apart.

'We have their names and addresses,' Rui told me, adding, 'We also have a list of English and German sex offenders living in the area from Interpol. We are following up every lead.'

One of those leads and addresses should have been Christian Brueckner and the Yellow House he rented for six years in Sitio das Lajes – which sits in a dead straight line between the two towns, overlooking the seaside resort. While he wouldn't have been there – as I will later explain – I'm pretty certain he would have been one of the German paedophiles on a watch list of the local police … or at least he should have been, given that he had already come to the attention of the local police and courts, in particular for child molesting, on two occasions.

Rui also told me that the PJ believed Maddie was 'most likely still in the area' and, intriguingly, that they believed she was 'being held captive really close' to the Ocean Club complex. He said they had a decent handful of sightings and believed the apartment was being watched for a few days before.

It was a great lead and I got straight on the phone to Lori, who phoned it in to the desk. She told me to wait in Portimao for her and Alban to arrive to try and get some more. But it was lunchtime by the time they arrived, and as the heat of the day descended, the majority of detectives appropriately melted away.

I could tell Lori was frustrated but we decided to grab some lunch at a cafe overlooking the square and within eye-shot of the police station. It proved more than worthwhile when an hour or two later, just as Lori and Alban were about to head back to Praia da Luz, the head of the PJ for the entire Algarve region decided to give an unprecedented press conference. This explained why a handful of Portuguese camera crews had recently arrived in the square, plus Ross Hindley (also known as Ross Hall), of the News of the World.

Unprecedented for a case like this, Guilhermino da Encarnacao, director of the PJ in Faro, was standing in the square, suited and booted under a blazing sun, with a dozen microphones shoved in his face. He must have been feeling the pressure. He said he believed Maddie had been taken by a sex offender, but there was also a possibility that she had been kidnapped for a ransom, given her parents were both wealthy doctors. In the first official briefing on the case, the police chief, best known for his wraparound shades and laidback appearance, said officers were working on the assumption she was being held between 3km and 5km from the resort. He said he believed she was still alive and added that after receiving '30 calls' from potential witnesses they had drawn up an artist's impression of the abductor.

'We have a prime suspect,' announced the grey-haired career detective, who died in 2010. 'A man has been seen acting strangely and we have a sketch, but we are not releasing it yet. We do not want to put the girl at risk. We believe the girl is still in Portugal, and probably nearby. I cannot rule out it was a paedophile who took her.'

He continued, 'There is all the evidence to show it was a kidnapping,' before going on to defend the police response, insisting that police were on the scene within ten minutes of receiving a call from Praia da Luz. He added that over 150 officers were currently working on the investigation.

We returned to the seaside resort before sunset to hear that the McCanns had been spotted walking between apartment blocks with their 2-year-old twins Sean and Amelie, carrying a bucket and spade. It brought it home to me that they were an ordinary family on holiday with two other small children.

By now we had been given more official information on the kidnapping by the British consul and the spokesman from the Ocean Club, who also represented Mark Warner holidays, as well as local workers and holiday-makers. The McCanns had been on the sixth night of their week-long holiday with three other families they knew from home. They were Jane Tanner and Russell O'Brien, Matthew and Rachael Oldfield, David and Fiona Payne and Fiona's mother Dianne Webster. Between them, they had eight children.

They had dined at the resort's tapas restaurant, some 75 to 80m from their apartment, taking it in turns to check on each other's sleeping children about every half an hour. (A staff member had made a note in the restaurant's reservation diary that the group required a table close to the apartments as they planned to dine without their children and check on them regularly.) Everything had apparently been fine at 9pm, but when Kate went back to the apartment at 9.45pm she found her daughter had gone. Running back to the group, she screamed, 'They've taken her!', before they and around 100 locals, staff and tourists took part in the long, late-night hunt, holding hands as they combed the beach and nearby countryside.

We also learnt that the shutters at the front of the apartment appeared to have been forced, while other sources told us the patio doors had not been locked by the McCanns, and were easy to slide open. One holidaymaker told us the McCanns were convinced they were being spied on and their regular evening schedule was 'probably being noted by one or more people.' It was very creepy.

Tellingly, a woman who looked after other apartments where the Mc-Canns were staying said the properties had become a 'hot spot' for burglaries. Giving her name as Paula Jones, she told Lori, 'We have a real problem with break-ins at the apartments because lots of holidaymakers don't double lock the patio doors. Burglars wait and watch the apartments so they know who is coming and going and they strike when tourists are out at the beach or in the restaurants.'

···

Around 50 men, half a dozen women and two bemused waiters buzzed between a handful of tables in the lobby of the Belavista. It was 10pm on Saturday and Her Majesty's press pack was well and truly letting its hair down, with stories filed and expenses to spend. The table in front of me was creaking from the weight of pints of lager.

They had come from every British national newspaper and each of the big TV news networks; an army of photographers, producers, fixers, translators and writers, all jammed in tooth by jowl with the decibels rising by the minute. I'd never seen anything like it and, quite clearly, neither had the waiters, receptionists or fellow guests. While extremely unedifying, I found myself going with the flow, despite a number of Portuguese hacks taking pictures of us, and looking decidedly uneasy.

By midnight the hotel insisted it was time to settle up, so the majority of us departed for a villa the team from *The Sun* had rented near the beach. Music was rigged up and the dancing and revelry went on into the early hours, when it was rumoured that two reporters from rival papers were having sex on one of the sunbeds by the pool. Thankfully I was out of there by then, because although The Mail and *The Sun* had asked me to stay on, I felt the need to come home for my daughter's second birthday. My wife and I had planned a small party with neighbours and a few close friends so I got some sleep before the long drive the next morning.

The journey gave me time to think over the case, and I found myself mulling over the anguish the McCanns must have been going through, particularly with a blonde, blue-eyed daughter of my own, just one year younger. I was close to tears as I crossed the futuristic Puente Internacional del Guadiana back into Spain, wondering if Maddie had been brought across this same bridge, restrained in a backseat or trapped in a boot. The optimism that she would be found was dissipating, especially after I confirmed with Spanish and Portuguese police that the border had not been shut until an alarming 48 hours after she was snatched. This is despite the fact the main A22 motorway, which straddles the coast into Spain, actually starts in the town of Bensafrim, just 3km shy of Praia da Luz.

This bridge, a one-hour drive from Praia da Luz, would have been the most obvious place to have put up a rapid police checkpoint. I saw how easy that was on various trips in and out of Spain into Portugal during the strict Covid restrictions of 2020 and 2021. I certainly found it ironic that my car was stopped and searched that Sunday morning, with police carefully checking the boot and grilling me on my movements, despite the very fact I had a press pass and told them I had been reporting on the case. But it at least gave me a chance to find out why it had taken so long to shut the border. 'The orders came in very late,' one GNR officer admitted. 'I don't know why they didn't move quicker.'

...

It was wonderful to see my wife and daughter again. Maria beamed when I came through the door and ran up screaming, 'Daddy's home! Daddy's home!' I gave her such a big hug and struggled to put her down. It was a lovely two days, but I couldn't keep my eyes off the news, and I was keen to return to Portugal.

By the time I got back on Tuesday afternoon Lori had been making headway. She told me she had also met Robert Murat, whom she found 'odd' and obtuse. She said he had told her about his failed marriage and how his daughter had moved back to the UK with her mother. She said she had grown suspicious when she heard him make what she thought was a deliberately loud phone call to his daughter back in the UK. She explained that his behaviour was reminiscent of the way Ian Huntley had behaved around the infamous Soham murders of 10-year-olds Holly Wells and Jessica Chapman in 2002. Huntley, a school caretaker, had taken a very unnatural interest in the case leading to him becoming a suspect. Eventually, he was charged with their murders.

These concerns about Murat had been enough for Lori to make a Monday morning phone call to the British consul and police in Leicestershire, the force that was now liaising with the Portuguese police on the ground in Praia da Luz. By Tuesday afternoon she'd had no response, so we decided to take a closer look at Robert and his life. We established that he lived with his 71-year-old mother Jenny in Casa Liliana, a charming detached villa on Rua Ramalhete, which was incredibly in direct line of sight and just 150m from the McCanns' Apartment 5A. His daughter, Sofia, also had an uncanny likeness to Maddie.

Speaking in confidence to one of the friends of the McCanns, we found that three of them had apparently seen him 'lurking' outside the apartment on the night Maddie had vanished. So when we found him hanging around outside the apartment on the Wednesday morning, we decided to go over and find out a little more.

He was decidedly vague. He told us he was an estate agent but happened to be freelance and had been dragged in to help the police with some translating. It seemed odd that they would so readily accept him into a key missing persons inquiry, allowing him to enter the apartment as well. Lori asked for his name, which he would only give as 'Rob' and said he didn't want to give a surname. When he noticed Alban taking a sneaky picture from a few feet away, he became enraged and insisted he delete it, which Alban pretended to do.

We left him and did more digging. I discovered he had a 33-year-old girlfriend called Michaela Walczuch, who was apparently a Jehovah's Witness and who, oddly, still lived with her estranged husband Luis Antonio, a swimming pool technician. The pair had a daughter.

I found out that Murat was born in London in 1973 to a British mother and Portuguese father, but raised in Portugal. He moved back to the UK as a young man, and lived in East Anglia, where he worked as a car salesman. He met and married Dawn Chapman, and they had a daughter in 2002. The family moved to Portugal in 2005 but Dawn became homesick and she and her daughter moved back to the UK, and the marriage broke down. Murat stayed, and had for many years, worked with the big American estate agency Remax in Lagos.

I popped into Lagos for a chat and was given one of Murat's old business cards by a former colleague, who told me he had left under something of a cloud and was setting up a rival agency called Romigen (presumably an amalgam of Robert and Michaela) and they were gathering properties for the launch. There didn't seem to be much love lost. His erstwhile colleague told me he was working with a Russian friend, computer technician Sergey Malinka, whom he described as 'something of an IT whizz'. Sergey's mother worked at the Ocean Club and he was also Russian, which if you live on the costas of southern Europe as I do, always raises a few eyebrows. It might not be fair, but Russians experience prejudice among the expat community because of their alleged connection to crime.

Nevertheless, Sergey was the go-to guy for all the expats in the Lagos area (which is thousands) to get their computers fixed. He also looked after a number of tourist rental villas, as well as a few boats. Could the pair have snatched Maddie and taken her to an empty villa or straight onto a boat? It seemed plausible, but we needed to find more.

We weren't the only ones to think something didn't add up. Unbeknown to us, Leicestershire Police had responded to the phone call they received from Lori and had sent an urgent memo to Portugal on the Monday afternoon asking for the PJ to take a look into Murat. The investigation had begun.

Chapter 5

The First Arguido

By Saturday May 12 – print day – we didn't have enough to pin anything concrete to Robert Murat. It was frustrating, but we could understand the newsdesk's requirement for caution, legally, and so we didn't hamper the police investigation. With the story at something of a dead end, I went home, agreeing to return the following week, if needed.

I was back in Ronda with my family when Murat got arrested. In a co-ordinated operation, police raided his home, Casa Liliana, before 6am on Monday, May 14, and by 7am they'd entered his girlfriend Michaela's house and three other properties that were linked to him.

By the time I woke up it was all over the national news networks and Sky reporter Ian Woods was reporting live from outside Murat's home. It looked like a massive breakthrough so it was frustrating that despite Lori and I appearing to have almost cracked the case, I was in Spain. I could only flick from channel to channel as Lori appeared on Portuguese and British TV, explaining her theories.

By late afternoon, police had completely sealed off the villa with a cordon. A green tarpaulin was erected around the two-storey home as forensic officers in white suits covered every inch. Dozens of police combed the grounds, while box loads of computer equipment and other electronic items were taken away for analysis.

As their investigation continued into the evening, Lori phoned me to say that she had seen Gerry McCann pacing up and down the balcony of the family's new apartment with a phone pressed to his ear. Curiously, we now know from Kate McCann's book that they had not been informed of the raid, nor kept in touch with any of its findings. The first they had heard about it was watching a 'breaking news flash' on television.

After scouring the house the forensic team drained the swimming pool and searched Murat's green VW van. His mother Jenny – who had also been closely involved in the search from the beginning and had been manning a stand giving out information and taking potential leads on the case – finally told a big pool of waiting journalists, 'They came in here but they have not found anything.' In her well-spoken cut-glass accent, she added, 'I'm okay, I don't know what is going on. I insist that the police issue a formal statement once this is over to clear his name.'

I wasn't surprised to receive a call from *the Sunday Mirror* newsdesk in London thanking me for my work and asking me to get back there as soon as possible. I left early the next morning and arrived around midday. I had hoped that by then something concrete would have come from the searches of the five addresses. But police were staying tight lipped and all we could get was a steer from Leicestershire Police that they were 'making good headway'. Looking through the PJ files (the nearly complete Portuguese investigative file) today, it is clear that detectives agreed that our theory was strong … but the truth is, they never really had any firm evidence.

The 61-volume, 11,223-page PJ files is full of interviews, detailed police activity and strategy surrounding the case. A must read for all armchair detectives and journalists, it has also fed many a conspiracy theory. Published by Portugal's Ministerio Publico on August 4, 2008, it was firstly made available as a DVD to journalists and later translated into English for the website *www.mccannpjfiles.co.uk*, which is an impressive body of work.

So good is this English resource that officers at Operation Grange (the Metropolitan Police's investigation into the case, which was launched on May 12, 2011 and is funded by the British taxpayer) allegedly preferred to use it over the original case files, which they found complicated and difficult to use.

Nevertheless, it is important to note that dozens of pages are missing from the files. These include up to 600 names of known paedophiles, both Portuguese and foreign, who lived in the area at the time and were likely a danger to children. In particular, in Volume 2 'a list of individuals connected with the practice of sex crimes with minors' had been removed, while in Volume 5, a list 'resulting from the search carried out in the PJ database related to foreign nationals linked with child sex abuse and paedophilia' had also been taken out. In Volume 15, no less than three separate probes into dangerous paedophiles had been removed, while in Volume 16 a probe into a French citizen was removed.

It was, however, still a prodigious body of work, with many sex offenders actually mentioned on top of many key clues and pointers. As Kate McCann noted in her book, she spent six months going through the files, describing the process as 'painful and time consuming'.

'Night after night, I read of depraved individuals, British paedophiles, Portuguese paedophiles, Spanish, Dutch and German paedophiles, and of the horrific crimes they'd committed,' she wrote. 'The police went to visit some of them, looked around their apartments and recorded merely "No sign of the minor". Was that enough to eliminate these vile characters from the inquiry?

'If more had been done, there was certainly nothing in the files about it. No description, no photograph, no alibi, no DNA. Just "No sign of the minor".'

•••

The first official suspicions about Robert Murat were raised on Monday

May 8, when a fax arrived from DC Sophie Hardy from Leicestershire Police based on Lori Campbell's concerns. In the six-paragraph missive, DC Hardy wrote that Murat, whom she described only as 'Rob' and as 'an interpreter', had allegedly given 'conflicting' accounts of the night Maddie went missing and was 'also going through a messy divorce' with his 3-year-old daughter currently back in the UK. She added that he had allegedly made a 'big show' of calling his daughter in front of the journalists and Lori felt he was being deliberately 'too loud'. She requested that Portuguese police give Lori a call to eliminate him from their enquiries, which I don't think happened.

It was hardly earth-shattering, but when added to another phone call that the PJ received that evening, it must have got the juices flowing. Coming at 8pm and noted officially by Inspector Manuel Pinho, it was from a woman speaking in 'correct Portuguese', suggesting it may have been an expat, but who did not want to give a phone number 'for reasons of safety'. She said she knew who had abducted Madeleine, that it was a man 'who knows how to keep quiet' and is 'quite close to the police'. When asked who she was referring to she said it was an individual who resided in Praia da Luz, who had an English mother, who spoke Portuguese very well and whose name was 'Robert'.

She said he had been in the area since the disappearance, supposedly 'with the intention of helping the investigation'. She continued that he was a regular user of online internet chats of 'a pretty heavy sexual nature' but she did not substantiate further. She added that most of the emails he sent to acquaintances abroad, especially in the UK, 'were encrypted' because of the 'content they possessed'. She added that she believed he could have had 'sexual motives' and the 'opportunity' to snatch Maddie, as he knew the area well and could easily be 'collaborating in this type of crime'.

Police decided to watch Murat more closely, and on May 11, officer Pedro Veranda made references to Murat's 'unusual curiosity' about the investigation. In a report, he stated that Murat had 'insistently and repeatedly questioned [him] about the identity of possible suspects', as well as 'the strategy' of the investigation and the work being planned for the coming days. He added that it was 'suspicious' that he had such an enormous knowledge of the dynamics of the 'Ocean Club Garden', referring to the tapas restaurant and the movements of the McCanns backwards and forwards to the restaurant, and presumably the pool and tennis area, during their holiday. And he concluded that he had 'tried persistently to influence the investigation.'

Next it was the turn of Chief Inspector Reis Santos to have a quiet 'informal' chat with Murat on May 12. His report didn't give the circumstances or exact time of the conversation, but did give some interesting pointers that could still be relevant today. In particular, Murat told him that the recent reward of one million euros leading to the safe return of Maddie was 'likely to have the opposite effect' and would lead to more abductions, in particular carried out by Russians, who were 'particularly cold when it comes to questions of money'. This mention of Russians must have had Chief Inspector Santos' ears prick up, knowing by now, I assume, of Murat's close friendship with Moscow-born Malinka.

Intriguingly, he also told Santos about various foreign paedophiles living in the area, particularly in the nearby village of 'Baroes' ... paedophiles who could be 'interested in abducting children.' He was almost certainly referring to Barao de Sao Joao and nearby Barao de Sao Miguel, a short drive from Praia da Luz, where a number of new age travellers had been living for years. But how could he know there were paedophiles living there?

He also went on to discuss a number of cases of abductions of children that took place near to where he had grown up in Norfolk. He mentioned one kidnapper who had released his charge after pressure from the media, as well as another who murdered a 10-year-old and buried her near an air force base in nearby Suffolk.

A decision was clearly made to deepen the investigation, as by 1pm on May 12, a trio of police officers were trailing Murat's every move.

A case log is available to read in the PJ files, which shows officers Manuel Pinho, Joao Carlos and Luis Pereira were following him around the resort from 12.40pm that day. They describe how they followed him into town and then to the stand where his mother was sitting on Rua 1 de Maio, set up to receive information from the public who may not want to give it to the police. Murat was driving a green VW Transporter van and later that day headed into nearby Lagos to get another rental car, a Hyundai Getz, using his British driving licence, registered from his former home in Hockering, near Dereham in Norfolk. Later that day he picked up a woman (assumed to be girlfriend Michaela) and took her for dinner at a local beauty spot, west of Praia da Luz.

The restaurant D. Dinis, in Praia da Cabana Velha, sits close to Barranco Beach, the other side of Burgau, and is a popular spot for van lifers to park up overnight. It is also, coincidentally, where Christian Brueckner used to regularly park his distinctive yellow and white VW van around that time. It might even have been where the German was actually staying on the night of Maddie's disappearance, having lost his rented Yellow House after going to prison in 2006 convicted of theft. Indeed a photo of the vehicle, taken on Barranco Beach, was released by German police in June 2020 as part of their appeal for witnesses to his movements (see photo section). It is not known, however, if Murat talked to anyone else that night while in the restaurant, but by midnight he had taken his date home to Lagos and headed back to his house in Praia da Luz.

The following day (May 13), Inspector Joao Carlos filed a five-page report on his reasons to suspect Murat to the District Court in Portimao. It was anything but convincing, but it listed five addresses that he believed needed to be searched in connection to the probe into the missing girl.

He started his report by recalling the circumstances of how Madeleine had first been discovered as missing. As well as detailing the chronology of the night, he pointed out how one of the McCann's friends, Jane Tanner, had noticed a man (dubbed the 'Tannerman') carrying a child up the road at around the time of Maddie's disappearance (as we now know, walking towards Murat's house). After stating that the police had followed all leads 'with titanic force', he went on to discuss an 'unusual situation' with an individual, whom he identified in full as 'Robert James Queriol Eveleigh Murat'. He wrote: 'This individual, voluntarily, approached the GNR [local police] alleging he was an interpreter of the English language. He said he could be useful in helping to translate interviews.'

Without any apparent check of his claims, the detective confirmed Murat was sent to speak to the detectives at 'the locale', meaning, we must assume, Apartment 5A. Then 'on this day and on the following days', he helped in various police tasks, in particular involving British tourists and staff at the Ocean Club.

While the report is neither explicit nor detailed, it demonstrates how quickly and seamlessly Murat was officially accepted by police and absorbed into the investigation. It doesn't look like they asked for any official proof of him being a translator (it turned out he actually had been one back in the UK) and one must ask, did he perhaps know any of the senior police at the scene? It seems even odder when, just a few days later, Inspector Carlos is noting Murat's 'strange behaviour' around the media and that he 'did not want to be photographed', clearly referring to the attempt by *the Sunday Mirror*, as well as stressing that other journalists alleged he could be involved.

The report added that Murat was the father to a little girl, the same age as Madeleine, and was in the middle of a divorce. It said he knew the area extremely well and that the McCanns would have passed his house on foot with Madeleine on various occasions. Furthermore, it claimed, without a shred of apparent evidence, that Murat had been able to 'sway' locals and holidaymakers into believing certain things. What things, I do not know. Finally, Inspector Carlos stated that when his colleagues had finally confronted him about his 'incoherent' behaviour and various discrepancies, Murat 'appeared very nervous' and insisted he was happy to withdraw from any further help if necessary.

He concluded that given Murat had allegedly been seen around Apartment 5A on the night in question, had been visiting websites 'of a sexual nature' and used 'encrypted communications' in his emails, a search warrant should be granted for five properties. Four of them were in nearby Lagos, with one being the residence of Michaela in Rua Adelina, plus three more in Rua D. Joao Moniz Nogueira, Rua Garret and Rua Lima Leitao.

The report also asked to search three vehicles, his VW Transporter, his mother's Peugeot 205 and his rented Hyundai Getz. It also asked for the court to grant the right to seize phone records of both his mobile and home number, as well as his mother's and girlfriend's.

It was a comprehensive list of demands and it was duly delivered by the judge under article 1 of law no 5/2002 of the child trafficking act.

It was a rapid turnaround, and by the following day they had a complete record of his mobile phone calls from Vodafone, as well as his home calls. They identified three mobile numbers they believed were of relevance (911948359, 914168557 and 918224078), with one belonging to Sergey Malinka. But the search at his home and other properties yielded very little. And after a full day of investigations, which included sending his computers off to be analysed, they could find no obvious link to the missing girl. An official report stated that they finished at 9pm and 'nothing was found of relevance to the case' in each of the places searched.

Yet, despite all this, the following day, on May 14, Murat was officially made an arguido, a term that doesn't have a direct translation into English but is very poignant, particularly around the Maddie case. Indeed, this is probably where most English speakers will have first heard of the word, if they have heard it at all. This formal status meant that he would be officially treated as a suspect in the crime. It also conferred various rights, such as the right to remain silent and the right to legal representation. For this reason it was possible – and it does happen – that someone being questioned as a witness, with less protection from the law, might declare him or herself arguido if they think the police suspect them.

And so began a frantic few weeks of digging into the background of Robert Murat by police on the ground as well as the media in Portugal and at home in the UK.

It is now known from the PJ files that in Portugal police seized a series of documents from Murat's house, including a list of phone numbers, a cash slip and a couple of his and Michaela's new Romigen company business cards. But the most bizarre thing taken back to police HQ in Lagos was a cutting from *The Guardian* newspaper, a review of a new book on Casanova entitled *Lock Up Your Daughters*, which can only have been of interest due to its supporting standfirst: 'A new biography reveals Casanova as both a fraud and paedophile.' Why Murat (or his mother) had specifically cut out and kept this cutting in his house we shall probably never know.

It also quickly emerged that three of the, as-they-were-now-known, 'Tapas 7' (Fiona Payne, Russell O'Brien and Rachael Oldfield) believed – and testified in police statements – that they had seen Murat around Apartment 5A on the evening in question, a claim strongly denied by him and by the alibi he was given by his girlfriend and mother.

In her book, Kate McCann contested how devastated she felt when Fiona told her on the day of the arrest that she had seen Murat outside the apartment on the night. She said she didn't want to hear their speculation on what might have happened and that she had 'gone from being cautiously optimistic to being very, very low.' She also revealed how Jane Tanner had been taken on the most bizarre, unofficial and highly dubious identity parade, which featured ONLY Murat, the night before his arrest.

In the strangest cloak-and-dagger operation, she and her husband Russell had been taken in a van to watch as Murat walked past the apartment escorted by the police. Connected to Jane's likely sighting of the assailant, the so-called 'Tannerman' whom she saw walking away from the apartment with a child in his arms around 9.30pm, the police had tried to cleverly bring the two together again. But Jane was unable to make a definite identification and, despite media claims, she never did sign anything to that effect.

Reporters were sent to his previous home in Norfolk and to doorstep his unsuspecting wife Dawn and daughter Sofia, who lived in Hockering. But, despite rumours that she had told the press off the record that he had been abusive to her, neighbours and former friends couldn't have been more supportive of him. His cousin Sally Eveleigh told *The Guardian* there was 'absolutely no way' he could be involved and he was merely sometimes 'over-helpful', while a villager Geoffrey Livock, 71, said he did not know anyone who disliked Murat, adding: 'Like we were saying in the pub last night, he would rather help than hinder anyone.'

The media in Portugal were more shameless. The Portuguese style of reporting, like its policing, is alien to the more transparent method of story-gathering in the UK. This is how it works: the media report everything they want, while the police tell you nothing and help you with nothing. It is disconcerting and leads to plenty of highly libellous, outrageous and disgraceful reporting. Although, as far as some of the British tabloid editors might be concerned, it gave them plenty of material to play with for their own editions.

Likely spoon-fed by the police – probably for money, which is usually the way – the Portuguese media published a series of salacious stories on Murat, who had spent over half his life in the country. The reports included his peccadillos online, which allegedly involved sadomasochism, bestiality and gay sex, all of which were mentioned or hinted at in the PJ files, I later discovered. They are still there.

Although hard to prove and verify today, it certainly did not include child pornography, at least not that the police or media could find. That however, was not necessarily the case with his close friend Sergey.

Chapter 6

Unexplained Phone Calls

Sergey Malinka was arrested two days later, on Wednesday May 16, at his home on Rua 25 de Abril, some 300m from the Ocean Club and just metres from the village church, Lady of Our Light, which the McCanns visited regularly. He was taken to Portimao Police Station at 8pm that evening, just minutes before the McCanns had left the church after praying for their daughter's safe return. His grilling came, rightly, after police had spotted and analysed the phone records of Robert Murat around the time of the disappearance, in particular a couple of late calls on the night in question, at least one of which was made to Malinka at 11.30pm.

A search warrant was issued for his third-floor apartment, signed by Judge Silvia Maria Goncalves Freitas at Portimao's Tribunal de Familia e Menores family court. Within minutes the press were camped outside the home he shared with his mother Svetlana, a cleaner at the nearby Ocean Club, and his father, a carpenter. A further warrant was issued for his office in Lagos. A total of six officers arrived in the afternoon in two cars, one carrying Malinka, whom they had presumably picked up from his office. During a four-hour search of both properties, overseen by Chief Inspector Rogerio Bravo, they seized various computers, including a Sony Vaio laptop, as well as nine 'mass storage devices' (such as discs, memory sticks and cards).

Given his job as a computer technician, it was surprising what little of interest was found. However, they did find pornography on some of the 27 CD ROMs they analysed, including, allegedly, 'bestiality'. What they don't reveal in the PJ files – which has many pages missing – is who these discs belonged to and, what exactly they might have included.

Photos of Maddie were found on one computer but these were the images that had been sent out to locals in order to help try and locate her. In two reports issued later on, police announced that 'nothing of interest has been found with relevance to the case.'

As soon as I had arrived back from Spain on the Tuesday afternoon, I had begun digging into the 22-year-old Russian. He fascinated me. When I found his office in Lagos, a typical backstreet computer lock up of little significance, late on Wednesday, it was in disarray as, irritatingly, it had been emptied out by the police a couple of hours earlier. We had heard rumours that police were looking for a Russian 'with a sexually violent criminal past',

31

but Malinka didn't appear to be that man … and he had denied it to the *Daily Mail*, insisting he had no criminal record and had been properly checked out by the Portuguese authorities. Born on May 30, 1984, his passport showed a handsome, fresh-faced man who had been living in Portugal for nearly seven years. Chief Inspector Amaral sent it to the Russian consul, Oleg Gostev, to be confirmed as genuine, which it is assumed to be.

In Goncalo Amaral's 2008 book *Maddie: A Verdade da Mentira (Maddie: The Truth of the Lie)* – which he wrote on retirement from the force and which must be viewed as extremely sceptical – he claimed that Malinka was, at the time, seeing a 33-year-old woman, some ten years older than him. Amaral wrote; 'The wife of one of his associates, of British origin, states that in 2006, he boasted about having had sexual relations with a minor, aged 14, and related how the father had surprised them. He allegedly stated that currently he maintains a relationship with an older woman and her daughter at the same time.'

He added: 'Interviewed, he refuted these allegations, he claims that it's vengeance on the part of his associate, unhappy with the way their shared company worked out.'

What is particularly interesting is the time that the police in Portimao finally decided to officially interview him, given they had first picked him up much earlier in the day in Lagos. Brought in as 'a witness' and not a suspect, the official time stamp of his interview showed that it was already 10.30pm when inspectors Joan Carlos and Luis Pereira finally got going.

Malinka, who must have been exhausted, informed them that he was fluent in Portuguese and had a Portuguese girlfriend, so he didn't need a translator. They went on to ask him about his friendship with Robert Murat, whom he said he had met the previous summer, via his Portuguese neighbour Rui. He had been recommended to Murat due to his IT and designing skills and was contracted to create a website for his new real estate business Romigen. He said he had developed his skills working for an IT company called 125 Computers, in nearby Mexilhoeira Grande, but had left after three years when he fell out with the boss over his salary. Curiously, while there, one of his clients had been Robert's mother Jenny and he had actually visited the Murat residence to fix her computer.

Currently working freelance, and spending much of his time driving around between clients in his Audi A4, he had been paid 3,000 euros for the Romigen website, but made a point of telling the inspectors that he had 'refused' to join another unspecified business of Murat's. Most of their meetings had taken place in Murat's bedroom in Casa Liliana, or at the nearby Baptista supermarket, but he gave remarkably little insight into his new client. He insisted their last meeting had been on April 30 at Baptista, to solve a few teething issues with the website. However, Murat said they had met again on May 2 and his girlfriend Michaela said they met on May 3 (she later changed this to May 2). Nevertheless, Malinka claimed that he had not spoken to Murat again until May 11, an entire week after Maddie went missing.

On the day in question, he offered up nothing of real interest, insisting he had spent the day undertaking 'the service and repair of computers', some of it on the road. He said he did not recall which customers were visited, but that he was home by 6pm, dined with his family and then spent the evening in his room playing computer games and, perhaps, doing some repairs on a client's computer.

He told police he only learnt about Maddie's disappearance when he saw a photo of her pinned up in a shop near his home the following morning. He claimed the shopkeeper was unable to tell him what had happened and so he went about his normal daily business. Asked why he did not help in the local search efforts he insisted he had 'too much work' to do.

Crucially, when asked about the phone call he had received from Murat at 11.40pm the night Maddie went missing, he said he did not recall having received such a call but added, 'If this actually happened, it will have been to arrange a meeting with him for professional reasons.'

He said he was 'not protecting' Murat and could not think of any information that could help police in the continuing search.

A total of three phone calls made by Murat to Malinka and Michaela were logged in the official police files and they all took place within a ten-minute period approaching midnight on the night Maddie went missing. Yet despite being questioned little over a week afterwards, all three failed to remember them, with Malinka and Murat repeating this in the Netflix documentary more than a decade later. From the phone records we know that Murat spoke to Michaela at 11.30pm, then phoned Malinka at 11.39pm for 30 seconds, and then phoned Michaela back.

Yet, somewhat incredibly Michaela also confirmed twice in police interviews that she did not remember the calls. 'She does not recall having spoken on the phone or exchanged messages with Robert until the following day,' read one of the police statements on May 16. 'But she admits that it could have been done without thinking, not recalling the reasons for that.'

Initially Murat claimed the phone call to Malinka was a 'pocket dial' made in error. He later changed his story: 'It lasted 30 seconds, so we must have talked, but I honestly can't remember what about,' he said. 'He was setting up my website, so it was probably that.' Malinka also had no memory of the phone call but according to a press report, his grandmother Lilia, who was in Russia, confirmed the Malinka and Murat spoke that night.

It was the early hours of the morning before police allowed Malinka back out on the streets. When I finally got to speak to him, after coming out of BCN Bank in central Lagos on the Friday, he brushed me away and told me he was 'completely innocent'. I had spotted him going into the bank in the heart of the town late in the morning completely by chance and decided to stick around to quiz him. I also got to take some photos as he came out (see photo section).

They didn't bring his mother, Svetlana, in for questioning until 8pm on June 20 – six weeks after Maddie had gone missing and more than a month after her son had been arrested. It was part of a series of interviews with staff that worked at the Ocean Club and Inspector Carlos Dordonnat was tasked with speaking to Svetlana, an employee of the Ocean Blue Villa Management and Rental company based in Praia da Luz. But she was anything but helpful.

Appearing as a witness, and with a Russian translator, she confirmed that she had worked for the cleaning firm for over five years and that she regularly cleaned in the Ocean Club. However, she said she didn't even know which apartment the McCanns were staying in, nor had she learnt about what had happened until two days after the events.

She added that in the eight years she had lived in the Praia da Luz area 'at no time' had she 'ever been aware of abnormal situations' and that the area was 'very quiet'. It was evasive at the very least given that we now know there had been dozens of burglaries in the block of apartments she cleaned and, crucially, a number of attempted and actual sex assaults on children over the years.

The only other information of note in the PJ files section on Malinka (and we must assume quite a lot has been redacted) was a note referencing 'paedophilia' given to the police some months later by private detective agency Metodo 3 (M3), who had been working on behalf of the McCanns. The Spanish agency, based out of Barcelona, had been tasked with looking into dozens of alleged sightings around Spain, Portugal and Morocco and digging deeper into potential institutional and police cover ups and involvement.

The operation, run by Julian Peribanez, was given £50,000 a month, of which around £8,000 was allegedly their fee. It was funded with the huge number of donations that had flooded in from private individuals, including Richard Branson and double glazing tycoon Brian Kennedy. M3 claimed to have 40 agents working in six different countries by the end of 2007.

Their first operation came when Peribanez teamed up with Kennedy's son Patrick to launch a secret investigation into Malinka. Why Patrick was involved, I do not know: maybe he was keen to help and needed a job. The pair followed him around Praia da Luz and Lagos, despite it being strictly forbidden under Portuguese law. They stuck trackers on his car and spent hours doing stakeouts. 'It looked like he was trying to get somewhere in a rush,' Patrick told the in-depth Netflix documentary in 2019. 'I didn't care about permission from the police … quite frankly I didn't care and neither did M3. We just wanted to get on with it.'

But they were unable to find much of interest and eventually resorted to the bizarre, perhaps desperate, tactic of trying to bribe him into talking. 'I started with 100,000 euros and went to half a million ... but Malinka said, "Don't offer me money because I don't know anything and I can't give you anything,"' Peribanez admitted in the same documentary.

The sinister firebombing of Malinka's grey Audi A4 outside his apartment in Luz some months later on March 20, 2008 has long been suspected of being the work of M3, although there is no evidence and it was strongly denied. (I find it hard to believe, but stranger things have happened in this case.) In the sinister late night attack, the word *FALA,* meaning 'speak' had been written in red capital letters on the pavement next to it.

Malinka told the press that he had slept through the bombing, which left the car a total write-off. ''I'm not scared. It's just a car,' he added. 'At least I wasn't inside it.'

While it has not been substantiated, the Russian also allegedly had a van set alight close to his home, although this was some time before Maddie went missing. If true, it's a strange coincidence.

What is also strange, and undoubtedly intriguing, is the existence of a note in the PJ files that points to paedophilia on a computer at Malinka's house. A man in relation to this content is noted as 'Cristian'. The file is not dated, it doesn't give any surnames of the characters involved and doesn't reveal if the police followed it up or found anything of relevance from the witness called 'Alison'. Like too many leads on this case, it quite simply, draws a blank. The note reads, and I reprint it verbatim: 'Alison informs us that 4 years ago her boyfriend Cristian was spending two nights at Sergei (SIC) Malinka's home when, upon going to send an email from one of Sergei's computers and upon joining an attachment, he saw paedophile material.

'When asked for explanations, Sergei told him that it was a client's computer and that he would denounce the fact to the pertinent authorities the following day.'

The statement lists Alison's phone number, which, annoyingly, has been redacted. It also notes that a transcript of the full conversation 'is attached'. It isn't. It has also been omitted.

We can speculate that this is an English expat called Alison, who still lives in Praia da Luz, who was a girlfriend of Christian Brueckner. She might have also dated another local man, a German called Christian Post, a good friend of Brueckner's. More on them later.

What we do know for sure is that Sergey Malinka won substantial damages of £100,000 from the UK and Portuguese media for the false claims that he might have been involved in Maddie's disappearance. He has long claimed he was beaten up by police in order to give out false information and, as he told the Netflix documentary had it not been for one late-night pocket dial from Robert Murat he would never have been investigated. 'One missed phone call pretty much ruined 10 years of my life,' he said.

Chapter 7

The Links

Robert Murat, Sergey Malinka and Michaela Walczuch have never fully explained why their phones connected late in the evening of Maddie's disappearance, nor agreed if they met up to talk business on May 2 or May 3 at Baptista supermarket. Yet, all charges were dropped against Murat the following year and Malinka and Michaela were never officially made arguidos. An alibi given by Robert's mother Jenny placed him at home all evening and a lack of any concrete evidence or link to Maddie at any of his homes or offices put an end to the police investigation in September 2007.

The following year he took the UK and Portuguese media to court winning a healthy settlement of £600,000. Since then both he and Malinka have been careful about speaking to the media, and the last time they properly spoke publicly was during interviews with the Netflix documentary. Michaela has hardly ever spoken at all, not even when Portuguese media falsely claimed in early 2008 that she had become an arguida.

Looking at the PJ files from the days around Murat's arrest on May 14, 2007, it is apparent the police had scant physical evidence that he might be involved. During a long interview that began at 10am that day at Portimao Police Station, it is clear he was consistently open and helpful with Inspectors Joao Carlos and Luis Pereira. Confirming he understood why they had arrested him and the significance of being an arguido, he waived his right to a lawyer and translator as he understood Portuguese 'perfectly'.

He talked about his background in the UK and Portugal, his Portuguese father who had died when he was three, and his extended family in Britain. He was frank and open about his lifestyle and employment history, which included working as a double glazing salesman, a car salesman and even on the search and rescue of shipwrecks. He pointed out that he had no criminal record and had never been in front of a court before.

The questioning moved onto his recent life in Portugal, where he had arrived in 2005 with Dawn and their young daughter, Sofia. He told them how Dawn had not settled on the Algarve and by August had moved back to Norfolk, and that they were in the process of getting divorced. A good father, by all accounts, he detailed at least five visits back to the UK to see his daughter since she and Dawn had returned.

Then the police shifted up a gear and began to ask him about his current set up with girlfriend Michaela, and his digital footprint. He told them how they had met at Remax and about their new business, Romigen. He admitted to having six email addresses, while she had three. He also confessed to watching internet porn, in particular a site called Red Clouds, but insisted he did not access it daily. He confirmed he did have some pornographic photos on his computer, but that they were pictures of women over 18 years old. He had no photographs of men or anything extraordinary: 'Just naked women, not sexually explicit, not remembering if they were using phallic objects,' according to the report. 'He has no record of violent sex, or sadomasochism or submission. He does not have images of rape, or fetishes with children or animals.' He also denied that he used any encrypted external server or encrypted content, despite the claims of the so-called witness.

He spent a good hour explaining his movements on the days prior to Maddie's disappearance and gave a detailed account of his exact whereabouts on May 3, which began when he left home at 10am in his VW van to visit Michaela in Lagos. She was at home alone and they talked about the website for their real estate project 'for a long time'. At midday they left home to take lunch at a Galp petrol station on the A22, and then to pick up Michaela's daughter from school at 3.30pm, before going to meet a friend Jorge and his son at Lagos Marina. After a long meeting about Romigen, they dropped Jorge and his son at the bus station between 6pm and 7pm. After dropping Michaela off at home, he returned to Casa Liliana around 7.30pm, where he had tea, read a newspaper and ate a cheese and ham sandwich with his mother in the kitchen, before she went to bed at about 10pm or 11pm.

He did not see Michaela again as she was 'at a Jehovah Witnesses' meeting between 8pm and 10pm, 'which is why he didn't phone her, because she turned her phone off.' He continued to insist he did not remember calling her after 10pm (despite phone records confirming otherwise), but 'accepts that it was a possibility'. He also remembered hearing a police siren and commenting on it to his mother, but he did not leave the house to investigate. He went to bed around midnight.

While his mother, Jenny, officially backed up his alibi, his movements were contradicted by a number of guests at the Ocean Club that week. Sisters Jayne Jensen and Annie Wiltshire told the *Daily Mail* in December 2007 that they saw Murat outside the McCanns' apartment half an hour after the alarm was raised. Their testimony was allegedly backed up by a British barrister on holiday with his wife and children staying nearby. The pair, from Kent, met police three times over the following two days, also claiming to have seen two blond men (more of which later) on the balcony of an apartment near the McCanns a few hours earlier. They also made several follow-up phone calls to the authorities.

Despite this, they weren't formally interviewed until six months later when they spent 11 hours with British police and later met private detectives at M3 before giving an official statement. Estate agent Jensen, then 54, claimed that she saw Murat light up a cigarette on the street corner opposite the McCanns' apartment. 'I had semi-given up smoking and was thinking I could do with a cigarette when this bloke just along the pavement from me lit up,' she said. 'I noticed him but didn't think anything more of it.' The next day she was introduced to Murat, who ended up translating for them when they spoke to the local police.

While admitting she found him 'odd', she insisted she was not conducting a 'witch hunt' against him.

Other witnesses who placed Murat near the McCanns' apartment that night include Mark Warner nanny Charlotte Pennington, two tourists who contacted M3 independently, and three of the McCanns' friends, part of the Tapas 7, Fiona Payne, Rachael Oldfield and Russell O'Brien.

But friends and family of Murat insisted he was not there. His mother Jenny said, 'People who say he was outside Madeleine's apartment that night are telling lies. I challenge them to tell Portuguese police what they're telling the McCanns' investigators.'

It is not known how quickly the Portuguese investigation got a psychological profile of Murat from the British police. We know from Inspector Amaral's controversial book that the investigation had brought in the UK's experienced Child Exploitation and Online Protection Centre (CEOPS) to 'develop his psychological profile'. And that, alongside other profilers and specialists, Amaral claimed the report stated there was a 'nine out of ten chance' Murat was guilty.

He also referred to a statement from one of Murat's so-called childhood friends, an ex-convict, put on file by British police, that 'he had an affirmed penchant for bestiality'. He recounted how this 'friend' had told him about his attempts at sexual relations with a cat and a dog, 'subsequently killed, he states, with cruelty.' He also mentioned the 'attempted rape of a 16-year-old cousin' and described Murat as 'someone violent with behavioural problems, a sexual pervert, sadist, and misanthropist'.

Despite this, Amaral went on to state that he and his department were 'somewhat sceptical'. 'According to the English profilers, there is a 90% chance that he is the guilty party. That seems to us to be a bit too easy,' he wrote. 'We think that drawing conclusions based essentially on the statement of an ex-convict is rather dangerous.'

Of the three late night phone calls between Murat, Malinka and Michaela, Amaral wrote in his book *Truth of a Lie*: 'We will never know the content of these conversations, no one will give us plausible explanations. The answers are evasive: "I no longer remember" or "that was about the website for the estate agency."'

At least that's one thing he got right.

•••

It is difficult to know how to approach Robert Murat's girlfriend Michaela Walczuch. The dark-haired German lived in nearby Lagos with her estranged Portuguese husband Luis Antonio, with whom she had an eight-year-old daughter. The couple had met at school on the Algarve and married when she was just 19. It hadn't been an easy marriage and they had split some four years earlier and were openly talking about divorce. An apparently laidback man, who ran a swimming pool business, Luis seemed to allow (or at least put up with) his wife bringing her dates back to the house. She certainly gave the impression to police that they had an amicable relationship.

She had been brought up in a family of Jehovah's Witnesses in Germany, before some major, slightly unclear, upheavals saw her moving to Portugal when she was 12 years old. She told police that she had moved when her parents had become 'very ill and were dying'. She said she was brought to Portugal by her maternal grandmother to live with an aunt who had a house on the Algarve.

She stayed within the Jehovah faith (in my opinion, a religion that lacks transparency and has been mired in controversy) and attended meetings up to four times a week. The area was, in fact, full of Jehovah's Witnesses and had two churches in Lagos, with Michaela mostly attending Lagos-Baia.

She told police that while her husband was also a Jehovah he had stopped going to church, after she had 'betrayed' him. She added that for this reason, she had not been able to take part in the congregation for the last three years, suggesting she had been having other affairs, aside from Murat, whom she said she met in March 2005. Indeed, her husband later confirmed that she had been having an affair in 2003 and had temporarily moved out.

Michaela was adamant that she was not involved in the Maddie case, and there is little evidence to suggest she was. In her statements she insisted she had been at Bible class for two hours on the evening Maddie went missing, along with her daughter. She confirmed that she would not have been home until around 10.45pm that day and probably went straight to bed. As noted, she said she did 'not remember if she spoke to Robert again that night, nor if they exchanged messages.'

Nevertheless, over the years she has been continually linked to the disappearance. In 2014 she was again interviewed by British police in their thorough cold case review of that year. The most damaging allegation is from a lorry driver who believes he saw her dropping Maddie off to a man in the nearby town of Silves two days after she went missing, on May 5. This sighting had been revealed to the press by M3 and had previously been given to the PJ, who had investigated it. The driver, Manual Gautier, told the PJ: 'I saw a woman delivering a child to a man on a road, in the Silves area.

'What surprised me … was the fact that the child was wrapped up in a blanket, which is not normal, during an afternoon in May, with the heat that was felt in the Algarve, at that time of the year.'

It was between 5pm and 6pm and he said one of the cars involved was a grey Audi, which was the same as Malinka's. And when the private investigators gave him several photos to look at, it is claimed he picked out one of Michaela.

There were no other witnesses to the sighting and it must be taken with a pinch of salt, especially as the police are said to have checked all CCTV cameras for that day on the nearby Via do Infante motorway in the Silves area and a few other cameras in petrol stations nearby. But it's food for thought.

•••

When it comes to Murat, I have to conclude that the likelihood of his involvement is very slim, despite the many witnesses who contradicted his alibi and the number of questions that remain unanswered. Certainly his ex-wife Dawn has never once doubted her former husband's innocence. 'I have known Robert for 13 years and was married to him for six and he would never, ever hurt a child,' she said in late 2007. 'He's the parent of a daughter, almost the same age as Madeleine, and he would never put anyone through the misery the McCanns are going through because he couldn't bear to think of something like that happening to Sofia.' She added that no one 'has ever produced a shred of evidence linking him with Madeleine's disappearance. This has totally ruined his life and he does not deserve that.'

Dawn revealed that, just months after being made an arguido, he had secretly travelled back to the UK to see his daughter, whom she describes as 'the most important person in his life'. So sure was she of his innocence that she had no qualms to let her daughter stay over with him at his sister's Devon home. And, as noted, not one of his former neighbours in Norfolk had a bad word to say about him.

It emerged that his lazy eye was in fact a glass eye, after he lost his in a motorbike accident as a teenager. And what I have also recently discovered is that he apparently did have clearance to work as a translator in Portugal, having worked as one in the UK before, earning £150 a time for Norfolk Police. While this was never confirmed to the press at the time – nor even the McCanns – it appears that behind the scenes he was actually sanctioned by the British Embassy in Lisbon. So, in hindsight, it looks as though Murat is innocent.

As a footnote, he went on to marry Michaela on April 17, 2009.

The civil ceremony, held on a beach just a few kilometres from Praia da Luz, was witnessed by 50 relatives and friends, including his daughter, mother, and brother Richard.

Chapter 8

Now the McCanns Are in the Frame

Having failed to put up roadblocks, protect the crime scene (by allowing two dozen or more people in the apartment on the first night alone), check all the guests at the Ocean Club, conduct thorough door-to-door enquiries and demonstrate a total lack of urgency to find Maddie in the early golden hours, how would the bungling Portuguese place make amends? By pointing the finger at the McCanns, of course.

Statistically, they were right to take a close look at the parents, with the majority of children killed or abused at the hands of their families. Percentage-wise the amount of sex crimes committed by family and friends is well into the 80s, even 90s. According to the global Rape, Abuse & Incest National Network (RAINN), 93% of juvenile victims of sexual abuse knew the perpetrator, 59% were acquaintances and 34% were family members.

Chief Inspector Amaral had every right to shine a torch into the relationship between the McCanns and their three children, plus the parents' private lives as well as the private lives of their friends. But there was one big caveat: they were English professionals – most were doctors – on a tennis holiday in a foreign country that none of them hardly knew. Add in the timings, as well as the lack of an obvious motive and surely any credible police force would quickly realise they were barking up the wrong tree.

I am not going to dedicate thousands of words to the disastrous probe into the McCanns' potential links to the disappearance. Largely because so much has already been written about the mistakes that were made by the police, in the media but also in Kate McCann's excellent book, Madeleine, as well as the detailed benchmark tome on the case by Anthony Summers and Robbyn Swan, Looking for Madeleine. Much of the couple's incisive analysis went on to become the basis of the comprehensive eight-part Netflix documentary, broadcast in 2019 with some of my own input and analysis.

I have never wavered in my belief that the parents were innocent. I laid out my argument in a long feature I wrote for the first anniversary of Maddie's disappearance in May 2008. I repeated it again on the tenth anniversary in 2017 and nothing has come close to changing my view. Not even the so-called evidence from sniffer dogs – who allegedly scented her body and blood in the apartment in two places, particularly behind the sofa, as well as in the McCanns' rental car. Some of their explosive findings might well have some critical relevance today, as we shall see.

Kate and Gerry became official suspects on September 7, 2007.

The warm tide of support had turned cool throughout the summer, as it became obvious the police were probing them instead of any other potential abductors. As the police cranked up their interest in the couple, media groups around the world started to question them under the guise that 'the public needed to know'.

Initially, they were perfectly reasonable questions about whether they had drugged their children to help them sleep. As any parent will tell you, there are various cough medicines and supplements that help children sleep – we often used Calpol (or Dalsy, as it is known in Spain) for our own kids (as well as daughter Maria, our son Albert was born in 2008). There were claims that, being doctors, Gerry and Kate may also have had various sleeping pills that could have done the trick.

Could Maddie have overdosed? The suggestion that they were drugged was certainly supported by the fact that Sean and Amelie had slept right on through the maelstrom and drama of the night, including Kate's screams and all the dozens of visitors traipsing around Apartment 5A. Detective Amaral still points to anomalies like this, and did so at length in his controversial book, although surely it is not acceptable for a police officer to write a book about an (ongoing) investigation. And hardly a year since the disappearance! He reportedly made well over half a million euros from the book, which has been the subject of numerous court cases with the McCann family and they are currently appealing the matter with the European Court of Human Rights. Remarkably, a website, 'Projecto Justiça Gonçalo Amaral' has been set up to fight his corner.

He still insists they were to blame because of their 'crime of exposing and abandoning defenceless children', and in an interview with *Nova Gente* magazine recently said, 'The fact that they lost their daughter did not give them the right to sue anyone or to be compensated. They can't escape their guilt, which is enough to rob them of their sleep, to provoke a lack of appetite and even rage, but against themselves and not against someone who only wrote down what happened.'

Amaral is also highly critical of the way Kate McCann advised her friends and husband that Maddie had gone missing. In February 2021, he told the three-part Discovery Channel series *Prime Suspect: The Madeleine McCann Case* that rather than screaming the resort down from the apartment, Kate ran back to the group at the tapas restaurant to tell them she had 'been taken'. This, he says, was a bizarre reaction to finding your daughter has been snatched and makes her 'very suspicious'.

As if this disgraced policeman would know what it would feel like. How many parents of snatched children has he interviewed? How would he react?

Curiously, in the same series, he denied briefing journalists off the record about the claims he made about the McCanns killing their child. This pitted him directly against Portuguese national TV reporter Sandra Felgueiras, who told the programme definitively that Amaral had told her over dinner that the McCanns had killed their daughter – by accident – in the apartment. To say he looked sheepish when confronted with this during the documentary would be an understatement.

The media had naturally gone haywire that September day in 2007 when the McCanns had been made arguidos. Once again hundreds of journalists camped outside the villa the McCanns had by then rented in Praia da Luz, and followed their every move between there and the PJ headquarters in Portimao. 'It became the biggest story of the spring and just carried on into the summer,' explained *the Telegraph's* seasoned Madrid correspondent Fiona Govan, who somewhat unbelievably had decamped for nearly three months to the resort that year. 'It is easily the longest time I have spent on a story and certainly the biggest case I have ever covered,' she told me.

'What happened to the McCanns was awful,' insisted Fiona, who interviewed the McCanns on several occasions. 'People in Spain and Portugal were convinced of their guilt based on the fact that they had left their children to go out for dinner with friends, because that just isn't the culture here. And then the way the police treated them was a disgrace.'

I couldn't agree more. Once they were pronounced arguidos, I spent a week in Praia da Luz, looking at the feasibility and motives behind the claims. Finding the police arguments decidedly flawed, I reported on it fairly in *The Olive Press*, but downplayed it if anything. I was not going to inflict on our readers what I believed was one of the biggest potential miscarriages of justice in European history.

The next time we really took a look at the case was when I wrote the detailed first-person piece on the first anniversary of Maddie's disappearance in May 2008, insisting the McCanns didn't do it, but a paedophile did. Two months later, in July 2008, I was proved right when the police officially lifted the arguido status and Amaral was shortly sidelined.

There had, apparently, been so much evidence that the McCanns had killed their daughter, not least from the sniffer dogs who detected Maddie's blood. But when the DNA samples were analysed in a British lab, the results came back negligible. So vague was the connection that it is now accepted that, as well as Maddie and all her family having a match, half the lab technicians would have also had a match. As the boss of the Forensic Science Service lab team, John Lowe, had cautioned at the time: 'Elements of Madeleine's profile are also present within the profiles of many of the scientists here in Birmingham, myself included.'

Detectives, journalists and web-sleuths have also long highlighted a so-called 'missing hour' on that fateful night when Gerry McCann could not be accounted for after playing tennis. The truth is after his three-set 'men's social' event he had gone back to the apartment for a shower and a glass of wine before going out to dinner.

But the conspiracy theorists (and police at the time) insisted that Gerry had disappeared at 7pm after playing tennis to go off to move or bury his daughter's body, before coming back to have dinner with his wife and friends at 8.30pm.

It was ludicrous to believe that the couple could have conspired to do this. In the first place, why wouldn't the McCanns just have admitted it was a horrible tragic accident if she had indeed died while being medicated to go to sleep? Furthermore, how could they have managed to behave so normally in front of their friends and all the staff at the Ocean Club that evening, assuming they had killed her?

It might also imply that all of the so-called Tapas Seven conspired with them to cover it up. But then again, the Portuguese media did report that the group had come to Portugal for a 'swingers holiday'. I have heard it with my own ears from Portuguese journalists, doctors, nurses and even police officers that they 'knew' the McCanns had a penchant for group sex. It made me so angry when this got parroted by locals in Praia da Luz, then more widely around Portugal, as well as across the border in Spain. The concept that, wink, wink, we all know what they were up to at the Mark Warner Ocean Club.

I have long argued that the window was far too small for Gerry to have got away with it. Let's assume he left the tennis courts at 7pm sharp, as his three tennis partners confirmed. He would have got back to the apartment at 7.05pm, then somehow have had to bundle up his daughter's body, without anyone seeing, and stroll off into the nearby countryside – or another property – to find somewhere to hide her.

It has been suggested she may have been kept in some sort of trunk freezer in a nearby rental villa until the McCanns hired a Renault 25 days later when they might have transferred her body to a safer, more isolated location. Or, as the Portuguese media reported, they drove to Lagos Marina, hired a boat and took her out to sea for a family burial. Yet Gerry didn't know the area well, hadn't visited any of the inland villages, and even if he had, how was he going to find a suitable place to keep his daughter's body for nearly four weeks?

Let's assume he buried her, just for a short time in a shallow grave. Where would he have got a shovel from? Furthermore, it was May and the land nearby was rock hard after a very dry spring, so digging a hole would have been a massive mission and certainly would have left him with blistered hands, if nothing else.

It was such a fix up – as you discover if you read the PJ files, as well as Kate's book. As if I needed any further proof that 'cold, steely' Kate had not been behind it, I recently spoke to the son of a woman who lived upstairs from Apartment 5A at the time. He told me his mum, a typical British expat who has lived in Praia da Luz for three decades, will 'never forget the haunting, guttural scream' she heard coming from Kate an hour after she realised her daughter had gone missing. 'It was both heartbreaking and terrifying in equal measure,' he said. 'She said there was no way you could put it on.'

Finally, let's not forget, British police described the apartment as the 'worst preserved crime scene ever'. I now wonder if this could have been deliberate on the part of the PJ? As I've noted, more than 24 people went through Apartment 5A during the night of the disappearance and it took a few hours before they even put up police tape. Could Amaral's claims that he had been out celebrating a birthday party that night – which explained his and other officers' lateness to the scene – have been a clever cover up by the disgraced detective? Was this all part of an alarming and much wider conspiracy? Read on.

Chapter 9

Inspector No Clues and Pushy Pereira

It was clear Chief Inspector Goncalo Amaral's claims that the McCanns were guilty was partly borne out of the frustration the police must have felt after failing to pin anything on Robert Murat, plus no firm evidence of any other suspects. They were also badly stung by the continual criticism in the British media that they were lazy and inept, not helped by Kate and Gerry's supposed snipes at their lack of progress in the case.

So desperate was Amaral to get a win, I now wonder if it was possible that the police even planted Maddie's DNA in the rental car the family had hired from Europcar a month after she went missing. Amaral is a badly-tainted detective, removed from the inquiry, while his friend and fellow former PJ deputy, Paulo Pereira Cristovao later went to prison for seven years in Lisbon.

Amaral was simply a desperate man, heavily under pressure for a conviction, as they had both been, coincidentally, a few years earlier in 2004.

It is a little-known fact that Amaral himself had actually been made an arguido in another still very murky case just ONE DAY before Maddie went missing. And he was later found guilty of covering up the beaten confession of a mother over her own missing daughter … a young girl who ALSO vanished up the road from where Maddie disappeared.

The similarities between the two cases are haunting, and I believe could potentially be linked. Both girls vanished without a trace and their bodies have never been found, while their mothers were accused of being involved by the very same police officers and were then later exonerated.

Let me explain.

Joana Cipriano was just eight when she vanished 10km away from Praia da Luz on August 12, 2004. She had gone missing from her village of Figueira, near Portimao, with no obvious motive or reason. The happy, spirited girl had been on an errand to buy tuna and a pint of milk from her local shop and was never seen again. It was 8pm and not even dusk on a Portuguese summer evening. And it was clear as daylight that detectives didn't have to worry about the world's press descending in on this case and – with her mother being from a poor working-class background – she was something of an easy target to fit up.

It is surely not just a coincidence that her mother, Leonor, was arrested by the same PJ detectives from Portimao who arrested the McCanns three years later. Picked up at 8am on October 14, 2004, she was held without access to a lawyer, and interrogated without sleep for 22 hours. Then, after a two-hour respite, she was interrogated again until 7am on October 16. Read that again, carefully. This is Europe, not Chile.

By the time she was released, as photos showed, her face was a mass of bruises, as was her body, claimed her lawyers. 'They tortured me so much, they left me black and blue from so much punching that I reached the point where I didn't know what I was saying,' Leonor would tell the media later. The police said the bruises came from when she 'tried to commit suicide' by throwing herself down the stairs at the police station, although there is zero evidence to support this.

The torture succeeded in forcing a confession, but the next day, when she was finally able to speak to a lawyer, Leonor withdrew it, insisting she was innocent.

The prosecution was built around the claims that Joana had been killed when she had interrupted an incestuous sex session between Leonor and her uncle, Joao Cipriano, after returning from the shop. Again, there was little proof of this, except that her uncle, something of a drifter, also confessed to the murder, saying he had cut up her body and fed it to his pigs. He has since confirmed he made the confession under duress.

It was a shocking case and, despite her claims of torture, Leonor was convicted and sentenced to 21 years in prison. As it was always believed to be a shaky conviction, this was later reduced on appeal to 16 years, with one appeal court judge insisting he was sure she was innocent. Were the others in on it?

The murder trial was coincidentally the first in Portugal to be conducted without a body, and it is incredible the conviction wasn't overturned completely after various police officers were later convicted of beating the confession out of her and covering it up. Five PJ officers were charged with a variety of offences including assault; three were acquitted, including Paulo Pereira Cristovao, while Amaral – who always insisted he was not present during the alleged assault – was found guilty of covering up for his officers.

He was convicted of perjury, having falsified police documents in the case, and received an 18-month suspended sentence in May 2009.

Fellow officer, António Nunes Cardoso, was also found guilty of having falsified documents and received a two-and-a-half year sentence.

As Leonor's lawyer Joao Grade said after their trial: 'I want to believe that the Portuguese police do everything the right way. But sometimes, if they really think someone is guilty, as they did with Leonor, they may find other ways to get what they want. It's only human.'

Perhaps unsurprisingly, in 2020, after Leonor and Joao had each served 15 years in prison, the Cipriano family came forward to demand Portuguese police probe the new Maddie suspect Christian Brueckner over missing Joana. Joana's stepdad, Leonor's partner, Leandro Silva, told *the Mirror*: 'The moment I saw police had a Madeleine suspect I thought about poor Joana and how he could be involved. I think the police handled the investigation so badly. That's why I'd like a new police team to re-examine everything and see if this German man is involved.' He had previously insisted in 2007: 'The only difference between the McCanns and us is that we don't have money.'

I do believe Brueckner could have been involved in the Cipriano case. He was in Portugal at the time, living in nearby Praia da Luz, he had a close friend in Figueira, I discovered, and was already heavily involved in sexual deviance; the following year being convicted of rape.

I also think Amaral unwittingly – or deliberately – led the investigation away from the real culprits in the Maddie case, as his team did in the Joana case, which was remarkably similar in genesis.

•••

Here is another curious aside in reference to Portuguese policing: in those first weeks on the Maddie case, I struggled to find a single journalist or independent investigator, Portuguese or otherwise, to commend the way the authorities worked. I finally stumbled across one person who did – expat policeman Roy Whitehouse. I had earlier been in contact with him a couple of times over various crimes on the Costa del Sol and, in particular, foreign paedophiles based in Spain and Portugal. The former Scotland Yard detective had moved to Portugal three decades earlier and become something of a specialist in tracking down missing people – particularly children – around Africa and South America, mainly Brazil and the former Portuguese territory Angola.

I knew he had an office in Faro, but was mostly based out of a rural villa somewhere inland from Portimao. We had only spoken on the phone, but I had found him to be knowledgeable, friendly and helpful in any enquiries relating to police work and expat criminals abroad. He was an invaluable source and aid during my various trips into Portugal for assignments.

I ended up quoting him in a few articles over the years, including around the Maddie case. But the one thing that had really puzzled me at the time was his staunch unwavering support for the PJ detectives during the clearly botched investigation. We had various arguments over it, but he was adamant they were doing a good job and he liked the silent approach that allowed the police to get on with their work entirely unfettered, and with no compromise needing to be made for the media. To be fair, it was similar in Spain. He insisted that the investigation by police chief Amaral was 'being well handled' and was 'solid and on the right track'.

It baffled me, until I discovered that Whitehouse had been the next-door neighbour of Brueckner and his girlfriend Nicole Fehlinger, who fostered troubled teenagers (more of which later) in 2007, in the village of Foral, a short 40-minute drive from Praia da Luz.

A career policeman, who become a detective constable and then a sergeant in the City of London, before retiring to set up his own private practice WIS International in London, and then opening an office in Portugal in 1992 with two bases on the Algarve and Lisbon, he had an apparently unblemished career. He joined the board of the British Portuguese Chamber of Commerce and became the President of the Council of International Investigators (CII), a security and investigation organisation with 400 members, all of whom are 'carefully vetted to ensure their trustworthiness.'

In 2013 his company picked up an award from the UK Trade and Investment ministry for its contribution to British industry abroad.

While WIS has now closed I found a number of websites that gushed about his skills 'undertaking business intelligence in Brazil and Angola' as well as his handling of 'investigations for a number of marks [clients] within Portugal.'

Could it be that he discovered something he shouldn't have and got silenced? Or could he have been involved in some sort of child sex ring himself?

The current Ukrainian owners of his villa in Foral gave me a tantalising clue. The son-in-law Yacha told me after his wife's parents bought the house 'in 2015 or 2016' they received a couple of visits from the police looking for Whitehouse. He said they were keen to find out where Whitehouse had moved and told them it was about 'tax not being paid on the sale of the house.'

'It was a bit strange and they came a few times,' Yacha explained from his home in nearby Albufeira, estimating the visits to have been in 2017 or 2018, which would coincide with the recent German probe into Brueckner. 'They asked if we knew Mr Whitehouse personally and all we could say was he wasn't a nice person. That was all.'

This doesn't add up. It makes no sense for the police to be probing a fairly innocuous case of tax, which is normally dealt with in Portugal by the tax authorities, who rarely knock on the door ... and if they did it would be a tax inspector, not two police officers.

Furthermore, Yacha's family weren't the only ones to describe this celebrated police officer as 'not nice'. When I asked a few of his neighbours in Foral, one described him as 'intimidating', while another, the President of the residents association, called him 'odd', adding that there was 'something very dark about Roy' and that she 'wouldn't be surprised if something bad had ended up happening to him.'

I wish I could ask Whitehouse, who was gay and had a younger boyfriend, but he died in 2017, the year German police started to probe Brueckner in depth. It's a hunch I can't prove – yet – but anyone interested should take a look at the research done by America's Rutherford Institute on 'predator cops', who protect and hide criminals and are often themselves paedophiles or involved in other unsavoury crimes.

•••

Before we start exploring Christian Brueckner, we should spend a moment looking at Chief Inspector Amaral's friend and former PJ detective Paulo Pereira Cristovao. This long-time critic of Maddie's parents – who like Amaral ALSO wrote a book about Kate and Gerry's alleged involvement and starred in the Netflix documentary (he also, bafflingly, wrote a book about Joana) – is currently spending at least five years behind bars.

The former police officer, who retired from the PJ in 2007 to lead, somewhat remarkably, Portugal's Association for Missing Children (*Associacao Portuguesa de Criancas Desaparecidas, or APCD*) was convicted of his involvement in a number of violent break-ins at luxury villas in Portugal in 2014. Pereira – who relinquished all links with the police after being acquitted of any involvement in the Joana case in 2009 – was accused of being the lynchpin behind the string of robberies of upmarket homes in Lisbon and nearby Cascais.

He denied giving his accomplices information about the victims at the 2019 trial, which saw a total of 16 people convicted, including two police officers from Lisbon's PSP division, who received jail sentences of up to 17 years each. The gang was led by a football hooligan called Nuno Vieira Mendes – better known as 'Mustafa' – who allegedly received the information from Pereira and passed it on to a relative who then got police officers to carry out the raids. They wore uniforms and carried fake search warrants. By flashing their ID, they were able to enter the properties, tie up or handcuff the owners and then rob their cash and other valuables.

In the most sinister robbery, on February 27, 2014, a couple and their daughter were kidnapped and the culprits took more than 100,000 euros. In a second robbery in April that year the gang managed to seize over one million euros in cash in two hidden deposits. 'It was Paulo Pereira who gave us all the information,' insisted Mustafa.

Pushy Pereira, who had left the missing children's association to become the vice-president of Portugal's leading football team Sporting Lisbon in 2011, was a 'lifelong friend' of Mustafa. At the trial in Cascais, Mustafa, who led the country's oldest football fan club, laid their relationship bare and accused Pereira of 'using' him. He pointed at him in court and spat out dramatically that 'his downfall in life' was 'meeting that man and doing him a favour'. He got six years for his involvement.

Pereira, who was said to have pocketed 40,000 euros from the crimes, appealed the sentence, although a new court hearing in June 2021 ratified his involvement and he will now spend the next half decade in prison. In any case, he did not completely deny his involvement in the scandal, telling reporters in December 2019, that he 'deeply regretted' his connections to the gang.

The former PJ officer is a highly controversial and troubled ex detective. Aside from the scandalous Joana case, he was convicted of embezzlement Sporting Lisbon's funds at Lisbon Central Court in 2016. For this, he somehow only got a suspended sentence of four-and-a-half years, despite being involved in at least two cases of misuse of Sporting's assets.

In 2019, while awaiting sentence for the villa raids case, it emerged that Pereira was still being probed over two other cases: A violent attack on various Sporting Lisbon players, as well as a separate case of cocaine trafficking.

But back to his role as head of the APCD missing childrens association.

There is little known about the organisation – a sort of quango with little obvious power or purpose – and what he did there. He appears to have spent his first year in the job insisting there was no major problem with missing children in Portugal. Having announced there were 'only six children still missing' in March 2009, he went on to attack the UK and Spain. 'It is much worse in Spain,' he insisted in various interviews, adding: 'In the UK there were 95 missing children alone at the time of Maddie McCann's disappearance.'

I believe he was shoehorned into the political position by someone on high. It was certainly a key role from which he could watch the mechanisms of the state and police as they probed or paid lip service to their efforts to deal with child abuse. This, after all, in a country where it was legal to possess child pornography until September 2007 (after Maddie went missing) and it was only made illegal to create and distribute it in 2001.

A long time apologist for the police investigation into missing Maddie, his new role enabled him to become a whitewash specialist for the sins and errors of Portuguese society.

I also discovered that around the time he left the police (or actually while still there) Pereira had apparently opened a detective agency, similar to Roy Whitehouse's WIS. However, there is now almost nothing I can find on this agency, which seems to have been airbrushed from history for one reason or another. Called Primus Lexis, it was termed a 'business research and consultancy agency' and was based out of the Almirante Reis area of Lisbon.

In the only interview I could find with Pereira about Primus Lexis, a promotional article from June 2008 still available on Blogspot Entrevistasentrelinhas, he told a journalist: 'I believe there is a market in Portugal for the type of work we do here and, on the other hand, there are no professionals who can do it within the law, knowing the rules.' He went on to claim that the agency, set up in 2007, already had 16 staff, including psychologists and lawyers, and had been growing at the staggering rate of '30% a month'.

He insisted it was the best agency in the country and worked 'well within the law' and 'without any illegality'. Why he felt the need to say this is anyone's guess. For some reason, he also stressed that the agency was meeting its fiscal responsibilities. 'This is not a joke, it is very serious, we have many customers, we deal with large sums, we have responsibilities, we pay a VAT bill every three months,' he said. 'We don't do anything illegal, not least because we work as we do in the police!' He added: 'I don't miss the PJ at all, I was exhausted of the way things worked, of the bureaucracy, of the low salary and above all, of the big lack of appreciation on the part of the bosses in recent years.

'When I left I insisted I never wanted to work for a boss again. I still have a lot of work, particularly as I am president of the Portuguese Association of Missing Children, I have television, I am writing a new book.'

How strange that in 2021 I could find no other trace of the company, no further mention or any links to any jobs or work it had ever undertaken.

Chapter 10

A Paedophile's Paradise

Cristovao's claims that his country didn't have a problem with child abuse couldn't be further from the truth. Going on the evidence of various recent inquiries into paedophilia in the country – in particular linked to PJ cover ups – I found the scale of abuse there alarming. Lawyer Pedro Namora, a former child abuse victim who today represents others in Portugal, has described the country as a 'paedophiles' paradise', with statistical and anecdotal evidence backing him up.

While it is a serious problem globally (*see Appendix*), Portugal appears to have a higher percentage of child abusers than many other European countries. I began to realise this when I started probing the Joana mystery, as well as the so-called Casa Pia and Rui Pedro cases, and the appalling 'Wonderland' probe.

I had first started to dig into the horrific Casa Pia case in the months after Maddie went missing. It came after journalist Lori Campbell and I had spent a few days trawling around the scruffy inland villages near to Praia da Luz, including Barao de Sao Joao, where we would later learn that Brueckner spent a lot of time. We had continually heard whispers, then claims, that this expat had been convicted of so-and-so, that priest was involved in this-or-that, until we got the impression that half of these inland settlements were brimming with paedophiles.

And then we were tipped off to look into the scandal involving Casa Pia, a state-run Portuguese institution for the care and education of orphaned children, which had surfaced in September 2002, after over two decades of allegations. The case, involving politicians, diplomats, lawyers and celebrities, which didn't finally come to trial until 2009, rocked Portugal to the core and has thankfully led to a rethink about how the country's society is structured and run.

Portuguese detectives had first begun to investigate serious child abuse allegations inside ten Casa Pia children's homes in the 1970s. In 1981, PJ detectives accused the caretaker of one of these homes of raping dozens of children over a period of 30 years. Police then accused perpetrators of supplying children to men both domestically – including various prominent public Portuguese figures – and to other countries. But no charges were formally laid and it wasn't until the late 1990s that some former orphans out of the 4,600 who lived at the homes came forward with horrific tales of abuse. The whistleblowing first became public from a mother of a victim called Joel.

Portuguese magazine *Visao* reported that Portuguese diplomat Jorge Ritto had been removed from his post as consul in Stuttgart some years earlier after he was caught in *flagrante* with an underage boy in a public park. He would later become one of the key figures running the Casa Pia sex ring, alongside the caretaker Carlos Silvino, better known as 'Bibi', Lisbon doctor Ferreira Diniz, as well as Hugo Marcal, a lawyer, who actually represented some of them. The most high-profile of those accused was TV chat show host and journalist, Carlos Cruz. But there were many others.

The boss of the Casa Pia homes, Paulo Pedroso, who had been the country's Secretary of State for Labour from 1999 to 2001, was himself suspected of 15 cases of sexual violence against minors. His case was eventually dropped and he won 100,000 euros in damages for being wrongly detained on paedophilia charges.

Even the country's socialist party leader Eduardo Ferro Rodrigues was dragged into the scandal when the newspaper *Expresso* reported in 2003 that four children had seen him at locations where sexual abuse was taking place. He offered to be questioned over the allegations and he was never formally accused.

As police were compiling evidence and prosecutors preparing for a groundbreaking trial in 2009, numerous senior staff were fired from the various orphanages, but the new Casa Pia director Catalina Pestana admitted in 2007 that there may still be paedophiles in the Casa Pia system.

It was into this country that the McCanns had come for a restful family holiday in the spring that year, at a time when a man sitting on the terrace of a holiday apartment next to them could still legally watch child sex porn on his laptop. Child prostitution was still very much on offer to holidaymakers in the country then, at it certainly had been over the previous decade.

Indeed in the 1980s and 1990s, Portugal was very much a haven, or hotbed, for child sex abuse, as is Cambodia, Vietnam or Cuba today. In a comprehensive poll of tens of thousands of Europeans in 1998, the EU's European Coordination Office found that an alarming 86% of the Portuguese population believed the country was a destination for child sex tourism.

And only a few years before the Maddie case, a child sex abuse charity 'Innocence in Danger,' criticised the Portuguese police for their reluctance to investigate paedophilia. 'Time and again complaint files are lost, witnesses are seldom interviewed, and suspects are let off the hook by totally inept search methods,' said a spokesman. The frustration was backed up by British sex crime specialist Ray Wyre, who said Portugal attracted large numbers of child sex abusers from around the world, including the UK. 'British paedophiles have always operated there,' he told *the Telegraph* in 2007. So what were Pereira and Whitehouse on about?

Denial, is the word. Just seven years earlier, in 2000, several foreigners – mostly British – were reportedly arrested in the historic town of Sintra, near Lisbon, for taking around 50 young boys (aged around 11 to 13) to a secluded villa. According to expat newspaper *Portugal News*, the men in their fifties, who presumably either lived in the upmarket area or had holiday homes there, had used the boys at their leisure and occasionally took them away 'to the Algarve' for holidays. A few years later, 46 men were arrested for links to child sex offence in Lisbon and Sintra, which seemed to be something of a European epicentre for abuse.

In 2001, the most sinister online child sex ring in global history was found to have dozens of Portuguese members. The Wonderland Club was launched by two paedophiles in the US, and one of its high profile victims was 11-year-old Portuguese boy, Rui Pedro Teixeira Mendonca, who, in 1998, was kidnapped from his home in Lousada, in the north of the country while riding his bike.

An investigation named Operation Cathedral had been first launched by British police after a tip off from US detectives probing the 1996 rape of an 8-year-old girl broadcast live to its hundreds of members by webcam.

It emerged that to join the club, whose USP was the raping of children live on camera, members had to supply or self-produce at least 10,000 new images or films. These are some of the most evil individuals in history, and I find it particularly sickening that after thousands of hours of investigation by over 1,500 police in 13 countries, the majority of the members received less than three years in prison.

A total of 1,263 victims were catalogued by the various police departments, led by the now-defunct National Crime Squad, in London. Tragically only 17 of them have ever been identified, seven in America, six in the UK, one from Chile, one from Argentina and one from Portugal, the aforementioned Rui Pedro.

Surprise, surprise, the subsequent Portuguese police investigation into his whereabouts has been mired in criticism by both the media and the missing boy's family. Despite countless confessions, semi-confessions and evidence to suggest he was snatched by a local 22-year-old lorry driver and a prostitute, what is certain is that the tragic boy ended up appearing in a film on the Wonderland Club website, paraded in front of its members, brutally raped, at an unknown location in Europe. Both the pictures and video evidence were gathered by police.

It is not known if Rui ever made it past the country's borders, if he was brought for a 'holiday' on the Algarve, or if he is still alive today ... but in 2019 his family finally got some closure when they managed to have him declared legally dead so they could move forwards.

A cursory search on Google brings up countless cases of child sex abuse in Portugal and many have uncanny (and alarming) links to the expat community. These include the case of Ulrich Schulz, a German 'New Age' musician and DJ, with the stage name, Oliver Shanti, whose music has been included in two of the popular Buddha Bar compilations.

Schulz was arrested and extradited back to Germany in 2008 from his home in Portugal after being wanted for more than 116 child sex abuse offences. He lived in the village of Vila Nova de Cerveira, where he set up an ashram and was worshipped by vulnerable followers, who called him 'Jesus' and 'the Messiah'.

Despite the obvious alarm bells, he had even been honoured in recognition of his contribution to the local community. However, unbeknown to locals, the wealthy Schulz – who had made millions recording 'chill out' music with among others, the London's Royal Philharmonic Orchestra – had abused hundreds of young members of a sect he had formed in Bavaria in the 1980s. 'We simply could not imagine that he could be suspected of paedophilia,' said Vila Nova mayor, Jose Manuel Carpinteira, pointing out that the musician had donated several vehicles to local emergency services.

It is this naivety, or a willingness to turn a blind eye, that seems to have become something of a trait of so many senior figures in Portugal. Take the case of the Irish Catholic priest recently arrested for decades of child abuse on the Algarve, who admitting he had moved there to be more 'secluded'. Father Oliver O'Grady had first been sentenced to 14 years for crimes of sexual abuse in California in 1993 before being deported to Ireland.

From there, he was somehow able to move to Holland undetected and began working as a volunteer in a parish of Rotterdam, where he organised children's parties until 2006, when he was arrested following the admission in the Oscar-nominated documentary *Deliver Us from Evil* that he had raped and abused more than 25 children

Incredibly, his behaviour was allowed to continue, and in 2010 he was again arrested after he accidentally left a laptop on a plane with over 280,000 images and six hours of child abuse videos. Following three years in jail he was deported again, but ended up living on the Algarve, near the village of Loule, where he was found in 2019. Once again, it doesn't look as if the PJ investigated any of his local relationships or even what he had been doing, or for how long, in the village which is just 16km from Foral, where Christian Brueckner was living on and off from 2007 to 2016.

Portugal's laissez faire attitude to child sex abuse is best illustrated by a scandal in 2015 when it emerged that a man who ran an 'after hours' creche for busy parents had been charged of abusing children for years – yet he was still allowed to continue looking after them while on bail until his trial.

Had it not been for the intensive campaigning of the victims in the landmark Casa Pia case, it is very likely Portugal would still be considerably further behind. Lawyer Pedro Namora, who as a former Casa Pia orphan witnessed 11 rapes on children while they were tied to their beds, is certain that elements in the establishment and police force conspired to suppress both the Casa Pia and Maddie McCann scandals, fearing damage to the country's reputation. 'Portugal is a paedophiles' paradise and if all the names come out, this will be an earthquake in Portugal,' he claimed in October 2007.

'There is a massive, sophisticated network at play here – stretching from the government to the judiciary and the police. The network is enormous and extremely powerful. There are magistrates, ambassadors, police and politicians - all have procured children from Casa Pia. It is extremely difficult to break this down. These people cover for each other, because if one is arrested, they all are arrested. They don't want anyone to know.'

It was a scary and damning claim, but if anyone knew, it was Namora. He had watched for decades as his former orphanage friends sank into alcoholism, drug addiction and death brought on from their traumatic childhood experiences. 'I was the only one who made it. What could I do? I couldn't keep silent,' he told the *Daily Mail*, in an in-depth look at the similarities between the Casa Pia case and missing Maddie in 2007.

In the hard-hitting interview, he told journalist Vanessa Allen how he had received death threats for continuing in his attempts to blow open the country's child sex rings. He had even had warnings about his own children, after he had taken up fighting on behalf of the orphan Joel in the Casa Pia case. During one sinister phone call, a stranger firstly offered to pay off his mortgage if he backed down, and then threatened to kill his family if he didn't accept, and went on 'to list his children's schools, hobbies and pastimes'.

But by then, with the wide-reaching interest in missing Maddie, the global media was shining a spotlight on Portugal and there was nowhere to hide. Namora was leading the way, under the rallying cry that Portugal had done too little for too long to deal with its paedophile problem, which he believed was growing. He was right.

With the world's press now probing the country's lax laws and with an increasing army of foreign paedophiles arriving on its shores to prey on the high numbers of poor, abandoned children, authorities decided it was time to make a change at the top of the Maddie investigation. Growing tired of his insistence that the McCanns had killed their daughter without any evidence to back it up, Chief Inspector Goncalo Amaral was formally ordered to step down on October 2, 2007.

The excuse given was that he had told the newspaper *Diario de Noticias* that the British police had only pursued leads helpful to the McCanns. In another outburst he had told Portugal's ex-Formula One racing driver Pedro Lamy, that he was sure the McCanns had drugged their daughter and accidentally killed her. Anyone interested in his continued arguments (and there are millions of conspiracy theorists out there) could pick it up on the many TV chat shows he's appeared on and, of course, his best-selling book.

In the Autumn of 2007 the Maddie case was handed to the urbane, educated Paulo Rebelo, the methodical Lisbon detective who had previously led the complex Casa Pia inquiry. He was the right man for the job and he had quickly recruited his own men from Lisbon, bringing in child sex abuse experts and homicide specialists, as well as computer analysts, which he dubbed 'the cleaners' to ensure no stone was unturned. Rebelo also allegedly made an angry private attack on the 100 officers involved in the original inquiry, which he cut back to 40 specialists whom he trusted implicitly.

He swiftly launched Operation Predator, a series of coordinated raids on the homes of up to 100 suspected paedophiles based in the Algarve area, seizing their computers and any other suspicious items.

Although he made no obvious breakthroughs, sources told the Portuguese press, that he believed that 'Russian child traffickers' might be involved. He might turn out to be correct.

All that remained was for the wheels of justice to slowly turn on the dozens of evil pederasts, who had corrupted the country's state-run orphanage network for decades. When the judgment in the Casa Pia trial finally came round on September 3, 2010, a panel of three judges ruled on what was one of the longest-running cases in Portuguese history, lasting more than five years, with testimony from more than 800 witnesses and experts. Six of the ringleaders were handed average-length sentences, which some might argue were light.

The stiffest sentence went to driver Carlos Silvino, who got 18 years, while Carlos Cruz got seven years, Hugo Marcal, six years, Manuel Abrantes, five years and Jorge Ritto, six years and eight months.

For me the most shocking - and appaling - sentence went to the doctor Ferreira Diniz, who was handed a seven-year stretch. Diniz was a wealthy GP, who helped select the children – his favourites being deaf and non-verbal as they couldn't complain – who would be sold for sex at private villas and sex parties around Portugal. So clinical was his job, and so well-rehearsed, that he would check them for sexually transmitted diseases before helping his colleague Silvino to take them to the clients.

An ebullient, colourful character, he was often seen driving his red Ferrari to Casa Pia football matches, where he would single out boys. He was accused of abusing 18 children himself and during the initial stages of the trial, he reportedly refused to answer questions put to him by the prosecution citing patient-doctor confidentiality.

The story made global news and came as a major wake-up call for a society that had long been in denial about its sexual peccadilloes.

It was a fitting closure for one of the most alarming chapters in Portuguese history. But it didn't solve the mystery of Maddie.

Chapter 11

Searching the Border

While the Portuguese police turned their focus on the McCanns, I started looking into numerous leads in Spain. There were so many popping up, almost by the day … and that was just across the border, an hour or two away. By the end of 2016, police in the UK and Portugal had to sift through over 8,600 reported sightings of Maddie in over 100 countries, including Tasmania, Dubai and Canada.

Between 2007 and 2013, my newspaper *The Olive Press* looked at more than a dozen links to the case around Spain. We knew there was a strong probability she had been spirited away across the border on the night of her kidnap, or the following morning.

Gerry McCann has himself said he believes there is a 'very real possibility' his daughter was taken across the border, and it is a theme Kate took up in her book, while the pair even visited the border city of Huelva in August 2007 to campaign for help. This is, after all, one long straight coastline that simply continues into Spain. There are no great mountainous boundaries and it has been a mostly fluid border, hardly manned since the 1980s.

There are numerous crossing points between Portugal and Spain stretching from the southern tip at Vila Real de Santo Antonio to the northern Atlantic border at Seixas, near Galicia. Known as The Stripe (A Raia in Portuguese, La Raia in Spanish), it is, at 1,214km in length, the longest uninterrupted border in the European Union and since 1995, when both countries joined the Schengen Agreement, it has been entirely open. Border checks are rare, and, apart from the recent ones due to Covid, when the border was actually shut for a number of months, it was only manned during the 2004 UEFA Euros, the 2010 NATO summit in Lisbon and Pope Francis' visit to Fatima in 2017.

There are around a dozen main road crossings, a few river ferry crossings and even a zipline (a world first) between Sanlucar de Guadiana and Alcoutim. However, in 2020, when I investigated a feature on the separatist group Euskadi Ta Askatasuna (ETA) for the background to a feature on the BBC drama Killing Eve, I also discovered there were dozens more local tracks crossing the border

The main crossings are between Madrid and Lisbon at Vilar Formoso – Fuentes de Onoro, Caminha and Braganca in Galicia and, of course, Vila Real de San Antonio to Ayamonte. This is the busiest one for tourists, who move back and forth from the Algarve onto the Costa de la Luz and then the Costa del Sol, with Sevilla about half way.

This was an obvious place to find Maddie connections and we looked into at an expat British DJ called Christian Rideout, who had left Portugal a year after Maddie went missing and allegedly moved to Sevilla. Going by the name DJ Shifty, he had grown up near Praia da Luz, where he had been known to have made lewd comments to a number of young girls.

We then spent a few days looking at the evil Swiss paedophile Urs Hans von Aesch, who had killed himself after snatching and killing a toddler remarkably similar in appearance to Madeleine in July 2007. The 67 year old – who had sexually abused then murdered Ylenia Lenhard, 5 – had lived for two decades in the village of Benimantell, near Benidorm, and was believed to have been on holiday near Praia da Luz when Maddie went missing.

Usually driving a white van, police found diaries at his home written in English that catalogued his desires to snatch and rape young girls, as well as photos of girls in swimsuits. In the case of Ylenia, an autopsy revealed that he had knocked her out using a substance called toluene, a dissolvent used in paint. A white van with Spanish plates was reportedly seen parked up near the McCanns' apartment in Praia da Luz a few days before she went missing.

We also probed a gypsy kidnap gang, allegedly based out of Sevilla, that had tentacles across the border on the Algarve.

The likelihood that she was smuggled across the border gathered strength in 2012, when a Portuguese taxi driver came forward to say he had picked up four adults and a young girl, who looked like Maddie, from Monte Gordo, on the Algarve, and taken them to the border town of Vila Real de San Antonio, from where they had got into a blue Jeep. The driver, Antonio Castela, was certain it was May 4, 2007, just a day after Maddie went missing and a day before police finally closed the border.

That same year, in September 2012, we reported how a businessman had seen a girl he thought was Maddie on a flight from Germany to Ibiza. And he sent a photo to justify it. Our exclusive got followed up in 12 countries, which showed how much interest there still was in the story, five years on. While I was concerned that it was sensationalising the case a little, we were delighted when the McCann family spokesman Clarence Mitchell praised the sighting by German businessman Frank Bode. It later turned out the girl was merely a lookalike. And she most certainly was.

We also spent a fair deal of time looking into long-time suspect Raymond Hewlett, a British expat, who claimed on his deathbed that Maddie had been kidnapped to order by a gypsy gang 'for wealthy couples unable to have kids or adopt.' The convicted paedophile – who lived for many years in Andalucia, as well as on the Algarve – allegedly told his son about her fate by letter as he lay dying of throat cancer in hospital in Germany in 2010. His son Wayne told *The Sun*: 'He said he had had nothing to do with taking Maddie but did know who had. He said a very good gypsy friend he knew in Portugal had got drunk and "let it out" that he had stolen Maddie to order as part of a gang … . They took photos of children and sent them to the people they were acting for. And they said "Yes" or "No".

'Dad said the man told him it was nothing to do with snatching children for a paedophile gang or for a sexual reason. He said there were huge sums of money involved. And he totally believed what this man was saying.'

Nonsense. He was much more likely to have been involved himself: Hewlett, who was convicted of the rape of a 12-year-old girl after knocking her out using a rag soaked in paint thinner was known to be in the Praia da Luz area around the time of her disappearance (although a credit card allegedly showed him to be in Lisbon earlier in the day) and spent many years living between three Algarve towns, as well as across the border on the Costa de la Luz, in Cadiz, and Malaga's Costa del Sol.

The father of six, who had three convictions of child abduction in the UK, had travelled to Morocco 'on a business trip' from Faro port a month after Maddie went missing. He always claimed that while he was on the Algarve at the time Maddie went missing, he was 100km away in the border town of Vila Real de Santo Antonio. We will never know for sure: evil paedophile Hewlett would be used to covering his tracks and cannot be regarded as a reliable source.

Hewlett was definitely one of the most likely suspects and we had visited a series of campsites on the Costa del Sol and Costa de la Luz looking for him in 2009, but never got lucky.

Easily one of the most intriguing claims I followed up in Spain was the case of the nightclub bouncer from Angola, who said Maddie was snatched by a paedophile ring that eventually took her to the US. As unlikely as it may sound, Marcelino Jorge Italiano had worked as a security guard on the Algarve for years and was running for his life, he told me, having fled to Spain after attempting to blow the whistle on one of the most powerful paedophile networks there.

It was early February 2011 when we received a call from him, claiming he knew what had happened to Maddie. Our receptionist, Pauline, had taken the call and found him incredibly hard to understand and, in her opinion, half mad. While he was difficult to understand, speaking a mix of pidgin Spanish and English with a strange Portuguese accent, it was clear that he was not simply making it up. He sounded genuinely upset, and said he'd twice been beaten up for trying to investigate the toddler's plight.

He told me he had uncovered a huge dossier of information on the big paedophile network and that not only had he reported it to the Spanish National Police but he also had a lawyer, who was representing him in Spain. I immediately assumed he was after money, but he insisted he was not, saying he merely wanted to expose the 'evil gang' of businessmen, lawyers and police that he claimed had attacked him for confronting them. Above all, he wanted to get his information to the McCann family.

I arranged to drive down and see him the following day in Huelva, where he was living, to hear one of the darkest, most revealing stories about the Algarve's dark seedy underbelly. He named names, which made it highly libellous, so I knew I would have to check the claims… although at least he was also making them to the police.

Marcelino Jorge Italiano – a 6ft 4in giant of a man, who played semi-professional basketball for the local Huelva team – bowled up at the cafe wearing a charcoal suit and smart blue tie, carrying a big leather briefcase, brimming with paperwork. Engaging and organised, the first thing he did after shaking my hand was grin and show me the big gap in his smile where he claimed he had lost a tooth to a beating from the gang that was behind the abduction of Maddie.

He spared no details as he laid out the information he had picked up and the things he had seen while working as a doorman and bouncer on the Algarve. He told me the gang was based around a Faro nightclub owner and two other businessmen who had connections to the Casa Pia orphanage network in Portugal. He said they were well connected to the Portuguese judiciary and police, and they also had high-level legal connections in London. Most alarming of all, he claimed the gang might have snatched as many as a dozen children around Portugal – a good number via Angola – and they were still functioning to that day.

'They prey on the weak and vulnerable,' he said. 'They are ruthless. I have been attacked twice for trying to investigate it. I know these people were involved in the snatching of Madeleine and I have been told that Madeleine may now be in America.'

They were remarkable claims, which I thought were outlandish at first. But he was adamant that he had proof, which he had handed over to the National Police in Huelva with his lawyer the previous week. Although concerned about saying too much, as he was 'genuinely worried' for his safety AND for mine, he did eventually give me the names of the two prominent Portuguese businessmen he said were behind the gang. He added that 'the police now know everything' and have their names, plus half a dozen of their colleagues. He said he had even provided police with photographs of them at a birthday party in the Algarve that he had attended. He added that much of his information had been verified by an ex-wife of one of the businessmen and he had documents on their movements that were particularly damning.

After speaking to him for a couple of hours, I asked if I could meet his lawyer, who was duly called. An hour later we met for a coffee near her office. She looked a bit brow-beaten, but told me she believed Marcelino was credible and that she had sat with him as he detailed his claims to the police. The National Police had told her they would be sending the information to their Portuguese counterparts in the following days, and would be keeping her informed. I asked why they wouldn't have been better off passing this over to London and she said because the police force responsible for the Madeleine case and other sex crimes on the Algarve was the PJ. I feared the worse.

I knew I had a dynamite story and I had to let the McCanns know, but at this stage, in early 2011, Operation Grange had yet to be launched, and the

UK only had a skeleton staff looking into the case. It was mostly being handled by the family's own team led by Dave Edgar, and they were struggling to keep on top of the huge number of leads that needed to be followed up.

When I called the McCanns' spokesman Clarence Mitchell in London, I wasn't really sure what to expect, but he was remarkably receptive to the information. Always friendly and approachable, I had known him since the early days of the case and he was helpful and quick in getting an answer from the McCanns on such matters. This time, he was even more forthcoming and told me he had already heard of one of the ringleaders, as well as various potential links to the Casa Pia case. I told him I would be seeking to publish the story in *the Olive Press* the following week and he said he would run it past the rest of the team and Gerry and Kate.

The next day he called back and said: 'We are taking this seriously and see it as extremely credible. We are actually aware of one of the names you mentioned and are already investigating the claims. We actually plan to come over and talk to Marcelino over the next week or two. The claims about links to the Casa Pia case are intriguing and you definitely wouldn't want to discount them. We have heard other claims that Maddie might have been taken to America. Gerry and Kate are grateful for the information and hope it leads somewhere.'

Having got the usual 'no comment' from the Spanish police, we ran the story on the front page the following week, and it was picked up by *The Sun*, who also put it on their front page the following day. 'Maddie is in US ... I know who took her' screamed the headline, describing Marcelino as both 'an investigator' and 'amateur sleuth' for some reason and printing his picture alongside Maddie's. Ominously I have been unable to track him down again and wonder where he may be currently living… or did he continue digging and eventually put himself in a shallow grave?

The following year, in 2012, the hunt for Maddie heated up again when we received a tip off that a 'groggy' blonde girl had been seen with a German family at Marbella's Cabopino campsite on May 6 in 2007, three days after Maddie went missing. It was particularly suspicious that the family had booked their van in under a number plate that was obsolete from Germany in 1974, and had paid a supplement for 'an extra child'. The 'girl had seemed completely out of it,' fellow camper Karen Sissons had told us, adding that the family seemed odd.

We went straight down to investigate and, not for the first time, I genuinely believed we might have been close to solving the mystery. It emerged that Karen had reported the sighting to police forces in three countries at the time and, after stressing the huge public interest in the case, we managed to persuade the campsite to give us the name of the family. We passed it on to German newspaper *Bild,* who were able to track down the family, a Swiss family called Mayer, living in Bern. The father, Karsten, confirmed that yes, they had stayed there at the time, yes, they did have a similar-looking daughter and a similar age to Maddie, and yes, she was tired and withdrawn at the time. But crucially, it wasn't Maddie.

It was so disappointing, and I was perhaps more deflated with this news than I had been on any other lead I have followed up over the last decade and a half. But such is life in journalism. You just keep following the leads and one day, well one day ...

Either way, by 2012 when Operation Grange was launched in the UK, the story very much had a life of its own again. It had legs, as the Fleet Street adage goes. And the sightings of Maddie in 2012 were spreading like wildfire along the Costa del Sol, into the inland Guadalhorce Valley and then east along the Axarquia coastline, between Malaga and Granada.

In the summer of 2012 we had at least 10 different readers come forward to say they believed they had seen Maddie. One, Yvonne Tunnicliffe, claimed she was '100% certain' she had seen her in 2009 being dragged around a supermarket in Alhaurin el Grande by a 'gypsy man speaking Portuguese'. We found it, but alas, the shop's CCTV had long been erased.

Then expat Rose Johnson was convinced she had seen Maddie at an isolated beach restaurant, Merendero, near Torrox, east of Malaga. The former cleaner, who had lived in Spain for a decade, said the blonde, blue-eyed girl, then around eight, was acting strangely and was clearly distant from the dark-haired family she was sitting with. As they left, Rose noticed the family getting into a people carrier on Portuguese plates. She had reported the sighting to the police, who confirmed to us that they had followed it up via their specialist and violent crimes unit UDEV. But nothing.

The following year, another British expat said he was sure he had seen Maddie the same summer in nearby Nerja.

We had received so many calls and emails on the hunt east of Malaga that I dispatched two journalists, Eloise Horsfield and Wendy Williams, to look into the various sightings over a weekend. To this day we have never managed to rule out the frequent alleged sightings of Madeleine in the areas known as the Costa Tropical and the Axarquia. And it should be pointed out that both areas have a good proportion of new age travellers and both areas border on the Alpujarras region of Granada, where, as I shall explain, Christian Brueckner spent a considerable amount of time.

•••

Such was the excitement during this frenetic hunt in 2012 that inevitably mistakes were made. One of these was an alleged sighting of Maddie around the Axarquia. A reader had called us to say that while he was having lunch the previous weekend a blonde girl had come over and hung around their table in a restaurant and claimed her name was 'Maddie' and 'acted mysteriously'. When Wendy Williams explored further she discovered a blonde-haired blue-eyed girl who happened to be the daughter of an expat British couple, and their home was called 'Casa Madeleine'.

It was clear by now that this was not THE missing Maddie, but Wendy knocked on the door anyway and was invited in for a chat with the girl's father, which she understandably perceived to be an interview. He was an *Olive Press* reader, it turned out, and it had been a good-humoured chat.

As she left she was invited to take a picture of the house, but not one of the daughter, who had an uncanny resemblance to Maddie and would have been about the same age.

We ended up running what we thought was a light-hearted story on our wild goose chase by mentioning her lookalike as a short teaser to a bigger feature on International Missing Persons Day that month. Under the headline 'Maddie? Yes, but not the right one', we ran the story with two pictures, one of the village in which they lived and one of the name of the house, which inadvertently also gave the house number.

The girl's mother, who had not been at the interview, was not happy. She phoned the paper demanding a retraction and apology, which perhaps we didn't deal with quickly enough or seriously enough. Soon her partner joined the furore and a long letter arrived complaining that strange people had started stopping outside their house to take pictures and they were worried about their daughter being snatched. They even made reference to a dangerous paedophile who had the previous year snatched a child in the nearby town of Velez Malaga.

While Wendy and I apologised profusely (and I remember exactly when and where I parked up near Guadix to take a long, heated call from the mother) we certainly didn't expect to receive a legal letter from the Federation of Association of Journalists of Spain (FAPE), the Spanish equivalent of the Press Complaints Commission.

Indeed we didn't actually receive one, but FAPE had supposedly sent one to our office outside Ronda, which being in the countryside opposite my home was infamously erratic for receiving post. Incredibly, FAPE hadn't felt the need to send another letter, or indeed call or send an email. But the following year we discovered we had been sanctioned by the organisation and rapped over the wrist on two counts of the country's press code. One, that we hadn't gone far enough to protect the identity of a minor, despite not giving her name, or picturing her; nor had we given the family the correct 'right to reply', which of course made no sense whatsoever.

I thought that by letting a journalist with a notebook, tape recorder and camera into his home, the father was more than tacitly giving permission to be quoted. But what really grated was FAPE's inability to get our side of the story. For an association that supposedly represents the morals and values of a country, I still find that baffling.

Our complaints and a demand to add our right to reply fell on deaf ears. It felt like a kangaroo court. Wendy blamed herself and felt the family in question were hounding her. She had been one of our best reporters and it was sad to see her lose her confidence, and it was certainly one of the contributory factors of her moving to live in Australia the following spring.

If nothing more it summed up the deep emotions that the Maddie case brought up in so many people and just how far reaching it was.

Chapter 12

The Yellow Brick Road

It was perhaps inevitable that the conspiracy theorists and paedophile supporters would unite and attack my work, as they have the McCann family and those surrounding them so often over the last 14 years. McCann spokesman Clarence Mitchell told me he described the creative and imaginative things made up about him and his clients as 'the yellow brick road', as it was fantastical and never ending. While *The Olive Press* has come under frequent criticism due to our reporting on the case, I was shocked to discover that I had personally become a subject of considerable vilification at some point in the middle of 2008.

It started after I penned the article blaming a paedophile, and not the family, for Maddie's disappearance on the first anniversary in May 2008. Because I believed the McCanns were entirely innocent, my reporting was picked apart and discredited in a number of sinister and creepy blogs, in particular, the Jill Havern forum, run by a shady collection of individuals, with connections to Spain, I later discovered.

One long post on this forum, spearheaded by a retired senior British policeman, who was living in my very own town of Ronda, has the heading: '*Disgraced Olive Press editor, Jon Clarke, and his THIRD version of the same story*'. In it, this former Nottinghamshire detective – or one of his aliases or colleagues – suggested, among other things, that I worked for the McCann family directly, or possibly MI5, and that I might have been involved in snatching Maddie.

As well as claiming I was on first name terms with the local GNR police officers in Praia da Luz, he (or one of his colleagues) Photoshopped an image of me (labelled 'JC') running away from the Ocean Club with a toddler in my arms. This same former detective, who works alongside Jill Havern (a controversial blogger by night and driving instructor by day), has also dedicated no less than four chapters of his book about me. *Called What Really Happened to Madeleine McCann?*, one entire chapter, '*Jon Clarke, Entrenched Lies*', is based on the fact that I might have got the name of a street wrong when I reported that I found a road crew digging a trench the morning after Maddie went missing. Another chapter (which can also be found on his blog) is '*Clarke, Lies and Videotape*', while two more are '*Fake News*' and '*On Lies and Conspiracies*'.

This man – a former career detective of three decades long – has published well over 10,000 words on my movements in Praia da Luz and Spain, which, in my mind, paints him as a creepy stalker with a warped obsession with me. While mostly well written (to give him his dues), the main problem is that in all his outlandish claims, he has continually published pictures of the WRONG man.

It would be boring to write more than a chapter on this man and his gang of trolls, but I think it is vital that I name him and that readers can make their own minds up about why people like him exist and what is the best way to deal with them. He is Peter MacLeod, who served with Nottinghamshire Police for 28 years, before becoming chief inspector and then temporary superintendent at West Bridgford Police Station. Why he left in the 1990s is open to conjecture and it would be unfair to print any of the gossip from the local expat scene in Ronda, or where he lives now, east of Malaga.

There is almost nothing about him online and the only story outside of his links to the Maddie case (and there are quite a few) is of him teaching a group of children to row an ancient Greek ship called a trireme, off the island of Poros, in Greece, in 1987. What is easy to find are his regular posts criticising the McCanns and anyone who might dare to support the couple online.

Using the initials 'PM' or 'P Mac' (or when he is feeling more brazen 'PeterMac'), he started slamming into me in May 2008 claiming that I might have been in Praia da Luz BEFORE Maddie was snatched, hinting I might be involved in a huge cover up, being orchestrated by MI5 or MI6, with my own 'personal handler' (or controller).

It happened to many other reporters too, including Lori Campbell, who is described as the 'world's worst journalist' on the Jill Havern Forum, and Sky News crime reporter Martin Brunt, who it was claimed also worked with the secret services and had made so much money from the McCanns that he had bought a villa in Luz. 'They've thrown everything at me. Every accusation you can think of,' Martin told me. 'It is alarming and depressing.'

In my case, everything I had ever written or done came under the spotlight. There were hundreds of posts about me and my newspaper, as well as, unfairly, some of my staff. And the fact that even today, over a decade later, these articles still pop up on Google when you search for anything about me or *the Olive Press*, concerns me greatly. Worse, they menacingly nudge people towards where I live, with my family, and the implication is simple: stop reporting or run the risk of something happening to you, or them.

Here is an excerpt, which illustrates what evil, vitriolic minds are behind this filth. There are many sections far more personal and sinister, but this passage sums up their point:

'Clarke was highly paid for what he did, and is clearly still paid for it. An audit trail might lead back to his handler and ultimately to whoever is coordinating the campaign, and they might not be willing to be exposed by a 'maverick' suddenly breaking ranks and going 'rogue'. Given that some deaths are already associated

with this case, he might feel he is in physical danger … and no one would blame him for not wishing to join the late Dr Kelly or Brenda Leyland [a Maddie Twitter troll who killed herself after being exposed by Sky News].

That does not condone his continuing mendacity, his serial invention of new versions, new stories, new sightings, nor stop us condemning him for having done it in the first place.

But given that his personal reputation has been destroyed … perhaps he should do something … . He is trapped. In the same way that the McCanns are trapped by forced and jemmied shutters, which weren't. In the same way Kate McCann is trapped by curtains wide open, and curtains tight closed.

Can we feel sympathy? Towards the McCanns for the death of their eldest child – undoubtedly. But for little else.

To Clarke in his present predicament, if he refuses to correct, apologise and explain? More difficult.

To Jon – to Kate and Gerry – to the Tapas friends – It is never too late to do the right thing.'

Initially, I couldn't work out who this 'PM' was but then this same PM sent me an email out of the blue criticising my continuing coverage of the case and informing me that he too had recently been to Praia da Luz to investigate the case and that he was involved in a strong, factual book, which 'definitively' showed the parents were to blame.

Bang! It was a horrible sudden realisation that my critic was Peter MacLeod, better known locally as 'Peter Plod', who had actually been in my home, had met my wife and kids and with whom I had even been skiing in the Sierra Nevada, near Granada! He ran a guesthouse with his then-partner Claire on the outskirts of Ronda and we had some mutual friends and acquaintances.

I immediately phoned him for an explanation for his ridiculous attack online. I felt so angry and somewhat betrayed. 'The point is Jon, you've got it completely wrong,' he insisted, in his matter-of-fact, holier-than-thou tone. 'Paedophiles do not snatch children like that. It is so, so rare.'

'But did you need to be so critical of me as a reporter and put it all over the internet?' I demanded, asking if it was fair when *The Olive Press* had exposed so many crooks around Andalucia. This had been one of the paper's key thrusts since launching, and over the years we have had a hand in the arrest of no less than three of *Crimestoppers Most Wanted* criminals – two almost single-handedly. Surely being an ex-copper he would appreciate that?

He agreed that, yes, perhaps the posts were a little over-critical and maybe they needed to be toned down and he promised to do something about it.

But in response, he merely corrected some parts of them and by way of explanation sent a sinister letter to my wife and I, written in the form of a tabloid newspaper story about a local newspaper editor whose children get kidnapped. It was way too much to bear and I got straight in my car to speak to him at his hotel.

It was an angry confrontation in front of Claire – who has since left him

– as well as a couple of guests. When I'd finally calmed down, he invited me into his office for a beer, where I could see that he had become fixated on the case. There were dozens of dossiers and folders on Maddie as well as huge piles of pamphlets and brochures, which I had read about and were libellous of the McCanns.

He said he had struck up a close 'alliance' with the main author, lawyer Tony Bennett, a Eurosceptic who worked for UKIP, and that he had helped him with the brochure called *What Really Happened to Madeleine? 60 Reasons Which Suggest She Was Not Abducted.*

Described as 'sickos' and 'stalkers' in the British press, Bennett – who with the support of MacLeod and Havern presumably– had even distributed the pamphlets around Rothley, Leicestershire, where Maddie's parents live. In her book, Kate McCann said this 'grieved me more than I would have expected' fearing that any unpleasant gossip 'might poison the atmosphere at the twins' new school.' The McCanns were forced to take legal action, and Bennett was ordered not to repeat his allegations and pay the court £400. It made little difference and the group continued 'insinuating' she and Gerry were involved merely being a bit more careful about what they wrote. Bennett was later given a three-month suspended jail sentence for breaching a court order banning him from publishing material linking the McCanns with their daughter's disappearance.

I still have a copy of one pamphlet MacLeod gave me that day, *The Madeleine McCann Case Files* with a foreword from Tony Bennett, no less, which he sells for £3 in the UK and £5 elsewhere. MacLeod publishes parts of it online – supposedly as a *'FREE e-book by PeterMac'* – and I'm pretty certain he and Bennett made a fair bit of money from it and any related pursuits.

It is strange that MacLeod has dedicated so many years to this case, continuing to insist that the McCanns are involved. Even in March 2019 he appeared on an Australian podcast - one that did extremely well for the popular network - to once again claim that Maddie had not been snatched. It made headlines and a friend of the McCanns told *The Sun*: 'Spurious allegations discussing what might have and might not have happened that night have been made umpteen times. Anybody can do a podcast … and one spouting off about what they did and subsequently said is something quite frankly they will ignore. What would he know?'

Exactly… and one might turn the tables and ask who is MacLeod's 'handler'? And how much is he getting paid?

•••

There is one intriguing postscript to Peter MacLeod, which is very close to home for me. My wife told me about it as I was writing this chapter in early 2021 and it nearly took my breath away.

It concerned a visit MacLeod had made to our farmhouse when we had briefly separated for a few months a couple of years ago. She wasn't in, but a friend of hers who was staying opened the door to this rather unusual man, now in his early seventies. Apologising for turning up unannounced, he said it was just a casual, friendly visit and he would pop back another day and handed her his business card and two bags of chocolate coins 'for the kids'.

It was the first contact my wife had received from him since the letter he had sent her describing the abduction of our children in the mock-up newspaper story many years earlier. She didn't get back to him and never saw him again, but to this day, finds the visit strange and unnerving.

Chapter 13

'Is That You, Daddy?'

In the summer of 2016, I got a totally different call out of the blue from a researcher for a TV production company in London. His name was Rory and he said his company, Pulse Films, was developing a documentary on Maddie and it would be the 'most comprehensive' film ever made on the case. It was all fairly mysterious and he didn't want to tell me much more on the phone. He said he had read a couple of my articles on the case and had seen my byline had appeared from the very beginning. Would I be interested in being interviewed and potentially helping more? We had just launched a new paper in Gibraltar and were looking at launching a new edition that autumn in Mallorca so I was fairly noncommittal. I was plenty busy enough.

A couple of months later he called again and said he was planning a trip to Malaga with his boss Caroline Marsden, who had been a producer on *Panorama* and before that *Dispatches*, two highly respected current affair programmes on British TV. I agreed to meet them for lunch, when Rory told me that the top-secret production was being made for Netflix and it was scheduled to be a series. It was not the usual fly-by-night shoestring doc (I later learned that it was said to have been the most expensive documentary series ever made, costing over £1 million per episode, more expensive than the *BBC's Planet Earth.*) It was a detailed relook at the case and they were setting up interviews with dozens of people. He said they would be filming for 'at least a couple of months' all over Spain and Portugal, as well as Morocco. He said they might need me to come with them.

I could tell that Rory was holding back most of what he knew, which gave me the sense that perhaps they held some bombshell information. I told them I would be happy to help, figuring that any information I gave them might just end up being a key part of the jigsaw. I had no idea where it might lead. I signed a non-disclosure agreement (NDA) which meant I was sworn to secrecy.

It wasn't until October 2017 that they finally bowled up in Malaga with two camera crews and a new employee Carl Hindmarch, an esteemed director and producer. It was one of the strangest experiences I have had as a journalist as they filmed me from the first hour they met me in the morning until the minute we arrived in Praia da Luz the following day. It was exhausting to be fielding questions for hours on end and I was caught off guard by how emotional it felt to be back at the Ocean Club after five or six years. I actually had to hold back tears after recalling the first press conference from the Mc-Canns when it became clear their daughter had been snatched. By now, my daughter Maria was almost a teenager, and I couldn't imagine not having been able to see her grow up.

I acted as a de-facto tour guide, showing the film crew a variety of key locations. I took them through the Murat episode – where he lived and why we had suspected him – and ended up making an impromptu apology to him for effectively ruining his life. The visit to Praia da Luz brought back so many difficult memories that I was delighted to be able to finally leave a few days later.

By the spring of 2018, it had all gone quiet. Eventually Rory told me that while filming had gone well, they were having issues with the family not wanting to appear. I heard nothing more until early 2019 when a story appeared in one of the British tabloids that the Netflix team had fallen out with the McCanns. It was sketchy on facts, but it was clear that neither Kate nor Gerry would be involved in the documentary.

Worse, in early March that year, the McCanns released a statement to say the documentary could 'potentially hinder' the search for Maddie. I wondered what the filmmakers might have found. Would there be anything groundbreaking? Would it solve the crime of the century?

A couple of days before it was broadcast, on March 15, 2019, Netflix's American press office rang me to ask if I would be happy to give any press interviews. I agreed, but insisted in return I should be allowed to run something on our website about the documentary and *The Olive Press*' involvement in it. It was agreed and they gave me some key details of the documentary but, typically, on the day we had written the story (which was scheduled to go out at midnight) there was a last-minute legal hitch and Netflix put the release back by a day.

It was too late to suspend the story, so I awoke to a series of angry messages. By 8.30am the story was suspended and set to run again that night. But we were threatened with legal action and the NDA I had signed was sent over, as if I needed reminding.

But by now, the cat was out of the bag. The whole world knew what was coming, and it was followed up by all the newspapers in Britain and many around the world. I felt uncomfortable initially, but in many ways it was the perfect pre-release publicity and everyone was talking about what would be in the eight-part documentary, *The Disappearance of Madeleine McCann*. When it finally dropped the next day, it turned out to be a comprehensive, taut and detailed look at arguably the world's biggest missing person mystery. Watched by more than 20 million people in the first month alone, it was that year's most-viewed Netflix documentary in the UK and Ireland. It is fair to say it was something of a hit, even if its reviews were generally lukewarm. I realised how much the case meant to the British public when I was persistently badgered by people who had seen the documentary and wanted to know what I 'really thought' had happened to Maddie.

While the documentary didn't have a knockout punch, it did raise a number of key issues surrounding the case. Largely that the police had been totally inept, the family were almost certainly innocent and that southern Portugal was awash with weirdos back in 2007. The only defining conclusion was that a paedophile network was almost certainly behind Maddie's disappearance.

It revealed the huge number of strange people hanging around the Ocean Club resort in the weeks leading up to May 2007. They included the 'ugly' pock-marked German, who spoke English, the unusual foreign pair speaking in hushed tones on the balcony below, two mystery blond men hanging around outside and the strange group collecting for an orphanage that did not exist. Then there was the 'creep' with the surgical mask and the attack on a holidaying British family in Praia da Luz, which actually happened a good deal more often than was let on at the time.

Heavily suppressed by the authorities and, in particular, the tourist industry, there is also a suggestion that the police far too often turned a blind eye to sex attacks on tourists. The information we now know about the Algarve back then would have been enough for many families to have cancelled their holiday in 2007. The coast was simply awash with depravity.

We know that following Maddie's disappearance, two British detectives, Graham Hill and Joe Sullivan, from the UK's crack child abuse department CEOPS were flown over to give their expertise and look, in particular, at an army of British paedophiles who were in the area at the time. By the end of 2007, they had helped Portuguese police eliminate at least 52 potential British suspects from the case, while the German, Dutch and other forces helped to eliminate many more.

Some of the most frightening, who could have also been around at the time, include British cousins Charles O'Neill and William Lauchlan who committed multiple offences, and are today serving life sentences for the murder of a woman, Allison McGarrigle, who was threatening to expose them. Known as the 'dirty rats', they had been living near Benidorm, on the Costa Blanca of Spain in 2003 and 2004, before flying to the Canary Islands in 2007 and were known to have visited Portugal on various occasions. Convicted of the abuse of six children in the UK and one in Benidorm, the depraved cousins who were in a sexual relationship together, masqueraded as window cleaners to enter homes and scout around for potential victims.

There was also David Reid from Northern Ireland, who was living in the small resort of Carvoeiro, just 37km from Praia da Luz in May 2007. The convicted paedophile, who had spent three years in jail for molesting his four daughters, had been working as an entertainer at the bars up and down the coast and was known to have visited Praia da Luz. He died in his early sixties in 2013, having repeatedly denied that he was behind Maddie's disappearance.

Critically, what is also now known is that there were AT LEAST 30 sex attacks on children in a 65km radius around Praia da Luz, in the two years leading up to May 2007. Nine British families alone told detectives at Operation Grange how their children had been molested by an intruder between 2004 and 2007. And Andy Redwood, who was leading the British operation at the time, said that 18 break-ins involving British children had been reported to them between 2004 and 2010. And these were just those reported. Of these, three had taken place in Praia da Luz, while 14 had taken place nearby, between Carvoeiro and Albufeira.

The number of attacks now known to have taken place on British children was a key thrust of the Netflix documentary. And two scenes that stick in my mind are the ones involving a 'creepy' charity collector and the oddball who crept into the bed of two young British girls. Both are documented in Summers and Swan's excellent book Looking for Madeleine, with the 'unkempt and scruffy' charity collector's visit taking place in Praia da Luz, between April 20 and May 3, just before Maddie went missing. It made for great TV.

It happened when the man had turned up at a woman's front door soliciting for a donation and spotted her 3-year-old daughter playing on the floor of her home. She had sensed his interest was unnatural, but when she saw the man hanging around in her street for much of the day it made her uneasy. The next day, at home, she came downstairs and found him standing next to her daughter in the front room, having let himself in. He fled when he saw her arrive. 'She thought he had got in through the sliding patio doors and believed – even then – that he had meant to take her daughter,' the book reported.

What is particularly intriguing is that he was part of a group of so-called charity collectors (up to four or five in total) which had been reported to police on no less than six separate occasions in the weeks running up to May 3. Going door to door, either alone or in pairs, they had been supposedly collecting for a 'nearby orphanage', although to this day nobody has been able to name the institution … and there is no orphanage in the nearby area. As we shall find out, there was however, a shady charity/institute that housed German orphans for years at a time.

The second harrowing scene took place in 2004, when a British family revealed that an intruder had sneaked into their villa in the middle of the night and got into the bedroom of their two sleeping daughters, aged eleven and eight. When the foreign-sounding man got into bed with the younger girl, she said, 'Is that you, Daddy?' and he replied 'yes'. Knowing it was not her father, she then asked, 'Is that you, Uncle?', as he was also staying with them. At this point the older girl woke up and saw the intruder lying in bed with her sister, 'wearing a surgical mask'.

Having seen the older child stir, he got up and tiptoed into the kitchen and then slowly let himself out of the glass patio door, through which he had got in.

The parents reported it the next day and the police said they believed it was very likely the same man who the family had spotted tampering with their patio doors on a previous day and that, while he was in the house, he had apparently wrapped some of their laundry around his shoes, potentially to avoid leaving footprints, as well as to move more quietly.

Of course, very little was done, with the break in brushed under the carpet, as were almost all other attacks at the time. As Kate McCann wrote in her book, she had read of five cases of British children being sexually abused on holiday while their parents slept in another room, all within an hour's drive of Praia da Luz, yet the PJ 'never mentioned any of them to us. In fact, some of them hadn't even been recorded by the authorities at the time they were reported.' DNA and fingerprint evidence was often not sought, and 'they might never have been brought to light if the parents hadn't been brave enough to come forward to the British police in the UK after Madeleine was taken.'

It was good to see the documentary conclude on a strong message about the huge and growing amount of child abuse online, the need for more money to be spent in policing child sex abuse and for countries to work harder together. What the viewers didn't know was that a couple of scenes from the film had led to important calls being made to both the British and German police. And two of these, as we shall find out, may lead to the cracking of the case.

In May 2019, it emerged that Portuguese police were actually hunting the oddball who wore the surgical mask, while British police were also allegedly looking for a mysterious 'woman in purple' seen outside the Ocean Club, who now allegedly lives in Bulgaria. In June 2019 there were new 'significant investigative avenues', according to Scotland Yard, and a source told *The Times* there was one 'critical line of inquiry' and a new 'person of significance' had been thrown into the ring.

The press then reported that it was a German paedophile who was being looked at, and speculation grew that this was 48-year-old Martin Ney, who had abducted and murdered three children, sexually abused dozens more, and was currently in prison. He was said to have been working on a project for the homeless with an evangelical church in Portugal at the time of Maddie's disappearance ... and certainly fitted the appearance of an e-fit issued of a man seen near the apartment in May 2007.

By the end of the summer this had fizzled out with police releasing no new information. The Ney connection seemed all but buried, when, in November 2019, Goncalo Amaral, spoke out in a Spanish TV documentary insisting that he was not the man being probed.

'It's true a German paedophile serving life for killing children has been spoken about,' he said. 'But the suspect is not him. It's another man. He's also in prison in Germany. He's also a paedophile.'

He may have been disgraced and off the case for well over a decade, but he still had some very good police contacts. Someone high up was keeping him in the loop. You had to wonder who, and why.

PART TWO 2020-2021

Chapter 14

Major New Suspect

It was the afternoon of June 3, 2020, in the midst of the global Covid crisis, with Spain having just been through the most draconian lockdown in Europe when I saw it on the BBC website. At first it appeared to be coming from Scotland Yard, but it was quickly apparent that the announcement of the new 'key suspect' had been released by German police. Moreover, an appeal was set to go out on German television at 7.15pm that evening, centred around a sex offender who had been living in Praia da Luz at the time of Maddie's disappearance.

Christian Hoppe, of Germany's BKA federal police, revealed that the man had two previous convictions for 'sexual contact with girls' and that he was currently in prison in Germany. 'We have evidence against the accused which leads us to believe that he really killed Madeleine but this evidence is not strong enough at the moment to take him to court,' said Hoppe. He reiterated however that the evidence was 'strong enough to say that the girl is dead'. My stomach churned.

'One has to be honest and remain open to the possibility that our investigation could end without a charge, that it ends like the others have,' he added. 'But we are optimistic it will be different for us but for that we need more information.' He said they were appealing for information about two vehicles owned by the man, who was now 43. One was a VW campervan, the other a Jaguar, which, as I will explain later, was suspiciously transferred to someone else's name the day after Maddie vanished. There were photos issued of both vehicles, the van appropriately pictured on an Algarve beach. For the record, the VW was a T3 Westfalia, an early 1980s model with white upper body and yellow skirting on Portuguese plates; the Jaguar was a dark 1993 sedan model registered in Germany.

The announcement came almost a year after Operation Grange was awarded another £300,000 of government funding, and Portuguese police announced that they were concentrating efforts on a foreign paedophile, who had been living in the area. It soon emerged from Scotland Yard that the unnamed man had been on Operation Grange's potential suspect list of 600 people, which had been created in 2013. 'Someone out there knows a lot more than they're letting on,' said Detective Chief Inspector (DCI) Mark

Cranwell, who was leading the Metropolitan Police inquiry.

What was particularly interesting was the difference in opinion of the two forces, with the Germans insisting it was a murder inquiry, while the Met continuing to describe it as a missing persons investigation, as there was no 'concrete evidence' of her death.

The new German appeal added that the man lived a 'transient lifestyle' and was living in his van for 'days on end' between 1995 and 2007. Crucially, police said he was staying in the Praia de Luz area at the time and even received a 30-minute phone call close to the Ocean Club at 7.32pm. As well as releasing his number (Portuguese mobile +351 912 730 680), they also published the number of the person who dialled him from outside the area (another Portuguese mobile +351 916 510 683). They said any information on either of these numbers or these people could be 'critical' to the inquiry.

In particular, they wanted the person who had made the call to come forward and be interviewed. 'They're a key witness and we urge them to get in touch,' said DCI Cranwell. 'Some people will know the man we're describing today,' he added, appealing to the public. 'You may be aware of some of the things he's done. He may have confided in you about the disappearance of Madeleine. More than 13 years have passed and your loyalties may have changed. Now is the time to come forward.'

It felt like a significant development and a massive breakthrough.

The McCanns were quick to back the appeal and were clearly not pouring any cold water on it. I had to get back to the Algarve.

•••

I had two problems. One, my passport was being renewed in the UK, and was already a month delayed due to the crisis, and two, the border with Portugal had been shut for the first time in nearly 50 years.

As I had discovered on a recent trip to Salamanca on a story for *The Mail on Sunday*, every crossing, even the various single track lanes, had been blocked with huge concrete barriers. To prevent the perceived threat of Covid from Spain, the Portuguese authorities were only allowing emergency vehicles and lorries to cross. Travel was strictly prohibited.

While I still carried a Newspaper Society press pass from *The Mail on Sunday*, I knew I would have to get something more official. Luckily James Mellor, the news editor there, was keen to help. I told him I wanted to leave the next morning, with *Olive Press* digital editor Laurence Dollimore as photographer and an extra pair of hands. It proved to be highly fortuitous in more ways than one.

The next day, Thursday, armed with official letters of introduction from *the Mail on Sunday*, and classed as a 'key worker' for the first time in my life, we embarked on what was easily the most surreal journey I had taken around the Iberian Peninsula in 20 years of living there. We crossed the imposing, futuristic Puente Internacional del Guadiana, which spanned the Guadiana River, around lunchtime and arrived at a police checkpoint completely alone. We'd hardly seen more than a dozen cars on the final 130km stretch from Sevilla and only one of four petrol stations we had stopped at had been open. The Iberian Peninsula was under total lockdown, after all, and 99% of people were stuck in their homes.

At the border – where I had never been stopped on more than 100 trips – I found myself facing a grilling from two officers from the PJ and two from their counterparts at the GNR. And they meant business. After being ushered into an impromptu layby, we were told to get out and take our passports and 'permission to travel' to a tent, where their boss was waiting to grill us further. It made no difference that we were journalists; they needed to see a letter explaining our reasons for crossing the border and, most importantly, our passports – mine, I didn't have – and driving licences.

My heart was thumping as I showed him a photocopy of my old passport and an email from the British Government explaining the delay. He told me that I definitely could not cross. With no option, I resorted to pleading and, eventually, he agreed to ask one of his men to make 'a phone call to Lisbon' for 'special permission' before pointing out that one of my car's wheels was resting against a big metal tent peg hammered into the motorway. I told him his men had guided us there before I tried to reverse without slashing the tyre. Too late. With an almighty pop, the front right tyre deflated in seconds.

Worse, we had no spare, such are cars these days, and the magic repair kit that was almost impossible to understand quite simply did not work, not even when two policemen helped us. We were stuffed and in total limbo, unable to go forward and impossible to go back, as my Spanish recovery service was refusing to come and get us, as we were 100m across the border.

And so began a two-hour shuttle of phone calls between us, our office and two different pickup trucks, which arrived as if by magic at the exact same time, one from Portugal and one from Spain. Both men joined the tug of war to decide who should take us to a tyre garage for repairs, each vying for their side of the border. But the decision was out of our hands as our insurers eventually ruled that the car needed to be taken to the nearest BMW garage in Spain, some 30km back the way we had come.

Fortunately, the phone call to Lisbon had worked; they had checked my credentials and as I had no arrest warrants and had been back and forth across the border for work, I was given the green light to carry on. Mindful that the chance of us arriving in Praia da Luz by the end of the week was reducing, we begged the Portuguese pickup driver to take us to the nearest town on his side of the border so we could try and hire a car. I agreed to pay him 20 euros to take us to Castro Marim, where typically not one of six rental car agencies were open!

We decided to switch to a taxi and took an 80 euro journey to Faro Airport, where we figured there must be some rental car offices functioning. And yes, there was … precisely one, Record Go, although the office was shut and they were working from home. Bizarre is not the word, seeing an airport like Faro, usually swamped with tourists, almost totally shut down, with just two flights arriving that day, I was told.

We waited for the local agent to arrive to be told that without an actual passport I could not rent a car. Thank God for Laurence, without whom we would never have got to Praia da Luz that night, as he whipped out his driving licence and credit card without delay or complaint.

We didn't actually get to the resort until sunset and with almost every bar and restaurant shut due to Covid, we were forced to stop locals randomly in the street to gauge their opinion on the new revelations. In a nutshell: they didn't think for a second that this German paedophile was involved, and predictably not one of them knew him. Their reaction was infuriating but not unexpected: it was typical of the hostility to the case – and the McCanns – that had built up over the last decade. The vast majority still felt the McCanns were involved and they blamed, at the very least, 'their irresponsible parenting' for damaging the resort's reputation and stymying its development. So deep had their antipathy grown that on the tenth anniversary of Maddie's disappearance in 2017, I learnt that posters put up to remind people of her had been defaced or torn down. It was a sorry state of affairs. We decided we might be better off heading into nearby Lagos for dinner and to find a hotel.

...

There was another reason why we felt we might get luckier in Lagos. We now had a name – Christian B – thanks to the British media who had finally decided to reveal this, and two addresses he had supposedly lived at near Praia da Luz had been published online that evening. One looked vaguely familiar, while the other had been named as Escola Velha or the Old Schoolhouse, in a hamlet called Monte Judeu, near the village of Bensarim.

The German newspaper, *Der Spiegel* had pitched in and announced that Christian B had worked in Lagos in various jobs, including catering, and we thought we might ask around to see if anyone knew him. The paper had some good contacts and had expanded further on his criminal record, revealing that he had been convicted on 17 separate occasions. Another newspaper, *Braunschweiger Zeitung*, reported that he had been deported from Portugal to Germany on a European warrant for 'another crime' in 2017. The German police meanwhile had added that he was known to have burgled hotels and holiday homes on the Algarve, as well as sold drugs locally.

His appearance also fitted with a series of sightings that had been recorded in the PJ files and on police statements many years earlier of a blond-haired 'pock-marked' man (Brueckner had acne as a teenager) hanging around the McCanns' apartment in the week Maddie disappeared, sometimes with a blond friend. One of the most convincing was from 12-year-old Tasmin Sillence, who saw the man twice. Firstly on April 30, in dark glasses, with his gaze fixed on the Ocean Club complex. Around the same time, the British girl had actually looked up and waved at a girl around Maddie's age playing on one of the terraces in the same block. Tamsin was able to give police a photofit picture, which was circulated at the time, bearing a striking resemblance to Brueckner; light-skinned, and around 5ft 9in, clean-shaven with short, possibly blond hair. She added that he was ugly – even 'disgusting' – and had a pockmarked 'pimply' face. She saw him again on May 2, the day before Maddie vanished, in front of the Ocean Club reception apparently staring at Apartment 5A.

British woman Carole Tranmer gave an intriguing statement to Portuguese and later Leicestershire Police. She had been visiting her aunt, Pamela Fenn, at her apartment which was above the McCanns, on the early evening of May 3 when she spotted a blond man on the floor below quietly leave an apartment and carefully close the gate of its garden while looking either side before hurrying away. 'It was his furtiveness that called my attention,' she told Leicestershire Police. Describing him as medium height, about 1.78m, of average stature and not muscular, she said he was not Portuguese but could have been Scandinavian or British.

She believes it was around 6 to 6.30pm, and before they drove back to their hotel an hour away. But given she hadn't arrived at the hotel until 8.30pm, it was much more likely to have been 7.30pm, or just before Brueckner received a phone call. When shown a picture of the prime suspect by *The Sun* last year, Tranmer said, 'That's the man I saw.'

Christian B was looking like a more likely candidate by the hour.

While we were in Lagos over the following days we were able to solve another mystery when we tracked down the owner of the phone number that had called Christian B for at 7.32pm, for 30 minutes, on May 3. The mobile's SIM card was registered to Diogo Silva who ran a restaurant in Lagos Port. We visited him to establish if there was any connection, but left convinced that there wasn't. The genial restaurant owner, a father of two, did not make the call, but someone had registered the SIM card in his name. A year later, I would ask chief prosecutor, Hans Christian Wolters – who would then be the main face of the inquiry – about this, and he would confirm that Silva was definitely not involved and that stealing identities to register SIM cards in another person's name was a common problem that has since been clamped down on.

By 10pm on that first night we had checked into one of the only hotels open in Lagos and were in a suitably hip expat watering hole in the heart of town chatting to a friendly group of Australians, English and South Africans, who had lived there for two decades. Over an excellent aubergine dip and a Caesar salad, they told us they ALL recognised Christian B's face, but couldn't quite picture from where or why.

It was frustrating, but the hunt was warming up

Chapter 15

The Threat

I awoke early to a detailed email from *the Mail on Sunday* newsdesk. A classic overnighter, it laid down the tasks the 'McCann team' would need to conduct, and a breakdown of the main lines that had come out in Friday's papers and online throughout the night. By now there were six of us working on the story, with senior reporter Abul Taher sent to Germany, journalist Andy Young on his way down to the Algarve and two staffers pulling things together in London. There were also two guys on the picture desk weaving their magic on social media. The paper was preparing to devote multiple column inches to the story, especially as the night before Wolters had said it was now a murder inquiry, announcing gravely: 'We assume that the girl is dead.'

Importantly, we now had a full name – Christian Brueckner – which the British and Portuguese press were naming despite the fact he hadn't been charged. According to his Facebook profile he liked Candy Crush and the composer Wagner, and had lived in Praia da Luz from 1999 to 2007.

In the memo from James Mellor in London, we were told that Brueckner had first become a 'person of interest' in a Scotland Yard cold case review that began in 2011, and started his life of crime with a burglary at the age of 15. It also emerged that he was currently serving a sentence for drug dealing and, most intriguingly of all, had been convicted the previous year in 2019 for the rape of an American pensioner in Praia da Luz in 2005. Somehow this vital and highly suspicious link to a serious sex criminal on the Algarve had missed the UK media ... and me.

A separate German police probe into him had apparently intensified in 2017 when he told a friend he knew all about the Maddie case. It came about when her face flashed up on TV screens in a bar during a report on the tenth anniversary of her disappearance as he was having a drink. He claimed to know what had happened to her (*The Sun* reported he had revealed to his drinking friend that he 'snatched her'), and then proceeded to show this friend a video on his phone of him allegedly raping an 'elderly woman'. More of which later.

I knew we needed to start talking to neighbours at the various houses he had lived at in the area. And before anyone else arrived, as the story was rapidly gathering speed, with new reports coming out in Germany, Portugal and the UK almost by the hour.

After grabbing an early breakfast, we drove over to Luz, starting with the Yellow House. Conveniently, German police had released details of two homes – and the interior of one – while one of the British tabloids had helpfully printed their rough location on a Google Maps overview.

I recognised the Yellow House immediately. It was along one of the dirt tracks I had walked up the morning after Maddie had been snatched. It had a remarkable bird's eye view across Luz and while just 650m from the edge of Praia da Luz as the crow flies, it felt completely detached from the tourist resort. Perched halfway up a hillside on scrubland, combining carobs, palms and wild olives, the small country bungalow was the very picture of neglect. Isolated on a bend below two bigger villas, it looked forlorn with filthy windows and building materials lying on its porch and the garden was badly overgrown. Despite being renovated over recent years by its British owner, the one-bedroom bungalow had a distinct air of melancholy.

Looking through the windows offered few clues. Simply furnished, a bag of golf clubs had been dumped just inside the front door seemingly by the owner in a hurry, perhaps, to catch a flight back to the UK before lockdown. It is an area known as Sitio das Lajes, which is reached off the busy M537 main road into Luz opposite the Orbitur Valverde campsite. It comprises around a dozen country homes and villas, lived in mostly by expats and is backed by the area's popular Boavista Golf and Spa Resort.

The track itself slowly narrows to a path that leads south west towards Praia da Luz's lovely beach, with various subsidiary paths dropping down into the village itself. Serving as exceptionally good exit routes from the resort, should one wish to rob houses or more, they were also the paths that the McCanns frequently jogged down while camped out during their long ordeal.

The neighbours, almost all of whom were German or Austrian, were not particularly forthcoming. Most didn't remember Brueckner aside from his many cars and vans that were parked in a layby just outside the house, as well as in the garden. 'It was like a scrapyard,' said one. 'He really loved his cars.' But they said he was a friendly neighbour, not brash or noisy, and anything but annoying.

One elegant Austrian woman, who gave her name as Salamanda, came out with her secateurs and a wheelbarrow full of cuttings to tell us 'what a lovely guy' he was, an 'excellent neighbour' who was always friendly and courteous. She went on to explain that she had sometimes had a coffee with him in Lagos. 'I was actually shocked when I heard he was involved in all this,' she told us. 'He was a good best neighbour, friendly and polite and I can't say anything bad about him. He was always nice and he helped me whenever he could. He was always laughing and joking and could certainly tell a tale.'

She said he had lived in the house for 'six or seven years' but had left suddenly in 2006 and she didn't know why. 'One minute he had simply gone, vanished,' she said. 'It was pretty odd and some of the neighbours actually went and filed a missing persons police report, which came to nothing.'

These neighbours, it turned out, were British and who had lived in the area for nearly two decades, running a stables and property business, including rental accommodation. They knew the owner of the Yellow House, a rather eccentric British man, who had asked them to clear the house up after an apparent burglary had left it in disarray a few weeks after Brueckner 'vanished' in early 2006.

'We went there to clean out the house because it had been burgled,' said Ruth Maclean, who had been living in the area since 1988. Along with her daughter Rosie, 29, and another friend, Ruth told Portuguese national TV that they had 'emptied the house' in May of that year. 'It was empty for some time and it was in a really terrible state with food in the fridges, rats, it was not pleasant at all,' she said. 'We just emptied the house. There was a massive mess, several computers all turned over on the floor, dirty clothing, blankets, everything just had to be ditched. We just cleared it up, emptied the fridge, the kitchen, cleaned all the surfaces.'

Unbeknown to them, Brueckner was serving an eight-month spell in prison at the time, and their clean up probably destroyed vital DNA evidence and clues to quite a few serious crimes.

Despite having their reservations about Brueckner – with daughter Rosie saying he used to make her 'feel uncomfortable' – they were still concerned enough to report him as missing. 'We just didn't know if Christian was alive or dead and so we decided to go and report him as a missing person,' continued Ruth. 'We went to the GNR police station in Lagos and made the report there.'

They were told nothing and heard nothing more (this was Portugal, after all), until we knocked on their door some 13 years later – although they preferred to give their testimony to Portuguese TV. 'I have never seen any activity around here, no excavations, no police, no searches,' concluded Ruth.

•••

It was approaching 10.15am when the first of six cars and two television vans wound their way down the narrow track to the Yellow House, leaving a trail of dust in their wake. I knew immediately who they were ... and as if by magic, out of this cavalcade stepped Her Majesty's finest press teams, one from each of the British tabloids, plus surprisingly one from *The Telegraph* and one from *the Times* They were soon joined by an upmarket-looking team from Germany's *Bild* and Portugal's *RTP* network.

After a brief chat with most of them, in the time-old tabloid tradition we made our excuses and left, realising that the dailies would hoover up anything that was left for the following day's editions. We needed to lead from the front and decided to head to Brueckner's other home, where he had apparently been living on and off, between spells in his VW campervan in 2007. But the Old Schoolhouse – appropriately named for a predatory paedophile – was not just hard to find, its current owners (a pair of expat Brits) were radically opposed to giving any comment.

Pic 1: Portuguese police arrive with sniffer dogs at the Ocean Club on May 4, while (Pic 2) detectives mill around outside the PJ headquarters in Portimao the same day

Pic 3: PJ boss Guilhermino Encarnacao briefs journalists in Portimao on May 5 that he is sure Maddie was 'kidnapped' but is still alive

Pic 4: McCann's apartment and street entrance today and (Pic 5), the much flimsier gate in May 2007

Pic 6: Robert Murat and (Pic 7) Sergey Malinka coming out of a bank in May 2007

Pic 8: Kate and Gerry McCann and (Pic 9) lead investigator Inspector Goncalo Amaral

Pic 10: *Netflix* documentary producer Carl Hindmarch with author Jon Clarke in Praia da Luz (left), while above (Pic 11 and Pic 12) two different police mugshots of Christian Brueckner

Pic 13: Christian Breuckner's Yellow House rental home (inset) overlooked the McCann's Ocean Club apartment complex circled (estimated) in Praia da Luz

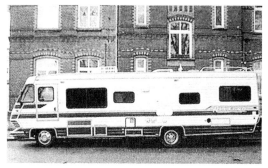

Pic 14: Brueckner's Tiffin 'winnebago' in Germany and Pic 15 and 16 (right) his VW Westfalia van

Diogo Silva
Assistant Mana...

Pic 17: Brueckner's Jaguar re-registered in Germany a day after Maddie went missing and (Pic 18) Luz Beach Cafe manager Diogo Silva whose name was registered to the mobile number Brueckner called in Luz on the evening that Maddie went missing

FRIDAY HAPPINESS
ASSOCIACAO
guest card
NO: 32

Pic 19: A 'pizza party' ticket, similar to ones where Brueckner regularly sold drugs, and (Pic 20), the Old Schoolhouse where German police believe he spent time around 2007

85

Pic 21: *Olive Press* reporter Laurence Dollimore shows photos to Brueckner's ex restaurant boss Tiziano Ilg, while (Pic 22) Roy Whitehouse and (Pic 23) his former Foral home

Pic 24: Foral residents association president, Christine Chinn and (Pic 25) the Foral home where Brueckner lived with Nicole in 2007 and later with the Stennards in 2016

Pic 26: Foral Villa Bianca homeowner Lia Silva beside Spanish-registered Mercedes for sale at her Foral home and (Pic 27) a rope left in the car footwell

Sat on a busy road in the hamlet of Monte Judeu, 'Escola Velha' was a typically attractive Algarve finca with the classic vernacular architecture. Sitting in the verdant Bensafrim valley, it was just missing a friendly Portuguese local to open the door with a smile.

The first time we knocked, we could hear a bell in the distance and some shuffling around, plus a dog barking somewhere at the back. Hitting the bell a second time, a man opened the door an inch or two and in a gruff northern English accent said, 'Leave me alone, I've got nothing to say.' An odd greeting, to say the least, on a bright sunny morning.

We drove up to the nearby hamlet with a cafe that oozed charm, and was still open despite lockdown. I realised that once you veered off the beaten track, life was carrying on pretty much as normal. It was definitely time for a coffee and when complemented with a pasteis de nata custard tart – the country's finest delicacy – it was a stop well worth taking. It turned out to be useful too, as we bumped into 62-year-old local farmer Fernando Lopez who remembered Brueckner and the home's former female German owner, who had sold up to the current British owners in around 2011, via Lagos' local estate agency Remax.

He told us that Brueckner had been 'a kind of handyman' doing odd jobs around the house and garden … and there were 'rumours' that he and the older owner – who may have been in her sixties – were romantically linked. 'It was just local gossip, but they definitely had quite an odd relationship,' he said. 'She was a good deal older, certainly around retirement age and he was probably in his thirties.'

He also mentioned that Brueckner hung around with a girl, 'a bit of a hippie', who wore 'flowers in her hair', but he couldn't remember much more, such as her name or where she was from.

Almost as he finished the sentence, the cafe went quiet as a news item came on the corner TV. It announced that Brueckner might have been involved in the May 2015 disappearance of a 5-year-old German girl, Inga Gehricke, known as 'the German Maddie', of which more later. Brueckner's face filled the screen, along with pictures of both tragic little girls.

The bar owner tutted and looked angry, while a Portuguese woman in her sixties chimed in with something about 'catching that bastard', or similar. 'I knew he was up to no good,' she said when we tried to interview her. While asking not to be named, 'for fear of reprisals', she told us he had been milling around the Monte Judeu area for a couple of years and confirmed that he drove a van and a Jaguar.

'He was around quite a lot of the time, sleeping on the sofa, and walking [his landlady's] dogs,' she recalled, sitting beside her daughter. 'She had quite a lot of them, some big, some small, and it was quite an operation to keep them exercised. Christian took up the task with vigour and I saw him walking them on lots of occasions.'

Annoyingly, her daughter stopped her from saying anything else, and she insisted she could not remember the German owner's name.

The conversation dried up and with no one else to grill, we decided to try the British owner of the Schoolhouse one more time to see if we could get a name and a number for the former owner. After all, one might assume that in an inquiry like this, it was in everyone's best interests to help out.

It didn't bode well. We returned to find two scribbled notes had been pasted on the front door and on the wall beside it, just in case you could somehow miss the first. Written mostly in Portuguese, it said: 'Journalists: Don't touch the bell or knock on the door. DO NOT BOTHER. DO NOT DISTURB. Thanks.' The name of the house, which was on a brass plate, had also now been covered by a blanket. These guys really didn't want to help. Sometimes expats can be that way.

I could see the small gathering of people that was growing across the road. Standing in the classic huddle of a press pack, the journalists had begun to arrive as the enquiries had dried up at the Yellow House. A couple of them had also got short shrift from the new owners, one who was called Martin they had established, but I figured it was still worth another go. Despite being a little nervous, I pressed the bell again. The door opened a crack and I explained to 'Martin' that I only wanted the previous owner's name and had been investigating the case for 13 years, yadda, yadda, yadda. He cut me off and said, 'Leave me alone. You've got two seconds to get off my property or else.' We got the message.

It was the sort of reaction I had learnt to expect. The hatred of the press, coupled with the antipathy towards the McCanns by locals and also now many expats was perhaps not surprising. Not necessarily due to the bad behaviour of the media or indeed the way the McCanns conducted themselves, but for a combination of reasons. One, that the police had made such a total hash of the case, in particular arresting the McCanns, and two, because I believed that a fair number of these expats had things to hide. They had come to Portugal to flee criminal pasts or continue with their crimes in a country that had disinterested police who were keen to turn a blind eye.

It was a hunch that would be confirmed over the next 24 hours.

Chapter 16

Van Lifers

After bashing on the doors of a dozen near neighbours in the hamlet of Monte Judeu and getting nothing more, with most of the houses empty or with owners who didn't have a clue, we needed to think laterally and came up with the idea of mechanics and garages. Christian certainly liked his cars and vans. He'd had a 'junkyard' in Luz and drove a VW and a Jaguar, so he must have appreciated the finer side of motoring.

Looking on Google Maps, we spotted a garage half a mile up the road behind Monte Judeu, towards Bensafrim village. It was called Cromax Mecanico and was run by a clean-cut chap called Vitor Martens.

Like so many businesses on the Algarve, it appeared out of nowhere after a tight bend on a winding line. You definitely couldn't miss it, with two 100m-long lines of cars on both sides of the road. And by cars, I mean wrecks mostly, plus a reasonable smattering of vans, at least one a VW campervan. It felt like a cross between Wembley Industrial estate and a gypsy encampment on part of London's green belt and it was typical of garages in this part of Portugal in that it was basically someone's house, with no sign, and unless it had been pointed out to you on Google Maps, you had to guess what service it offered. There are literally hundreds of these garages and breakers yards on the Algarve, with a number tucked away in tiny hamlets up narrow lanes that you would never stumble across by accident.

Vitor's customers obviously knew how to find him as we realised once we'd made it inside. As well as two rows of cars waiting to be fixed in the front yard, there were five or six vehicles up on lifts inside, and at least the same number of mechanics working on them. Vitor told us he had worked in the area for decades, but previously lived in the UK, where he had perfected his English. He was well aware of the case, with the police having visited his garage two years earlier looking for the distinctive white and yellow VW campervan Brueckner had been driving. He had told them he recognised it as belonging to a German man in Monte Judeu and had pointed the police to the house now lived in by Martin and his partner.

He said he had never repaired Brueckner's VW or any of his other vehicles as he 'used some German guy inland somewhere' (I later found out that this was Bernhard Piro), but was more than happy to give us a general overview of the area and the company Brueckner kept. He described him as 'a new age, traveller type' and he added that many people who lived in this part of the Algarve were 'very alternative, very hippy and pikey'. All his words.

'It's a very transient place especially in the summer and it's hard to know where these people come from, where they go or what they do,' he told us. 'It would be very easy for someone like Christian to come and go with his various vans and blend into the community here. The authorities just don't do enough to keep an eye on people like him. It is quite a disgrace.'

He said we should visit another breakers yard a few kilometres up the road near the village of Barao de Sao Joao. I remembered the name straight away. Lori Campbell and I had visited in May 2007, the month Maddie went missing, when we were investigating paedophiles in the area. Damn! It was so obvious. Christian WAS a drug-dealing, new age traveller type. Barao would be the perfect place for him to blend in on the fringes of this foot-loose, demi-monde community of dropouts and freedom fighters. He was probably also a regular visitor, I suspected, of the infamous Granada town of Orgiva, where thousands of travellers had based themselves for decades. He would fit in perfectly there.

'There have always been hundreds, in fact thousands, of hippies living around Barao for years,' explained Vitor. 'They all have ramshackle vans and trucks and most of them don't do proper jobs.' He was right, Barao was Portugal's Glastonbury or Totnes, and the community centred on a series of earthy cafes and bars, trinket and bracelet stalls, and until a few years earlier, it had an infamous flea market once a week that brought in travellers from all over the country and further afield. 'They came from far and wide to sell their stuff, but it became too much of a kind of commune with people hanging around for days at a time, often weeks,' continued Vitor. 'It ended up encouraging criminality and particularly drug use, including heroin.' Three years ago the authorities shut it down, 'much to the delight of most of the local Portuguese,' added Vitor. We clearly needed to visit and conveniently we'd have to pass by the garage Vitor had mentioned. We thanked him and set off.

The garage was a campervan graveyard, chock full of battered old vans and trucks. Hidden by two-metre high metal fences, we ambled in to find absolutely no one about. Or so we thought. In a far corner, we stumbled upon a small group of local Portuguese men, and one woman, huddled around a small wicker table smoking what looked like a joint. Deeply strange looking and overtly hostile, it felt like a scene out of the film *Deliverance,* as they eyed Laurence and I up suspiciously. It was clear they wanted to know what on Earth we were doing there in smart shirts and trousers.

I got out my phone and thrust a photo of Brueckner and then another one of his old van at the group of four. They looked bemused, baffled and ultimately all agreed they had no idea what we were talking about. It was uncomfortable and unsettling and we retreated rapidly to our hire car. Five minutes later we were standing at the bar of one of the five or six cafes in Barao de Sao Joao, again totally thwarted by the locals, who mostly refused to engage with us.

Not much had changed from 13 years earlier when Lori and I were last here. At the time it had been fairly impenetrable with most people – a mixture of Europeans from just about any country you could think of – intolerant of the media, with almost nobody agreeing to talk to us. This time they were even more unfriendly, with two or three locals actually walking away as we approached them, while two English hippies sitting drinking bottles of lager outside told us to 'get lost' and 'you journalists are all full of shit'.

One added that the new story was 'just another tabloid fake news fest'. 'Those wanker doctors killed their daughter, they set it all up, I don't believe a word about anyone else,' said the other, in a Home Counties accent. It took all my powers of patience not to tell them what a bunch of wankers they were. Laurence went off to speak to another hippie, with nasty looking scabs on his arms, who tried to pick a fight with him. I had to step in and drag him into a nearby cafe. The hostility was intense.

We later stopped for lunch at a different cafe, after which the owner insisted I delete some photos I had taken of her waiter because he had 'not given you permission'. Then pursued an ugly standoff as I told her angrily I didn't need permission and what was his problem anyway? Who was he hiding from? before finally agreeing when I realised I needed a receipt for the ridiculously over-expensive lunch.

The only upside of our short visit was bumping into Portuguese journalist Elena Figueras from the country's national TV channel, *RTP,* who was having lunch with her cameraman at a nearby table. I'd known her colleague Sandra Felgueiras from the very beginning in 2007. Between them they knew the case in Portugal better than anyone. I knew we must be on the right track.

I got Sandra's new number from Elena and gave her a call and it was great to hear her say there 'might just be something' in this Brueckner fellow, according to her police contacts. She told me she had heard he'd spent time among the footloose traveller community that centred on Barao and was 'probably' dealing drugs from there. She and her team were spending the day trying to firm up some old contacts of his to find out where else he may have lived.

Sandra was rather a controversial figure in the case, and had been somewhat ostracised after she had – wrongly – pointed the finger at the McCanns in a bombshell interview not long after their arrest. I could still not understand her rationale behind it, particularly as she had been there at the McCanns' first press conference and we had discussed the case at length in those early days. She told me she had simply been fed so many lies from the police at the time and was now beginning to think Chief Inspector Amaral had been 'a total failure'. 'He totally used me and my network,' she explained. 'Obviously I now regret that.' Her views on the McCanns had changed completely.

She still had excellent police contacts. She knew plenty of the detectives in the Algarve section of the PJ having cut her teeth as a regional reporter based out of nearby Faro. She also knew her way around the courts and had some great legal contacts. She was now producer and presenter of her own weekly crime show, *Sexta as 9 (Friday at 9)*, which was one of the national channel's most popular programmes. Blonde with blue eyes she fitted the mould of attractive current affairs presenters, so typical of southern Europe. But behind her wavy locks and bubbly persona, stood a steely determination to chase a story … and she was definitely not scared to roll up her sleeves and bang on doors. We agreed to stay in touch as the story developed and I agreed to be interviewed for her friday night show.

The trouble was the story was not developing fast in Barao. After another half an hour or so wandering around taking a few photos, we stumbled across a shopkeeper who recognised Brueckner and said he might have worked for a time at an 'unofficial' restaurant/cafe owned by a German called Walter a few kilometres outside town. He also ventured that his name was 'Holger' and not Christian. It was worth a look.

The place was up a dirt track, with the only clue being a simple wooden sign with the name 'Walter' on it. It turned out to be a series of ugly, ramshackle buildings and looked more like someone's house than a restaurant. Yet amazingly, it somehow scored a high 4.1 out of 5 rating on Google Maps and went by the name '*Abzweig zu Algarve-Metzger Walter*'.

It was closed, and a long-haired German living in a Kombi van beside it got out and told us to 'go away', but not before we had taken a few photos and had a quick sniff around, taking note of a pair of knickers discarded by the front door and writing down a few numbers of German locals, one called 'Holger' from notices on the door.

It was time to find somewhere to stay the night and I had spotted an attractive looking guesthouse on the outskirts of the village, which I thought might tick some boxes. Monte Rosa turned out to be an excellent find, with its expansive grounds, charming casitas and decent-size pool, not that we'd have any time to swim in it. Best of all, it was run by a far more friendly Dutch expat called Sandra Falkena, who had lived in the area for nearly three decades and knew Barao like the back of her hand. She introduced us to a journalist from Holland's respected *De Telegraph* newspaper, who also happened to be staying, oddly looking into an apparently (but now I am not so sure) unrelated case involving the recent murder of a Dutchman.

His name was Roy Klopper and he was as surprised as we were to find fellow journalists bowling up in Barao in the heart of lockdown. Roy told us the recent murder of a Dutch expat called 'Kelli' had made news in Holland (and a small story in the local Portuguese press) and was allegedly over a big drug deal that had gone wrong. 'We think it is linked to a big heroin deal,' explained the fellow hack, as he chain-smoked beside his girlfriend some ten years his junior. 'Typically nobody heard anything and nobody wants to talk. It is all very strange. But that is apparently normal for Barao.'

Sandra confirmed exactly that, saying the area had been awash with heroin and other drugs for many years and plenty of odd things went on. She was confident we could witness some of these alternative goings on – aka 'the scene' – with our own eyes if we were to go that evening to something called the 'pizza party' that took place every Friday at a huge inland estate, near the village of Monchique, a 45-minute drive inland from Barao. Run by a trustafarian-type hippy, who allowed these unofficial 'free for all, anything goes-type of nights' to take place, even during lockdown, allegedly.

She said there would be 'every sort of drug for sale' and he got round the rules by selling tickets for a meal – in this case a pizza – in advance, meaning as it was a private estate he could allow people in. She told us there were usually hundreds of people taking drugs and partying until dawn. She said we could get a lift with her friendly receptionist and handyman Hans, a 'van lifer' by his own admission, who predictably lived on the grounds in a caravan, when not drifting up and down the coast.

She wasn't exactly selling it but we decided to give it some consideration later in the day. First we had to hotfoot it to Albufeira.

Chapter 17

The First Breakthrough

We eventually got a good lead. Typically it came from London, via social media. It was a first name of a woman who was apparently a Facebook friend of Brueckner's. Her name was 'Wendy' and she was a British expat living on the Algarve, around Albufeira. The problem was she had just deleted her entire Facebook account, as had some of her family, so keen were they to distance themselves from Brueckner.

I was stumped but Laurence wrote a few posts on various Facebook expat groups along the coast, asking if anyone knew how to 'get hold of Wendy'. Even though we didn't say why, we were hit with a wall of silence, until around 7.30pm when a German woman called Petra from an Albufeira group messaged Laurence to ask, 'was it Wendy Baker?', who was involved in various animal rescue groups, which is typical of expats abroad. We dug around and discovered that the Wendy Baker in question had posted on quite a few occasions in the Albufeira area, but that was it. Luckily our German friend Petra was, by now, in a rapid exchange with Laurence and finally called him from Stuttgart, where she had fled during lockdown.

We asked a few gentle questions before dropping in the names 'Christian Brueckner' and 'Holger'. And bingo! Petra told us she had been following the case around the clock in Germany and explained that Wendy was a friend of hers, who had got to know Brueckner via an animal rescue charity, some 12 or so years before. She confirmed that Wendy had met him on various occasions and he was indeed 'going by the name Holger'. She added that Wendy's father had apparently agreed to take on one of his dogs, 'a big dog', for one reason or another and that it had apparently arrived 'looking malnourished'. Oddly, Brueckner may have even occasionally stayed at his house, 'perhaps to use his shower.'

It sounded intriguing so our next question was: 'Where could we find them?' Unfortunately, Petra refused to divulge any addresses, but she did tell us that Brueckner had been living for a number of years at an inland village, which she believed was either Tunes or Foral. She couldn't remember which one exactly, 'maybe both,' she said. It was enough for us to be hurtling at a rate of knots towards Tunes, which sat just off the old IC1 highway, directly north of Albufeira.

It didn't take long, maybe 20 minutes, but it was already starting to get dark as we parked up in the strange workaday town that didn't seem to have an actual centre, and was split in half by the main railway line between Faro and Lisbon. We went into every bar or restaurant we could find (and there weren't many) and thrust a photo of Brueckner in front of the staff. And … nothing!

After all the excitement, it was frustrating, but we figured we might have more luck in Foral, another ten minutes further north. It was by now approaching 10pm and to describe the drive to Foral as creepy would be an understatement. It was pitch black and the narrow winding lane tumbled back and forth under and over the railway track, through dark olive groves and past ruined fincas and shacks, almost none of which had a light on.

It really felt like the back of beyond and Londoner Laurence, the most urbane of city dwellers, who gets a nosebleed from the altitude on Hampstead Heath, was getting decidedly spooked. He started asking, 'what if this was the lane that Maddie was brought down?', and actually worked himself up into something of a state, when suddenly, bang, we were in the middle of Foral.

There was certainly no fanfare or 'welcome to Foral' signs to indicate that we'd arrived. In fact, we only knew we had because we saw a sign for the restaurant O Foral that sat on its main crossroads. We drove around for five minutes and found nothing more of interest so, given the time, we headed to the restaurant to plead for some dinner.

We were in luck and with two other tables, both comprising elderly foreigners, only just getting their main courses, we had time to relax.

It turned out to be something of a find, with an excellent wine list and a decent kitchen serving up great food.

We decided to play it gently, gently and befriended the owner, who told us how he had lived abroad for years, running restaurants as an expat, and had only recently returned home. While we were tempted to launch into the reasons for coming, it didn't feel right. It was past 11pm and the owner looked tired and clearly wanted to close his doors as we were now the only table left. To have grilled him about Brueckner there and then may have irritated him, and possibly ruined the chance to ask him – and other locals that may well have been warned about it – the next day. We were pretty sure we were the only journalists in town, and sometimes it pays to be tactical … and patience won the day.

It was past 1am when we got back to Monte Rosa. Perhaps unsurprisingly, fellow journalist Roy was still up, nursing a whiskey, and five minutes later, in strode the van lifer Hans with a small dog. He was fresh back from the 'pizza party' in Monchique and handed us a flyer for the event, which on this occasion was called the 'Friday Happiness Association' (see photo). He had been the 32nd punter through the gates and was eager to talk to us as he thought he had seen a dangerous felon at the event that he thought we should know about.

He said the man had been hanging around in the area for years, and claimed to be some sort of mystic but was actually a fraudster. He Googled the man's name there and then to find a Dutch website that claimed he was wanted, and a 20,000 euro reward was being offered for his whereabouts. We looked at each other wide-eyed, before realising it was late, he probably wouldn't still be there, we had no tickets and, well, quite frankly a double whiskey on the rocks was a much better plan.

Hans also proceeded to tell us excitedly about an old man of 'easily over 65' who was dancing and kissing with a girl of around 20 – 'maybe younger' – on the dancefloor. He said it had 'creeped' him out and it was time for him to go. To be fair he creeped us a bit too. I went to bed wondering, once again, what sort of place the McCanns had inadvertently stumbled into for a late spring break.

...

We were up and on the way to Foral soon after breakfast, stopping at two roadside restaurants at a busy junction on the approach to the village from a different direction to show photos of Brueckner and his VW van and Jaguar. We got a positive response at each; the first with the mother of the elderly owner remembering that Brueckner had been in to eat in the main dining room on a few occasions, along with his dog. At the second, Cafe Mariano, the owner told us he had often seen him and the VW van driving up and down and then told us he had actually been interviewed by national Portuguese television, RTP, the day before. We were definitely getting warmer.

We arrived in Foral to find the restaurant closed. Bloody typical.

So it was back to the classic method of putting in 'tread', literally going door to door to see if anyone could help. The good news was there were no other journalists around; the bad news that most of the houses were behind big gates and very few had bells. On top of that, at least half were empty as these were mostly holiday homes and the foreign, mainly expat owners were locked down in their respective countries, thanks to coronavirus. With their identikit-size plots and high metal gates and fences, it reminded me of *The Stepford Wives*.

Each of the owners had their own postbox in a central block by the O Farol restaurant. We went to have a look. There were many British names (Churchill, Sparrow, Field-Millard), with one having named their villa Hampton Court Palace, plus French, Germans and Swiss. Eventually, we found Christine Chinn, Foral's president, who was tucked away at one end of the village.

She told us a little about the area, which was now seeing increasing numbers of Eastern Europeans, Russians and Ukrainians moving in. More of a concept than a village, the settlement of Foral had been planned out in the 1960s as the perfect retreat for retiring city dwellers and foreigners. The brainwave came from original landowner Jose Carrera Gomez, who measured out 200 identical half-hectare plots, which could be developed as the new owners saw fit, using the land to grow produce for the local market.

'The area is famous for its citrus produce, in particular kumquats and grapefruits,' explained Christine, who had lived there for 45 years and now runs yoga retreats from her leafy property, Puri Puri. 'Many owners grew lettuce and other vegetables commercially, until cheap exports came flooding in from the US making it unprofitable.'

Other owners hoping to build their dream homes were devastated to learn that the land was mostly protected as it sat in a so-called rural national reserve, which meant that many were forbidden to build on it and, in the end, only around 80 were built. The problems bred resentment, with many frustrated owners caught up in the courts for years and some cases still unresolved. There had also been a fair amount of bad blood between owners and land feuds, in particular over boundaries, with one actually leading to murder over claims of some dogs being shot or poisoned.

'You certainly meet some funny people here,' said Christine. 'And the houses are quite set apart so many neighbours have nothing to do with each other, yet many others end up hopping into bed with one another.' She added that with so many foreigners moving to such a tiny community it was inevitable that 'many of them end up getting bored and unhappy which leads to affairs.' Then she added, 'I wouldn't be surprised if plenty of sinister things have happened here.'

It was a pretty frank introduction to the village by its very own president, but the one issue she couldn't shed light on was Brueckner. She didn't remember him, although she did recognise his VW van.

We continued digging. After receiving a brush off from a couple of British owners and a Russian, who all but ushered us off the property, we struck gold with some German pensioners Peter and Ingrid, who straight away knew why we were there. The former restaurateur and his rose-grower wife from Hamburg had, it turned out, been fixated on the German TV reports about the new suspect for the last few days. In particular, the previous night's report on hit TV show *Aktenzeichen XY … Ungelost* (Case number XY … Unsolved – Germany's Crimewatch) had convinced them that the new suspect had been a staunch fixture in their village back in 2007 and 2008, and again more recently. They seemed certain of it.

'I know they are investigating the Christian who lived here,' insisted Ingrid, while Peter, who shuffled around on walking sticks, held up his hand in a bid to quieten her. 'You don't forget that face and he was hanging around here for a long time with his battered old van,' she continued, before Peter cut her off dead. He was quite angry. Or worried. 'Who are you? Why are you here?' he barked.

We fished out our press cards and explained we were journalists investigating the Maddie case, and he calmed down a little, bidding us to sit down outside their small bungalow – one of the few that didn't have a high fence or gate. Evidently nervous, and in broken English, the couple began to tell us about this 'strange guy' Christian and his 'odd and scary behaviour'.

Insisting we would not reveal their surnames for fear of retribution, they started by telling us what a 'strange place' Foral was. How there had been a shooting behind their home and how they were particularly concerned about the movements of children, and potentially child abuse. I shivered. They expressed surprise that neither police nor press had yet to visit the village enquiring about the 'oddball' who had arrived and parked up his VW Westfalia van outside a near neighbour's house at some point in early 2007.

They had first come across Christian living out of his van opposite the house of an eccentric Portuguese neighbour, Eulalia da Silva, better known as Lia. He had also regularly parked his van outside the restaurant we'd eaten in the night before. 'When I saw pictures of the white and yellow van I knew immediately I had seen it in our village,' said Peter. 'It was often parked in the car park of the restaurant when the owner was living in the village.'

They spoke to Christian in their native German on many occasions, explaining that he was always friendly and happy to stop for a chat. 'The first time I met him he was hosting some sort of a party at O Foral,' said Peter. 'I often saw him in the restaurant and he would always say hello, nothing more at first, just a nod of heads. He had two dogs. A big labrador cross called Mool, and a little dog, Frau Muller [German slang for housewife], which was always hanging around and taking rubbish from the bins.'

'You don't forget names like that, or how annoying that dog was,' continued Ingrid. 'He was always off the lead and scrounging at the bins, or sniffing around cars. Christian didn't seem to care and I don't think he looked after them properly.'

They said Christian occasionally worked at O Foral and, more pertinently, that he was involved with local crime. 'Specifically the theft of some solar panels, which he tried to offload to us,' added Ingrid. 'But we also heard that he was involved in burglaries, so we politely declined. He was definitely a bad egg.'

They explained that the house he lived in at the time was being rented by a German woman called Nicole – a friend of Brueckner's – and her partner Romano. And that Nicole was a foster carer and therapist for troubled German teenagers. 'We were always suspicious of that,' said Ingrid, adding that one of her foster children, who lived in the home with her had run away and that, according to the grapevine, it was Christian who had been enlisted to track down the missing teenage girl … and she had eventually come back … pregnant.

'The police were involved and it was definitely a real scandal for the village. Everyone was concerned about where she had gone and Christian had allegedly gone off to track her down and two weeks later had somehow located her living with some gypsies, or Romanians, in a nearby town.

'That was the story, at least. Supposedly he went about carrying a gun and claimed to be some sort of detective. It was all very strange.'

Strange yes, but as testimonies go, it couldn't get more tantalising and we knew where to go next.

Chapter 18

The Knock

We quickly found the house a bit further up Rua Quinta da Larga Vista (Estate of the Long View Road) – plot 89 – at the next junction, some 200m from O Foral restaurant. From a distance it looked like an attractive coal pink villa, set back slightly from the road with mature grounds of cypress trees, willows and oaks, with a profusion of striking bougainvillea on the front wall.

It is no exaggeration to say that we both gulped as we walked up to the black rusting gate, which was padlocked shut, to take a look inside. A cross between the imposing home of the Addams Family and the ramshackle residence of Steptoe and Son, the courtyard had a handful of battered old cars, one of them up on bricks with a wheel missing, while a filthy child's pushchair lay on its side beside it. Next to that was a box full of old videos and CDs. Villa Bianca, as it was named, had a distinct feeling of neglect, not helped by over a dozen filthy dogs roaming around its front garden barking at us. There was dog shit everywhere.

I noticed that one of the cars, a black Mercedes, had Spanish plates (I later found out it was registered to a British couple, based in Alicante, on the Costa Blanca, although it was impossible to locate them or, indeed, find any link to them anywhere). Had it been stolen? Another vehicle, a grey transit van, was parked outside the front gate in a layby, where Brueckner had apparently usually parked his VW Westfalia. 'Could it be used to transport children?' queried Laurence tensely.

We decided to hold off knocking, in particular as there was no bell. But we were also hungry, wanted to get our story in order and – most importantly – line up our questions for whoever was living in the house now. Some 45 minutes later we were back, banging on the metal gate, above a cacophony of shrieks and yowls from the army of mutts prowling the grounds. After about a minute, a side door opened and a portly woman in a sarong and tight blue vest waved at us cheerily and came over. She confirmed that her name was Lia and asked us what we wanted, speaking decent English in an unusual Australian accent. 'There is no easy way to put this,' I told her. 'But we are investigating your former tenant Nicole, her friend Christian Brueckner and possible links to missing Maddie McCann.'

It was as if she had been waiting for this moment for years, as she did the most bizarre double take and then launched into a long monologue about the 'awful, traumatic years' that Nicole had lived there.

It was clearly a weight off her mind as she unloaded about the former German tenant, her various boyfriends and the strange goings on that left the house in a terrible state and her, many thousands of euros out of pocket. She told us she had inherited the villa from her parents in the 1990s when her mother had moved to a smaller house up the road. The villa had then been divided to create a small apartment at one side, in which she was currently living, while the main four-bedroom house was rented to an English couple (perhaps the ones with a car from Alicante), who were stuck in England because of lockdown. She declined to give us their names.

We gently guided the conversation towards Nicole's connections with Christian Brueckner and initially she seemed a little vague. But then I showed her some pictures of him on my mobile phone. 'Er yes, that's Christian,' she said, looking almost sick. Her tone changed. 'He was here for a while, but I don't really remember him.' It was obvious she was holding a lot back.

We changed tack to stop her drying up, and talked about Nicole. It worked. She told us that Nicole Fehlinger (the name was later confirmed from a rental contract she had kept) had lived in the villa from 2002 to 2009, but failed to pay the rent for 'at least five years' she claimed (although I think it was more like seven months: Nicole's father Dieter would tell me later that she moved to Foral in 2004 and left in 2010). Lia, a grandmother of three, who works as a taxi and minibus driver on the Algarve, had been forced to take her to court and it had been the 'most unpleasant' period of her life.

She said Fehlinger had moved in with a German man called Mathias and her 6 year-old daughter Jessica (from a previous relationship with a man called Andreas, who had committed suicide). Later I would learn that Mathias Hamel worked for his sister Barbara Hamel's yacht business Ouro Iates (Golden Yachts) in Vilamoura.

'Nicole was quite a catch for him. She was really stunning, a very pretty girl, and I think he was kind of setting her up in this place,' said Lia. 'Her name might have been on the contract but Mathias was paying the bills. That was the impression I got.' Lia said they rented the whole house, at a cost of 1,300 euros a month, plus bills, which is steep for Portuguese salaries. She was unclear exactly what they did to cover all those expenses. Or at least she didn't want to tell us.

She said the couple had arrived having lived with Mathias' wealthy sister Barbara in a big house in Goldra, a 20-minute drive away, but that they had fallen out and needed to move. She also revealed that they were with a troubled teenage boy (Thomas: of whom more later) she was looking after, via a German programme for wayward children. 'That was why they insisted on renting the whole house and wouldn't let me stay in the annexe as I had done before,' she said.

But the relationship didn't last long and Mathias left, leaving Nicole with just the income she was getting looking after teenagers – via the agency that had an office in nearby Messines – who would stay in the apartment annexe.

She soon started dating another man called Romano, who was half German, half Italian, with a dash of Romanian or Turkish, and who Lia said was 'abusive' to Nicole and beat her up. 'Romano was a nasty piece of work and she was afraid of him, for sure,' said Lia, adding he had moved in with Nicole in late 2007 or early 2008. 'At one point she had a broken arm and bruises on her face.'

She said Nicole had told her she had known Romano for years ('perhaps back in Germany') and the pair ended up having a baby together (a girl called Luana) but Romano was 'not a good father' and spent much of the time away. On the few occasions Lia had met him, he talked about his job as a builder, telling her he had big construction projects 'in Alentejo', a region an hour north, and that was why he was often away for days at a time.

Everything was stable until 2008, when one of the teenage girls in Nicole's care disappeared. 'All of a sudden this guy Christian was back,' recalled Lia. 'He came from Germany and the rumours were spreading around that he was a private detective of some nature.

'He used to have a gun with him, he wore it on the side of his hip, and everybody was really afraid of him and what was going on in the village. He was always wearing a leather jacket.

'Eventually, he ended up finding this girl and bringing her back. He literally showed up from nowhere [this is not actually correct as he had been hanging around Foral for over a year] … and found her with this group of Romanians (it was actually Ukrainians, I later discovered) and the girl was pregnant and therefore the organisation stopped all the kids coming in.

'Who the hell was he in the first place?' she said getting angry. 'I just know he was German and she [Nicole] brought him out here. I don't know where she got the contact from.' It was, to be fair, a little vague. And actually wrong, as they had met at a Christmas party I later discovered in 2006 nearby.

Lia said she finally regained possession of the house when Nicole fled Romano one evening in 2009. Lia believes she had been planning it for a while, and she took off when Romano was out. She packed everything up into her Jeep and a friend with a van came to help. 'It was blue and had Dutch plates on it,' she recalled. I asked if it could have been Brueckner but she wasn't sure.

Luckily, as Romano didn't have his name on the contract, he was forced to leave over the following days, which he did with the insistence of the local GNR police, whom Lia enlisted. Then Lia saw her beautiful home. 'It was a terrible state, a real mess,' she said. 'There was rubbish on the floor and I found a syringe and a spoon in the wardrobe, plus used needles. There was a brick of hashish in a shoe box, a big chunk. I was completely devastated when I found it, knowing there were kids there and troubled teenagers.

'I threw the drugs away, I can't remember exactly, but I think I burnt them. I realised if it was me that called the police it would be me that got in trouble.' She then had to go to court for the outstanding rent. 'The court situation took forever,' she said. 'It was such a joke.'

She never saw or heard from Nicole again, but a few legal letters arrived for Romano, hand delivered by the local GNR police in Messines. 'There were a couple of occasions when the cops came around looking for him,' she said. 'A few years after they left, I also had some letters for him from the courts in Lisbon. It must be serious if they were sending the police around to deliver letters. They really wanted to find him. I simply returned the letters and told them he no longer lived here.'

There was not much more to say on the matter so I asked her about the Mercedes on Spanish plates in the drive. She said it was for sale and realising it might be a good opportunity to have a look around the house, I told her I would like to have a look at it. It worked like a dream. She opened the gate and beckoned me over to have a look at the car, which 'only had a few hundred kilometres on the clock' and 'had just one owner'. She said it was in a great condition apart from the fact that it wouldn't move 'as rats have eaten the cables.' She said I could tow it away that day for just 1,000 euros and it was owned by a friend of hers 'who used to live in Spain.' It transpired he was English and that he wasn't around 'at the moment'. I assumed it must be her current tenants and asked, but she wasn't being drawn further.

As she opened the door, I got the shock of my life ... not with a rat sitting on the dashboard, but a metre of rope slung in the footwell of the passenger seat. Talk about creepy. I took a couple of photos before asking Lia if she could open the bonnet.

The five-minute inspection had given Laurence the opportunity to spin around the garden and take some pictures. I could tell he felt uncomfortable on his return and was anxious to leave, in particular, as he told me later, because he saw someone lurking inside the apparently empty house and the curtains twitched.

But just as we were beginning to wrap things up, a car pulled up outside the front gate with a middle-aged man and a lad of around 20 inside. They stared at us menacingly. Just as I was on the verge of panicking, thinking we might be about to get trapped, the car sped away leaving a cloud of dust. We would find out later it was a team from *The Sun* newspaper, who had got a tip off about the village. They had no idea the house had any relevance to the case.

It was now 5pm, and we knew we would have to move fast if we were to get the story into the next day's *Mail on Sunday*. The paper was going big on Brueckner and a picture of Lia's villa anchored a four-page Maddie special. Happy days.

Chapter 19

Man of Many Movements

The following lunchtime there were over 20 journalists camped outside Lia's door, trying to reach her over the cacophony of dogs. She however, was adamant, that she had nothing more to say and was angry that we had published a photo of her house without her permission. She was soon featured in every paper, with some pointing out her bizarre Australian accent, while the BBC did eventually persuade her to invite them in to interview her, albeit blacked out in silhouette.

We had got an excellent head start, and had already passed a copy of Nicole Fehlinger's rental contract to *the Mail on Sunday's* reporter Abul Taher, who was probing the story in Germany.

What struck me was that while Nicole now lived in Bavaria, she actually came from Wurzburg, where Brueckner had grown up. Abul tracked her down and we thought we'd struck gold when she agreed to an interview.

We, meanwhile, were talking to as many people as possible in and around Foral to try and piece together Brueckner's movements back in 2007 and 2008. Lia was thankfully soon back onside, having fallen for the charms of Laurence, and was helping as much as she could. She said she would happily allow police to dig at her property if it could bring even the smallest clue to the case, and we continued to ask her questions, but she wasn't much help, as she was either hiding her closeness to Nicole and Christian, or she couldn't remember much of what happened. Probably the latter

However, she did mention the strange former German neighbour Tiziano, a friend of Brueckner's, who had run the O Foral restaurant for a few years, and had been involved in a court case in 2010 also involving Lia, as well as Nicole and the mayor of nearby Silves.

Lia also suggested we talked to her friend Maria, whose two daughters had regularly come into contact with Brueckner and Nicole at the time. The Portuguese mother of two, who had lived in the village for 30 years, told us she had been very scared of Brueckner and Romano, who made up a sort of 'double act'.

'I was very scared of the three of them in fact, including Nicole,' Maria told us. 'Romano in particular struck me with fear, while Christian was clearly a bad man. Nicole meanwhile, claimed to be a psychologist but she would bully my daughter who had mental health issues and was bipolar.

Nicole would call her horrible names and treat her terribly … . What kind of psychologist would do that?

'Something was definitely not right and it made me really concerned, especially as she was meant to be looking after children, including her own.'

She confirmed that Romano and Brueckner were often to be found hanging out at the restaurant O Foral, when it was run by Tiziano. She said the pair even occasionally worked there, and at least one of the teenage girls Nicole looked after did some shifts there. She added that she had heard many stories about Brueckner carrying a gun and that she remembers he once allegedly wielded it during a fight at the restaurant. 'It was such a scary time with all those bad people around,' she said.

Other neighbours were more direct with some insinuating that there was child abuse at the property and that it might have been Brueckner who had got the teenage girl pregnant … and it was for this reason that the girl, Lina Valz, as we now discovered she was called, might have run away. 'There were a lot of strange people and when Christian arrived in 2007 they would hang around together,' said one. 'I didn't like the way they were. Particularly as there were always little girls around the property.' Having heard Brueckner might have been responsible for the pregnancy, she added, 'It makes us think that what they were doing [with the children] was not good.'

As pensioner Ingrid later told me: 'Nicole once insisted that I shouldn't walk around at night without a rape alarm or mace. She said it was dangerous even walking back to our house from the restaurant at night and it was only 400 metres.

'She said that there were many men out there that would rape her or I and that I had to take precautions. It made no sense to me in a sleepy inland village like this. What was she expecting?'

Around the same time, there were reports in the *Daily Mirror* from 'friends' of Brueckner that he allegedly gave underage girls drugs at woodland raves in return for sexual favours, and sold drugs from his van, which he parked up just outside Barao de Sao Joao.

Eventually, we tracked down the rural home of Brueckner's former friend and boss at the restaurant Tiziano Ilg, who lived in a remote villa, Quinta dos Dois, a mile outside Tunes. He had previously been a near neighbour of Brueckner and Nicole's in Foral and gave them, and Romano, work as waiters.

It took some digging but *The Sun* has since found a secret Facebook profile of Ilg, listed under a different name and with just 12 friends. In 2016, it posted a cryptic reference to Maddie, hinting she was dead. Responding to an online news story about her, he wrote: 'It's time to stop looking and stop imagining. We all know.'

I found another page of his on the photo sharing site *Flickr*, which had some pictures of him with a dog on his lap, apparently at a villa in the hills in the Algarve. One of him outside the villa, with the same dog, holding its paws as it stood on its hind legs looking uncomfortable, was used in various press reports.

Finding him wasn't easy and nor was it easy to get him to open up and talk, as he did his level best to avoid coming out of his big hillside villa to chat. We had to bang on his door a number of times and the second for a full five minutes before he came out looking sheepish. Wearing glasses and with a big pot belly, he told us he was a former German air force veteran, now in his seventies, who had lived in various places around the world.

He was surprisingly defensive of Brueckner, who had worked with him on and off for a number of months after Maddie had gone missing and 'possibly as late as 2009', when he had left the village, seemingly for another spell in jail. 'He was always charming, clean shaven and you would never have suspected he was up to no good,' said Tiziano. 'And there is no way of knowing if he had anything to do with Madeleine McCann today.'

He threw a new vehicle into the mix, telling us that when Christian had worked for him he drove an all-white VW LT van. 'A five tonne van and definitely not the yellow and white one he had before,' he said. 'He was definitely driving that one in 2009.'

He also insisted Romano was 'up to no good': 'He was not a nice man for sure. I was definitely wary of him,' he said, adding strangely, 'I don't want to say why. In fact I cannot say why.'

It was frustrating that he wouldn't elaborate further but he did at least confirm the mystery court case involving Lia and Nicole for which he had been ordered to attend in 2010. He said he turned up on the morning of the case, as he had been ordered to by the judge, but with no knowledge of what it was about, only to find it was settled. 'I didn't know why I had been dragged into it,' he said. 'I didn't know what it was about. I still don't. You should go and talk to the mayor about it.'

We did. Predictably with no luck at all. The town hall secretary told us he 'wasn't available' to talk, despite lockdown meaning no business was being conducted. The court in Silves wouldn't help further. Finally, on further pressing, the mayor's daughter returned a call and told us bluntly: 'He simply doesn't remember it.' We went back to Lia, who also dried up, feigning amnesia. It was frustrating, and a good time to spread our wings.

We decided to try and track down Romano using social media, and managed to find a trace in the coastal town of Vila Nova de Milfontes, where he had been apparently living for a time between 2012 and 2018. However there was no way of knowing if he still had a property there as his social media accounts showed that in recent years he had been spending increasing amounts of time in Switzerland.

We had gleaned the information via the birth records of the baby, Luana, he and Nicole had registered in Portugal together, as well as two Facebook feeds, which gave his full name (which I am not revealing for legal reasons) and one which had an Italian link.

The older page, dated from 2015, had a profile of the Balkan-looking man with a young child, while the second had him in a hat and mask with only his eyes showing. It marked him down as 'single'. His current location was given as Vila Nova de Milfontes and many of his 'friends' (they have since been hidden, along with his location) were from around the area, while his posts were mostly about expat animal charities, football, rap and tattoos, although one post he shared from a German friend called Simon, about 'pulling a child out of a well', made us look twice.

His more recent page gave little away but it did allow the visitor to see his collection of weird and wonderful friends, who came from all over Europe, including many from the Balkans, a few from the UK, some from Spain and a fair few from Portugal. Many of them had pictures of their dogs and cats on their profile pages. Romano had certainly been a regular visitor to Portugal over recent years, in particular visiting German-run animal refuge Tierschutz Esperanca in the town of Saboia, 20km north of Messines and close to Monchique.

We decided to drive to Vila Nova de Milfontes on the off chance we could find Romano or, at least, someone who might know him. Milfontes, as it is known, is an attractive seaside resort, halfway up the Silver Coast towards Lisbon, facing the Atlantic. While it was annoyingly out of the way, a good 90-minute drive north west, I had stayed there on holiday so it was nice to return to the attractive town that sits on an inlet with some breathtaking scenery and wonderful beaches.

Our first port of call was the local GNR police station where we asked if they could help with an address for Romano. We told them we were journalists investigating the Madeleine McCann case and immediately we were ushered into the captain's office and asked to sit down. He told us he recognised the name and sent someone off to look for a file. He added that he knew a number of Romano's friends on Facebook and there were quite a few 'oohs' and 'ahhs' from his staff, as they scrolled through the names. It was all going swimmingly until he noticed me taking a photo of his colleagues as Laurence scrolled through the Facebook page on his phone ... and then Capitan Clot went off the deep end and threw us both out.

I hastily apologised and showed him I was deleting the photo, but his face was red with anger as he ordered us to leave … and we were out on the street in two minutes. Frustrated again.

We were forced to resort to classic gumshoe; taking either side of the high road and walking into shops showing pictures of Romano until finally someone recognised him and told us he used to run a car-cleaning service on the edge of the town. Bingo! We headed there and, on arrival, we were told to contact someone called Torsten, his old business partner, who thankfully still lived in the town.

It turned out to be the shortest interview in history. After we'd insisted we couldn't tell him anything on the phone, he agreed to meet us for a coffee an hour later. He turned up looking incredibly nervous and shifty and once we told him we were trying to locate his friend Romano and said we were journalists, he jumped up and made to leave. It took all my powers of persuasion to get him to stay, insisting we wouldn't mention his full name, plus his coffee had already been ordered and was just arriving. He gave us exactly five minutes and was as evasive as hell.

'He [Romano] ran away, left in a hurry,' he said, confirming he had worked with him cleaning cars. 'He went back to Switzerland and is now in Basel. But he is hard to keep up with as he is always changing his number. I communicate with him via Facebook messenger and normally when he gets in touch with me.'

Asked what line of work Romano was in, Torsten pulled hard on a cigarette and tapped the table with his other hand: 'Dunno really. He works in scaffolding, he's got some sort of building firm. Over here he did a few different things. He was working with Nicole with the troubled German kids thing. Then suddenly he had this new girlfriend and he left.

'He was a good friend, but then we lost contact … he comes back from time to time and he was here last summer for two weeks. I saw him a couple of times. He's got three kids now, that is all I can tell you.' And with that he stood up and pretty much ran off towards a van that was being driven by a girlfriend.

Back in Foral, more neighbours and friends were queuing up to tell us about Nicole's troubled, chaotic life. One resident, Joao Paulo Pascoa, told Laurence that Nicole had a 'snobby' air about her. He often came into contact with her, as did his wife, a local school teacher, who taught Nicole's daughter Jessica. The friendly local, a skipper by trade, said he knew of many teens who stayed in her rented villa and most were 'not happy', including Lina Valz, who had run away. 'People say she was scared to live in that house,' he said. 'Heaven only knows what happened in there.'

Certainly, after tracking down various police documents surrounding Lina's disappearance in 2008, I realised there was a lot more than meets the eye. Thankfully, the records were still at the GNR police station in San Bartolomeu de Messines. It took a bit of coaxing but eventually the area's new chief of police allowed us to take a look at the paperwork, as well as, by coincidence, a later file kept on the arrest of Christian Brueckner in 2017 (more of which later).

The first official report on the disappearance of Lina Valz, who was 16 at the time, was filed on September 17, 2008 by Nicole Fehlinger.

In the carefully typed out report, it notes that Lina had been born in January 1992 in the town of Konken, in Germany. Alongside a clear colour photo, it noted her height as 1.65m, her green eyes and that she had two ear piercings and a silver necklace complete with an 'L' pendant. It added that she was a 'traumatised child' who had left her country to get away from 'mistreatment by her father'.

Nicole, whose job was given as a 'social worker', told the police that she was looking after Lina at her rented home Villa Bianca, via the *Instituto Algarve Projecto Reabilitacao Social (IAPRS)*. She said on the day she went missing she had seen Lina at the O Foral restaurant, where she had been working as a trainee, on the previous afternoon at around 5pm. She told police inspector Luis Manuel Silva Guerreiro that after her shift she saw her in the company of 'three Russians' who she suspected she left with, before later describing them as 'three Ukrainians'.

She said Lina had left the restaurant to come home for supper, and at 8pm had gone out under the pretext of meeting a friend to bring home to introduce to Nicole. She never came home. She suspected that she may have fled to the coastal resort of Albufeira, where, curiously, she 'ran away once before', although she didn't go into any detail. We were unable to find a missing persons report for that occasion.

The report was dated and signed by Nicole with a decidedly basic signature. Alongside it was an official form from the IARPS that noted Nicole as a 'worker' for the institute, listing her social security number and little more.

It is not known how much notice the GNR police in Messines took of the missing persons report. After all, she was 16 and had run away before, and teenagers frequently run away at that age. Badly understaffed, as we were to discover, they probably knew little about the IAPRS organisation at the time, which, as I will explain later, was probed over a number of discrepancies, before shutting down.

Indeed, the next report on Lina, a so-called 'witness inquiry' was filed with the teenager herself some two weeks later on September 30.

Also taken at Messines Police Station, it was made with the help of a translator – conveniently Nicole Fehlinger – who should surely have been kept outside the process given her closeness to the case. It might explain the shortness of the questioning and the brevity of the answers, as Lina sat alongside her 'tutora' Nicole.

Starting at 9.57am, the entire process was over by 10.51am, with Lina asked no more than seven or eight questions. She said she could not explain why she ran away, but confirmed she had returned 11 days later on September 27 of her own accord. She said that she had met just two Ukrainian men at the O Foral restaurant and 'decided to go for a walk' with them. She was only able to name one of them – Ivan – and said both lived in the nearby town of Algoz, near Silves, but couldn't (or wouldn't) give the exact address.

Why the police inspector did not press for the other man's name, or ask their age or what they did for a living is unclear, considering these two men (or was it three, as Nicole had claimed?) had driven 15 minutes to have lunch, presumably at the O Foral restaurant, and then left with a teenage girl in their car. Is that normal? Acceptable?

Lina told the policeman (at least according to Nicole's translation) that she had left with the men entirely of her own 'free will' and that they had brought her back when she said she wanted to come home. She said she had stayed at their home in Algoz, where she was not forced to stay indoors, but chose to do so, 'preferring' to spend the time watching TV.

She insisted – again, according to Nicole's translation – that she had not had any 'sexual relations' with either of the men and that she was 'not forced to do anything [she] didn't want to do.' Bizarrely, she also added that she had 'cooked for them' on various evenings.

There were no further questions and Lina signed the document, while Nicole signed a separate form the same morning confirming that she was happy for the 'case to be closed'. It was.

Chapter 20

An Alarming Confession

There are two distinct sides to Nicole Fehlinger. The caring social worker and mother, only too happy to open her doors to needy, troubled children … and the sexy, tattooed vamp, who liked to talk dirty and let a range of ruffians, wife-beaters and even paedophiles into her life. Photogenic – as can be seen from a series of pictures taken at her home in Foral and nearby beaches around 2007 and 2008 – with dark eyes, jet black hair, slim waist and long shapely legs, the 43 year old was never short of admirers during the decade she lived in Portugal … and allegedly had various lovers and boyfriends, including Brueckner, wrapped around her little finger.

Yet, when journalist Abul Taher managed to track her down, via her father Dieter, in Schweinfurt, Germany, she painted a different picture.

While we were being given sordid and uncomfortable information about Nicole's complicated life on the Algarve, *the Mail on Sunday's* security correspondent was being fed a picture of middle-class respectability. Working as a hotel receptionist in the mid-size Bavarian town, the mother of (at least) two children came over as 'professional and credible' Abul told me, although he said she 'was extremely careful about what she said'.

Managing to get the first interview with this close female friend of Brueckner's had been a coup for us, particularly with all the German, British and Portuguese press vying for it. But somehow it didn't work out. Whether we didn't coordinate properly on the questioning or she was simply a master of deception, she was always one step ahead and managed to pour cold water over her Brueckner connections, which, as we shall see, were far more intimate than she claimed. It was a total let down as far as I was concerned, given how much information we were unearthing on child neglect and other crimes concerning her associates.

To make matters worse, Abul told me the newsdesk had 'got cold feet' about using the interview after some 'legal problems'. He wouldn't tell me what they were (although I now know it was over a contractual complaint) but he reiterated that Nicole had insisted she 'hardly knew' Brueckner and was 'certainly not [his] ex-girlfriend'.

Initially I was a little angry with Abul, not understanding how she had pulled the wool over his eyes when so many former friends and neighbours were telling us the opposite. But these investigations are often fraught and complicated affairs, particularly when interviewees are soliciting for money and lawyers are involved. And I now know Nicole far, far better.

The interview had been set up via her father Dieter, a retired minibus driver (not ambulance driver as reported widely) who is divorced from Nicole's mother Sonja, on the condition that his daughter had anonymity. Abul had met her twice, once at her father's flat, which was also in Schweinfurt, and later at the apartment she shared nearby with her two daughters, in order to deliver a contract for the interview. Cautiously, she told him she had been 'living with [her] own boyfriend' at the time and had never dated Brueckner. Abul eventually agreed to give me a transcript of the interview to look at for clues for this book, and he also gave me a breakdown of what she had allegedly told him, while the picture desk sent me a photo they had taken of her, which showed a conservative, warm and open woman, apparently only too happy to help in the inquiry.

Nicole had insisted she and Brueckner were not childhood friends and that she had met him for the first time at Christmas 2006, which would tally with him getting out of prison on the Algarve a week earlier. 'She said she was visiting the house of a German friend, some 2km out of Foral, but she wouldn't give me a name,' explained Abul. 'She said they were a family and her daughter played with the couple's child, who was the same age.' I now know this was the Piro residence nearby.

Nicole claimed she had only met Brueckner 'about six or seven times' between then and 2009, when he left for Germany. She did, however, admit though that he had been to her house in Foral, where she moved in 2004 with a 'wealthy man' (Mathias). Prior to that she lived in a town called Goldra, after arriving in Portugal in 2000. 'She said Christian mostly came round in a Winnebago, and used to refill the water and recharge its batteries and sometimes would stay for an hour or two,' said Abul. 'Sometimes he slept in the Winnebago overnight parked outside.' (His van was actually a Tiffin Allegro Bay RV, which is often mistakenly referred to as a 'Winnebago' in conversation and in press reports).

She said she had opened a restaurant in Foral with her boyfriend (I assume this must be Romano) and that she had looked after German teenagers in her care via an institute in Portugal. 'She said it was paid by the German government and admitted that it ended after a girl in her care ran away,' explained Abul. 'She claimed it was her boyfriend and not Brueckner who had found the girl.'

She confirmed that she had ended up leaving Portugal in 2010 as her boyfriend became violent towards her, and then she fled with her two daughters, one from a previous boyfriend and one from Romano. She added that her own ex-boyfriend was evicted from the Foral villa shortly after she left, not Brueckner, as was reported in the media (I'm not sure what she meant by this as it was certainly not reported in the British media). 'Nicole said Brueckner never mentioned the Maddie case to her, but talked about friends in Lagos and Portimao,' explained Abul.

The interview threw up no surprises. In fact, the only really intriguing part was that the German federal police had already interviewed her three times about her links to Brueckner. They too must have suspected it was more than just a fleeting relationship. 'She told me she had been at the police station, brought in as a witness, and assured that she was not a suspect,' Abul told me. 'She insisted they were less interested in what she got up to with Christian, but more about the people who Christian knew and where they are now.' They knew there was a tight-knit German community on the Algarve and, according to Nicole, they just wanted her to tell them who Brueckner's friends were to help connect the dots.

When I asked Abul why the police were taking her information and evidence so seriously when she claimed to have only met Brueckner 'six or seven times', he admitted that it did 'seem strange' and she 'must have been economic with the truth'. He added she had definitely been evasive and she 'probably had a lot to hide' and that she probably know Brueckner more than she was letting on. 'The problem is when you get a sit down interview like that you can only go on what they tell you,' he said. 'I agree now we should have tried harder to get more out of her.

'She's quite a character, for sure. You wouldn't want to mess with her.'

Later he told me she seemed the type to have been involved in petty crime, although he would question whether she could have been in child trafficking. 'Of course you can never be sure,' he added.

While this interview was a damp squib, Abul landed a great scoop with Nicole's father, who had, by coincidence, also 'bumped into' Brueckner on a trip to Portugal in 2007. It was an extremely damning character assassination with Brueckner effectively admitting he was a drug dealer and even hinting that he may have been transporting children in his vans.

Dieter said he had met him when he had parked his huge RV outside his daughter's home in Foral, asking if he could recharge its batteries and fill it up with water. During a ten-minute conversation with Brueckner – who grew up in Wurzburg, where the Fehlingers lived at the time – Dieter was invited in to take a look around the vehicle.

Dating the conversation to spring 2007, certainly around the time Maddie went missing, he said the cream and brown house on wheels – which had a bedroom, bathroom and a kitchen – was on German licence plates from Hanover. Later he would tell me that it had an 'odd smell'.

'As I looked inside, I asked him, "Herr Brueckner, what do you do in Portugal? What is your job?" He told me, "I work, I get money, because I have a special business. I transport grass [cannabis] in my van."

'I was surprised, I did not believe it exactly. But Brueckner told me again, "I have 50kg of grass, and I transport it around Europe. Nobody can see it." I thought he was joking.'

'He told me, "I can transport children, kids, in this space. Drugs and children, you can transport them in this van, it's a safe space in the van, nobody can find them. Nobody can catch you."'

It was jaw-dropping stuff and it rightly made big news that weekend in England, and was followed up by hundreds of media groups worldwide.

I was perplexed by the apparent lack of alarm Dieter showed at the time, particularly given his grandchildren were around. He told Abul he thought Brueckner was 'merely bragging' about the size of his new van at the time and making most of the claims up. However, with evidence continuing to emerge about Brueckner's crimes against children, the German pensioner now fears he was more than capable of snatching and transporting youngsters in his vehicle.

'I believe he kidnapped Maddie and brought her out of Portugal in his big van,' admitted Dieter in the interview. 'At the time, I thought he was interested in my daughter – he was a bad boy. I felt, as a father, my daughter was not safe with such a man.' He then said, 'I want to kill Brueckner. My daughter was in danger at the time, as was her daughter (who was six at the time), because he is a paedophile.'

Dieter mirrored Nicole's claims that she had been visited by Brueckner in Foral 'about half a dozen times'. He said he had either been driving the van or his dark-coloured Jaguar. He said his daughter had fallen out of contact with Brueckner when she left Portugal in 2010, but did hear from him again in 2012 when he arrived unexpectedly on her doorstep in Bavaria.

How he got her address is anyone's guess, particularly when she had slipped under the radar as she had fled violent Romano and owed thousands in rent. It is more likely that they stayed closely in touch and, in any case, her father later confirmed to me that they had certainly met again years later when he phoned Nicole out of the blue and asked to stay with her because he 'did not want to be alone over Christmas'. According to Dieter, she declined, but he told me he thinks they 'kept in touch over the years'.

Dieter hoped that by speaking out, other witnesses might come forward and give evidence to the police. The week after giving the interview he himself was asked to attend a police station to give detectives his additional information. He told a German newspaper: 'There were two plain-clothed officers from the BKA. They interviewed me for about two hours. I told them everything – about the motorhome, the drugs and the children.'

He retold his story in early 2021 in Prime Suspect, the three-part Discovery Channel documentary on the Madeleine case and its connections to Brueckner. Filmed in his sitting room, with his face blurred out and only his rings (one of a skull and another of what looked like a scimitar visible), he recalled how his (unnamed) daughter had moved to Portugal 'in 2002' and left in '2009'. This time his story changed slightly, and he said he had arrived at his daughter's home in Foral to find Brueckner's RV already parked inside the gates and his granddaughter playing with him on the lawn.

Unwittingly suggesting that his daughter and Brueckner were by now a couple, he also recalled a lot more about the motorhome itself. 'I was visiting in March or April 2007 and flew down to help my daughter clean the pool. When we entered the main gate we saw someone with a big campervan inside. I didn't know him. We saw him with my granddaughter and he was playing with her on the grass in front of the bus.

'My daughter introduced him as Christian. We started to speak about the camper because it was so big. I went in there to look; there was a big sofa and a rotating seat and in front some sort of dancefloor and looking to the back there was another huge space. It really was a gigantic thing.

'He told me right away he wanted to smuggle weed in the camper. Real grass, weed – 50 kilos. "Where do you want to put 50 kilos?" I asked him. He said he would hide it so well, no one will find it. "It is so big that you would be able to hide a small child."'

Brueckner is certainly bold. How many convicted paedophiles with drug offences, talk openly about drug smuggling and child trafficking with the grandfather of the 6-year-old girl they had been playing with on the lawn?

It is interesting that German police have not commented on Dieter's claims and said only that Nicole is not a suspect. I wish I could be as sure. Just before this book went to press, I visited Dieter and he gave me news that would make me feel Nicole is more involved than she claims. In fact, he said he thought she was the key to the whole case. Read on.

Chapter 21

The 100,000 Euro Haul

Despite Nicole Fehlinger claiming she'd only met Christian Brueckner six or seven times, a Portuguese family accused the pair of working together, as thieves. Talking to the *RTP* network on Portuguese TV, they described Brueckner and Nicole as 'a couple' and accused her of being his 'accomplice' in burglaries on the Algarve. The mother and daughter from Lisbon said police had actually questioned Nicole over a robbery at their own villa in November 2007.

Julia and Isabel – who asked not to be named in full – claimed to have known Nicole well, having employed her for six months to work with Isabel's 2-year-old daughter who had learning difficulties. They had met around May 2007, having answered an advert she had placed in a local newspaper on the Algarve offering her services as a therapist to children with 'hyperactive problems'. They told the journalist Sandra Felgueiras' *Sexta as 9* programme that Nicole claimed she was a 'social worker' but offered no proof, aside from introducing them to the teenage Lina, whom she said she was officially tutoring, via the German government.

They should have heard alarm bells when it emerged Nicole would only be charging them the ridiculously low fee of five euros a day, plus lunch. Apparently, she described it as a 'symbolic' fee, which would 'cover her petrol', and insisted she didn't need to charge more as she got paid enough from the German government. They claimed that was around 1,200 euros a month and later I would discover it was even more than that.

She also said she was charging so little in order to get more experience of working with children with learning difficulties, and particularly of those belonging to expat families, as she wanted to understand how different nationalities lived.

It sounded plausible, and the couple were completely taken in by well-spoken Nicole, welcoming her into their family. She would spend hours with them at the house, as well as afternoons on the beach, and would even go on holiday with them. They shared photos of her at their house, and building sandcastles with the toddler. She was, by all accounts, an asset to the family. 'She was a calm, patient person and was never argumentative, quickly adapting to our needs,' explained Julia, adding that she would often ferry her granddaughter around in the car, as her daughter was unable to drive following an accident.

It was while working for the Lisbon family that Julia and Isabel came into contact with her 'boyfriend' who they are sure today was Brueckner. They first met him when he came up to Lisbon with Nicole later that summer, and he was also to visit their home in Albufeira. Despite displaying a placid nature to Julia and Isabel, Nicole was different with Brueckner. 'They seemed to get along well although it was clear that she was very much in charge,' said Julia to Felgueiras. 'He was a calmer, more reserved type, she was more domineering. She was the one who called the shots. You could see she told him what to do.'

They said that Nicole didn't talk about her husband Mathias at all. Indeed, they believe he was completely out of the picture by late 2006 (he was) when Nicole claimed to first meet Brueckner at the Christmas party near Foral. He had by, all accounts, returned to Germany to work and rarely came back to Portugal. The pair had certainly become estranged, allowing for Brueckner and/or Romano to jostle for position. While vague, it was suggested by the programme that it was Brueckner who was introduced as the father of Nicole's daughter Jessica.

Nicole was an integral part of the family throughout the summer of 2007 until there was a robbery at the couple's four-bedroom beach villa in Praia de Gale, near Albufeira, some 50km up the coast from Praia da Luz. Nicole ended up being a key suspect in the raid that saw the couple lose 100,000 euros in cash ... but today they are certain that Brueckner was involved as well.

They say that a man with a striking resemblance to Brueckner was seen by neighbours leaving the villa, Casa Magali, on the afternoon of Sunday November 4, carrying a rucksack and heavy tools that were probably used in the break in. What's more, the break in had taken place while the pair had been attending Nicole's daughter's birthday party in Foral. And furthermore, only Nicole knew about the hoard of cash that was hidden in a suitcase in the villa.

They went on to accuse Nicole on national television of being behind the robbery, by tipping off Brueckner when they were out of the house.

Court documents in Portugal unearthed by RTP, allegedly revealed that Nicole was brought in for questioning over the robbery and that she had been in regular phone conversations with Brueckner at the time. The couple told Sexta as 9 that they believed Nicole had specifically bought a pay-as-you-go mobile that week to call Brueckner about the money, so it could not be traced back to her normal number.

Moreover, they insisted that Nicole was the only person who knew about the cash as she had been in the car with them as they attempted, and failed, to deposit it at their local BES bank branch on Thursday November 1. 'It was too much money and the banknotes were too high in denomination and we were told to come back another day,' said Julia. 'We didn't tell her it was cash, but she must have worked it out.'

They are sure of this for various reasons. Firstly, because Nicole had watched them go in and out of the bank with the bag and had asked them to pull over soon after leaving the bank so she could go into a mobile phone shop. 'She actually told us she was going to buy a cell phone and she wanted a disposable one,' recalled Julia.

It was that very weekend – just three days later – that the theft took place while the couple were celebrating Nicole's daughter Jessica's ninth birthday at her home in Foral. Photos taken by the couple show the elegant mother-of-two lighting the candles on her daughter's birthday cake. In a light blue chiffon top and with her hair swept back neatly and tied in a bun, she is the picture of concentration, as her daughter and a friend smile for the camera wearing matching black Stetson cowboy hats.

If career criminal Christian Brueckner was involved, it couldn't have been hard to locate the suitcase that was stuffed with cash, mostly in 200 and 500 euro denominations. With his years of experience as a burglar he would have been in and out in a matter of minutes, and he would have been well hidden because, as I discovered while visiting, the villa was next to a dirt track, which provided an easy escape route.

It was only in July 2020, however, when RTP visited the property that neighbours recalled seeing a man with an exact resemblance of Brueckner slinking away down through the brush beside the house.

Intriguingly, they also remembered how they had seen a white van parked in the cul-de-sac around the time of the robbery. 'That was the day that everything ended,' recalled Julia. 'We had gone with Nicole to her house in Foral at 1pm. It was far from our home and we decided we had to come back early at 4pm after my granddaughter had a fall.' It wasn't a serious injury but the couple felt it was time to go home. 'She (Nicole) tried to stop us going but we disagreed and walked up to the restaurant [O Foral] and ordered a taxi to go home,' added Isabel.

They knew instantly that they had been robbed, with the burglar managing to get through a kitchen window. And they were immediately suspicious of Nicole, recalling how she had bizarrely followed Julia around the villa as she got ready to leave. They believed this was to see if she put on the alarm or not, before leaving for the party.

'She was right behind me the whole time I was getting ready to leave,' Julia told the programme. 'As we have a cat and we didn't want her setting off the alarm, we didn't turn it on that day. Looking back I could see she was being very attentive to see if I turned on the alarm or not.'

They also think it is significant that Nicole had brought over a cake she had baked that morning, and left it on an inside window sill, by the very window that the thief would end up climbing through. Could she have somehow tampered with the lock or loosened it in some way while it was obscured by the cake? Did she leave the cake as a signal for Brueckner who may have been hiding nearby, so he knew which window to try? What was most damning was a phone call Nicole had received in the car, while they were en route to the party. It was a short call, half an hour into the unnecessary-long drive to Foral and they only heard her say a couple of words, in German, the main one being *naturlich*, which means 'of course'. All the talking was by her friend.

'She said that word – *naturlich* – more than once,' recalled Julia. 'And when the conversation was over she told us it had come from Germany.'

They were so sure Nicole was behind the robbery they filed an official police complaint the following day. They told police they believed she had deliberately taken a longer route than necessary to get to Foral, ensuring that the robber had more than enough time to break in and search for the money. They gave them the full story and added they felt it was suspicious that Nicole had also suddenly turned up out of the blue that evening at about 9.30pm, ostensibly 'to check' if their daughter was OK. Indeed, why would she have left her own daughter at home on her birthday to come all the way to Praia de Gale (a one-hour round trip on a good day) to see them, merely over a small bruise on their daughter's knee? Surely she could have phoned or waited til the next day?

The police felt the claims were worth investigating and they referred the report up to Portimao Court. Ten days later Nicole was summoned to answer questions by police from the GNR. She completely denied knowing about the money being deposited at the bank, and said she had no idea what was in the couple's bag. She flat out denied being involved in the robbery or coordinating it in any way.

However she did admit to something which, I believe, is extremely pertinent to the case today: the person she spoke to on the way to Foral was 'Christian Brueckner'. She even provided the police with the phone number that her 'friend' Christian had called her on during the drive. A pay-as-you-go number (915 078 040), not entirely dissimilar to the one used outside the Ocean Club the night that Maddie disappeared in May that year. In further questioning, however, she insisted Christian was in Germany at the time of the call and was still there ten days later. This seems unlikely, and Julia and Isabel are certain that Brueckner was in Portugal at the time.

One would have hoped the police would have tried to locate Brueckner? At least speak to him on the phone. They had his number. But apparently not, and unbelievably the case was dropped by the courts a few days later. Julia and Isabel refused to give up though, and appealed to reopen the case, but the investigating judge and prosecutor refused, insisting there was no evidence to support their claims. It is quite baffling. A request to police to triangulate the calls and find out where Brueckner really was at the time of the call also fell on deaf ears.

Later, Brueckner's former friend Elke Piro would tell me that she knows '100%' that both were involved 'as Christian confirmed it to me.' Even Nicole's own father, Dieter, went on to tell me that he felt there must be 'some truth' in his daughter's involvement to the robbery, and he believes that it wasn't an isolated case.

It is as confusing as it is disgraceful on the part of the Portuguese police. Not just in their inability to investigate such a big, broad-daylight burglary, but the fact that the name Christian Brueckner, who had a string of convictions and – as I will explain – had only got out of a Portuguese prison ten months earlier, should come up again. He was also by then allegedly on a list of suspects over the Maddie case and detectives were meant to have been cross-checking the movements of all foreigners at the time, particularly sex offenders.

In December 2007, Nicole's errant husband Mathias returned to the Algarve. According to *Sexta as 9*, when he found how much money Nicole had somehow accrued during his months back in Germany, which was evident with all her brand new expensive furniture, he decided to ask for a divorce. The fact that she may have been seeing one or a number of other men, including Romano and/or Christian Brueckner, may have been the final straw.

What we know for sure is that two years later Nicole had a child with Romano and Brueckner was still a regular visitor to the house and was spending time with them. When questioned by Germany's BKA police on her movements in 2007, Nicole said she hardly saw Brueckner and spent most of her time with Mathias. Yet Julia and Isabel claim they were a couple and that Brueckner and Nicole had come up to Lisbon to visit them in October 2007. They said he was en route to the airport, claiming that he had to go back to Germany to get his 'teeth fixed' as he did not have social security in Portugal. 'We only had a short amount of time with him, before he went to Germany. He spoke little but he seemed calm. He just wanted to take care of his teeth in the best possible way,' said Isabel.

The last time Julia and Isabel saw Nicole was towards the end of November 2007, a few weeks after the robbery, when she turned up to pick up a car from outside their house. While they cannot remember the make of the car they do recall that it had no licence plates. Nicole had arrived with Lina and knocked on the door to ask if they could take the vehicle out of the drive. She had brought a new set of plates with her, which they believe were German.

There was understandably quite a lot of bad feeling and they were still convinced of her involvement in the robbery, and also brought up why she had a car without plates. They ended up arguing about it. 'She told us it had no licence plates because it had come from Germany where it was registered,' said Julia. 'And she could only come and pick it up once someone in Germany had sent her the plates. The whole thing was definitely strange.'

Nicole was unfazed and went about putting on the plates in order to drive away, but then an argument erupted between her and Lina. 'Lina was 'clearly uncomfortable with the situation' with the plates, said Julia and she began to 'shout angrily' at Nicole. At that point, Nicole lost her temper with Lina and started screaming back at her. 'In fact, she literally bundled her in the car,' recalled Julia, jumped in and drove off at high speed.

Why did Nicole have this car? What was it doing parked at Casa Magali and what was she planning to do with it? Was it a stolen Portuguese or Spanish car? Did it belong to her? Or could it perhaps have been owned by Brueckner? One assumes it was never checked for DNA.

•••

There is one uncanny final connection between Nicole and Brueckner worth mulling over. The pair are almost exactly the same age and were born into the same small German town of Wurzburg, within a week of each other in 1976 (Brueckner on December 7 and Nicole on December 15) at the University Hospital, an ugly imposing place on the edge of town. Wurzburg is a medium sized town of 127,000 residents, and the Fehlingers have not ventured far away, living in Schweinfurt, just 50km away.

Instead of having met just 'six or seven times', could they have been secret lifelong friends? It was a question I would eventually put to her father, and to which I would receive an intriguing response.

Chapter 22

Birth of a Monster

A classic sociopath, Christian Stefan Brueckner is a master criminal, who somehow largely stayed under the radar for most of his adult life, free to carousel the highways of Europe to indulge his sick fantasies. Despite an alarming 19 convictions in his home country, he has spent much less than ten years of his life behind bars in Germany. Mostly earning short sentences, for what the legal profession often dub 'minor crimes', he was able to leave prison in one country and pop up in another reinventing himself.

In what will prove to be a lesson for European-wide crime-fighting collaboration and, in particular, Europol, the perverted German was able to indulge his depraved desires almost totally without suspicion around the continent for the best part of two decades. Zig-zagging his way across the many Schengen members, he drove his vans with impunity in and out of Eastern Europe, up to Holland, down to Italy, and backwards across France and Spain on dozens of occasions ... with one goal: to find the next victim of his sadistic tendencies.

Although first convicted in a court in his hometown of Wurzburg at the age of 15 in 1992, for a burglary that landed him a light sentence, Brueckner had been on the local police radar from a tender age – due to his sexual behaviour around children. Schoolfriends described him as 'strange'.

His first run in with the courts had no effect on him, and the following year, in 1993, at the age of 16 he was sentenced to an eight-month suspended juvenile sentence for 'multiple thefts' and driving without a licence. A year later, at the age of 17, he was finally convicted of two separate sex offences – that of molesting a 6 year old and a 9 year old.

Brueckner had certainly not been dealt the kindest hand as a child.

Born Christian Fischer, his birth mother rejected him, leading to a short spell in an orphanage, before he was adopted by his parents Fritz and Brigitte Brueckner, who lived a 15-minute drive out of Wurzburg in the small village of Bergtheim. The leafy village with a population of just 3,800 sits in the north east of Bavaria on a flat plain of farmland and is remarkable for how very unremarkable it is.

Christian's parents had three boys, who are all understood to have been adopted. They lived in a grand four-storey home, with a pitched roof, Velux windows and a statue of the Virgin Mary in a portico above the front door.

The austere stone building had ancient foundations and, curiously, a cellar, with four small slit windows.

While on the surface life looked calm, Brueckner later told a social worker about an unhappy childhood behind doors. Beatings and punishment were the norm and Christian claimed that he and his brothers had been abused every day. In June 2021, I would visit his childhood home, and his mother Brigitte, and learn more about his harsh upbringing.

The boys were sent to the local primary school Grundschule Bergtheim, before heading to secondary school in nearby Wurzburg.

And it is there that an awkward-looking Christian, with a bowl haircut and gormless looks, started to come off the rails. A former classmate told the *Daily Mail* that Brueckner spent his days annoying the other pupils and getting into fights. 'I've only ever had one fight in my life and that was with Brueckner,' said the unnamed man. 'He spent a year talking about me behind my back. He would not stop making nasty comments. One day I exploded and told him to go back to the orphanage from where he had come. We all knew he was adopted, so I shouldn't have said that but I lost my temper with him. He jumped on me and we traded punches. A teacher pulled us apart.

'Everyone in my class hated him and they all kept their distance. But it wasn't just the children it was the teachers as well. I always knew he would turn out bad.'

In the early 1990s, his father suffered brain damage and was confined to a wheelchair following a car accident, and his parents decided they could no longer handle this wayward teenager. It was agreed that he should be sent to an orphanage in Wurzburg run by the charity Diakonie. It was here that things got worse, because while he smoke and drank like many adolescents, he also started to experiment with drugs. It made him more erratic and worsened his behaviour.

A fellow orphan who lived with Brueckner for two years from 1992 remembers him as an 'aggressive' troublesome flatmate, who attacked his carers and led a continual life of crime. The man, now in his late forties, told the *Frankfurter Allgemeine Zeitung* newspaper: 'The conditions in the flat were already violent, but Christian was one of the most aggressive of all. He once threw a glass bottle at a carer because he had saved him nothing to eat. It was awful, particularly as I got a splinter in my eye.'

Although the boys got ten marks pocket money a week, there was 'never enough food in the house' and the place was filthy. 'It was a really dirty place full of cockroaches and moths and the caretakers usually slept downstairs in the common room, but they changed often,' said the unnamed man.

'Christian had the largest room on the first floor and had a balcony. We often sat there and he frequently rolled joints. He was always getting into trouble and was often given curfews or orders to stay in his room. He hardly took any notice and was always breaking into local homes and sheds and once stole the minibus. He was always dressed in black and most of the kids were afraid of him.'

With bad acne, Brueckner struggled to find a girlfriend and needed to find a release. He resorted to easy gratification and started to prey on younger children. He was arrested over a number of child abuse and assault cases – including dropping his trousers and masturbating in front of a 9-year-old boy. In 1994, he was convicted for molesting a 6-year-old girl in Wurzburg, after grabbing and assaulting her in a playground the previous year. According to *Der Spiegel*, he had followed her into a bush, held her by one of her arms, taken his penis out of his pants, lifted her skirt and grabbed her between her legs. He only ran away when she screamed.

A little later he abused a 9-year-old girl, leading to being prosecuted over three separate incidents and charged with 'sexual abuse of a child, attempted sexual abuse of a child and sexual acts in front of a child'. It was quite a collection of charges for a man not out of his teens. 17 to be exact.

The court took the offences seriously and heard evidence from a number of the children's family members, and witnesses. In the end, a psychiatrist told the court that Brueckner would require 'intensive supervision' and the judge handed him a two-year custodial sentence in a juvenile facility, which operated as a halfway house, meaning he still had considerable freedom. When asked by the judge what he thought of his behaviour, he replied, chillingly, 'I don't think anything.'

The former flatmate recalls that day, in 1994, when he was removed from the orphanage to start his sentence: 'I remember the police turning up and taking him away. I thought it was for breaking into cigarette machines, I had no idea that it was over the molesting of a young girl.'

Despite this punishment, Brueckner had no intention of mending his ways and in the same year notched up convictions for drug dealing, driving under the influence and driving without a licence, the latter for which he was handed an eight-month suspended sentence.

While he was at the juvenile facility, he was given the chance to learn a trade as a mechanic. Throwing himself into his apprenticeship, he knuckled down and became pretty knowledgeable about cars and vans. He made it around half way through the required three year-apprenticeship, learning about all aspects of engines, but he was also working hard to learn how to drive and, as soon as he had passed his test at 18, and despite not having been officially released, there was only one thing he planned to do. Run away and live abroad!

Chapter 23

No Escape

Within days of passing his driving test at the age of 18, Christian Brueckner vanished. AWOL. He had been saving up the money he earnt doing odd jobs at a garage in Wurzburg, and had extra money from drug-dealing. Although he still had some time left of his youth custody sentence to serve, and was only half way through his apprenticeship as a car mechanic, he didn't care. He had recently found himself a serious girlfriend, called Silke, who had a similar desire to travel and they took off one day in spring 1995.

On his return to Germany after being extradited from the Algarve in 1999, he told the court: 'We knew nothing about Portugal. We went to Lagos because we simply liked the name. We had little money, but we had a tent with us and went off and camped in the wild.' While I have been unable to uncover the complete identity of Silke, friends recall her as being petite with dark brown hair. Although fiercely attracted to one another, the relationship was turbulent and on and off.

It is unclear exactly what he got up to in those early years on the Algarve, but from talking to locals around Lagos and Praia da Luz he worked in a string of low-paid jobs. I also discovered that he worked at a local English newspaper in telesales, having done a stint at a German newspaper before that.

He also used his skills as a car mechanic and got a series of temporary jobs at the numerous car garages scattered around rural Algarve. 'He certainly bought and sold a lot of cars,' a mechanic friend Bernhard Piro told me. 'He always had different cars and he certainly knew how to do them up and fix them. He knew what he was talking about.'

I had discovered the quixotic German Piro living a ten-minute drive from Foral. It had been a mission tracking down his rural, hillside workshop that spread around a copse of cork oak, carob and olive trees hidden up a narrow, dirt track in the hamlet of Barrocal. I had first turned up with Laurence, which was just as well, as it was an eerie, isolated place. It was a nerve-wracking doorstep to bash, having just discovered from police documents that Piro had not only visited Brueckner in prison, but had also offered up his home as a bail address.

I cross-checked the story with the reporters from the *Daily Mail* and *The Mirror*, who had both been sent packing on recent visits, as well as Martin

Brunt, from *Sky*, who had been 'practically chased off the property' when his cameraman had pointed the camera at Piro. The situation had not been helped by Portuguese journalist Sandra Felgueiras hinting that Piro might have been linked in some way to Brueckner's criminality, while others claimed that his breakers yard was illegal.

But somehow, Laurence and I managed to get on with the eccentric German, who looked like *Asterix the Gaul*, with a big shaggy moustache and a shock of white hair which shot out in all directions. Coming from southern Spain helped – as did living there – as he related to how tough life had been for most expats over the previous decade, and how the majority of us had to do various jobs to survive. He also appreciated how much we knew about the Maddie case and was impressed that we had already managed to speak to half of Brueckner's key acquaintances from Portugal and Spain.

That said, he was only really prepared to give one or two-word answers to any of our questions and, at best, affirmations of what we needed. Perhaps understandably cautious, he said he felt it was up to the police to give out the information 'when and if' it was needed. He was also angry that the Portuguese police had clearly leaked official reports of his involvement in the case, in particular visits to the prison, to the media. 'They dropped me in the shit,' he snarled. 'Why did they drop a private person into this? I am sure the German BKA said nothing, so why did the Portuguese police in Portimao?'

Talking beside a VW van (one of what looked like hundreds dotted around), he confirmed the police had first turned up two years earlier looking for Brueckner's now trademark yellow and white Westfalia camper van. Piro had it.

Like pulling teeth, we fed him 100 words in order to get two back … the majority of his answers being, 'I don't remember nothing.' But eventually he confirmed that he had been visited by two German detectives from the BKA, as well as two PJ officers and a liaison officer from the German embassy in Lisbon. 'They didn't tell me exactly why they wanted the van or what it was regarding,' he said. 'But I located it for them and they towed it away.'

Later, on a visit in the autumn, he confirmed that it was indeed the VW Westfalia van that had been part of the first appeal by the German police in June. And he told us he had bought it off Brueckner. Would he get compensation? 'What do you think? I'll get nothing,' he barked. 'The police do what they want and they asked me a lot of questions. But helping the police is one thing, helping journalists is another.

'What I will say though is helping Christian was a mistake … but either way, you will never get it correct. No one will, unless you speak to Christian himself. Only he can give you the right answers. Maybe after you have spoken to Christian in prison you can come back and ask me some more questions,' he said with a grin. I knew that was unlikely to happen over the Covid-ravaged winter of 2020.

I popped back to see Bernhard in January 2021. It was a bright sunny day, a Friday, the lane was completely quiet and it was the prettiest spring-like morning with a profusion of paperwhites and daffodils blooming along both verges.

I parked up in a layby opposite and called out Bernhard's name a couple of times with no reply. Then out came a dog, growling and barking and annoyingly refused to calm down. I decided to brave it and wandered onto the breakers yard to see if I could find Bernhard. Skirting around his house that sits in the middle of the large plot, past the swimming pool, which is now completely surrounded by cars, I heard a banging noise and there at the back of a two-storey workshop filled with at least 100 car wrecks was Bernhard, hard at it. He was fortunately in a good mood and greeted me like an old friend, then he started to open up.

Coming from Bruchmuhlbach-Miesau, in the Rhineland Palatinate state of Germany that borders France and Luxembourg, the father of two who is in his mid-60s had first visited Portugal for a holiday with his wife Elke in the 1980s and liked its ambience as well as the climate. After a couple more holidays on the Algarve, the couple decided to make the jump in 1993, with Bernhard setting up as a mechanic in Albufeira, where they became official residents. It was there that he met Brueckner.

'I first met Christian in around 1995 or 1996. He had not been here long and he seemed like a nice young man,' he told me standing next to the body of a 2CV he was bringing back to life. Brueckner had apparently tracked him down to help him 'fix a car' and was soon bringing 'a lot of different cars' to his workshop.

'He was with his young German girlfriend, Silke, at the time. They seemed like a decent couple and she was a nice girl. They had driven down from Germany and first slept in a tent on a beach in Lagos. He was definitely trying to make a go of it here, getting odd jobs wherever he could. I warmed to him.'

The young couple spent most of their time living in vans, largely around the Praia da Luz area between 1996 and 1997, before apparently spending more time inland in the hippy area of Barao de Sao Joao until in 1999 when, according to Portugal's *Expresso* newspaper, he was finally stopped by police on a random check and found to be handling stolen goods and was connected with other 'minor crimes'. I could find no other reference to these 'minor crimes' and no apparent police record still exists.

We can only speculate what they were, but he was to spend two months in prison in Evora – presumably close to where he was picked up on one of his regular journeys around Portugal towards Spain – before he was extradited back to Germany. While there is remarkably little information on the 1999 arrest, there was a series of mugshots of him at Faro Police Station from July that year.

The photos, released to the Portuguese media, show a pensive Brueckner, fresh faced and clean shaven. Wearing white trousers and a smart white shirt, it is perhaps hard to imagine that he was about to be sent back to Germany to serve the rest of a two-year sentence for molesting two young children, six and nine years old. Given the severity of these crimes, one might have hoped that police in Faro would have filed the pictures carefully in a folder marked 'Dangerous sex offender to watch on return'.

But this was Portugal in the late 1990s when there was no sex offenders register and it was not even an offence to watch child pornography. 'I only found out he had been extradited from his girlfriend Silke,' Bernhard told me. 'I bumped into her and she told me he had been sent back to finish a prison sentence. She didn't tell me what for and I am not even sure she knew. She seemed pretty shocked actually and I think she ended up going back to Germany soon after that.'

But Brueckner didn't stay back in Germany for long. He duly served the rest of his sentence and, almost as soon as he was out, made the long journey south again. Were his movements monitored or watched? Don't be daft.

Chapter 24

A Violent Stalker

Brueckner arrived back on the Algarve towards the end of 1999 and with money he had acquired along the way, was able to take on the rental of the one-bedroom Yellow House, just outside Praia da Luz. Owned by a Brit, who rarely visited the area, he was apparently able to secure a great value annual lease. And despite being away for much of the year travelling – I assume on business buying and selling drugs – he made a point of getting to know his neighbours, who were mostly German and Austrian. They knew when he was around as he would normally leave one or two vans on the track outside, and there were always a few old cars around the garden below the house.

He managed to get jobs working at restaurants and bars in Lagos and Praia da Luz, as well as odd jobs cleaning swimming pools, gardening and walking dogs. he even picked up errant golf balls at the club that sat just 400m behind his house. However, his main source of income was from buying and selling cars, drugs and other illegal substances.

He always looked smart. Friends and neighbours confirmed that he was a 'snappy dresser' who often wore a jacket and polished leather shoes. And he was never short of girlfriends or female attention, particularly during the tourist season from April to October.

But behind his respectable attire, and charm, he had a nasty temper. One British girlfriend, who dated him for a year from 2004 to 2005, described him as 'violent' and 'aggressive'. The Lagos-based woman from Berkshire, called Alison, started dating him when they worked at a restaurant together but ended up reporting him to police for a vicious attack on her in a local bar, and for stalking her.

She met 'Chris' not long after moving to Lagos in 2003, where she rented a small flat. The pair were waiters together at the Taberna de Lagos restaurant, now called Sal e Companhia, in the same road as her apartment. Brueckner took an immediate shine to the brunette, who, at 28, was two years his senior, and flirted with her relentlessly.

'At first I didn't actually like him that much,' she told the *Daily Mirror*'s Martin Fricker, who has spent many months on the story, mostly on the Algarve. 'Not for any reason, I just didn't like him. I knew he liked me in "that way" but I wasn't interested.'

But the pair became friends and in spring 2004, he made his move.

'Chris could be very charming, funny and smooth in the way he talked and he was always dressed nicely, holding the door open for women,' she said. 'We got together romantically and at first it was great. The relationship was very nice.'

Now in her mid-forties and a mother of two, she says she frequently stayed over at Brueckner's rented bungalow, where she recalled he kept various cars including his now-infamous VW van, a mustard yellow VW estate and his 'beloved' black Jaguar. She told Fricker, 'He wasn't sleazy in the beginning [but] easy going, even chivalrous and our sex life was normal. He wasn't into anything weird with me.' They had a whirlwind summer romance and he regularly took her to the beach, particularly the isolated ones on the west coast of the Algarve, above Sagres. She said he loved Indian food and cooked her German dishes at home.

But the pair began to argue, and he became jealous and aggressive with anyone she befriended. She recalled one incident, in late 2004, when she bumped into a male friend in the street. They were chatting when he stopped abruptly, 'like he was spooked or suddenly remembered something. She said, 'Someone later told me Christian had previously threatened the guy because he'd seen us speaking before.'

She added that he was a chauvinist who expected her to clean up after him. 'He lost it once because I didn't clean his house. I said, "I've got my own house to clean, I don't live here." He was like, "You should clean my house, you're a woman."

'He said he had two Portuguese girlfriends before me and they both cleaned his house, even though they never lived there. I remember saying, "But I'm not Portuguese," and he replied, "English women are all lazy."' He mentioned a former English girlfriend called Carol who was 'lazy like me'.

Alison said that during the winter he went back and forth to Germany, presumably transporting drugs or other illicit goods. 'He'd stay one week in Germany, then back to Portugal,' she said. 'I remember feeling suspicious, like something strange was going on, so I looked at his phone.

'I found messages in German from someone called 'B' saying 'Ich liebe dich' – I love you. It was a German number, and obviously he had been going back and forth to Germany, so I put two and two together.'

When she confronted him, he went 'completely crazy', leading to a huge fight.

He also flew into a jealous rage on New Year's Eve at the Metro Bar (now called Little Breakfast) in Lagos, where Alison retired after a late night shift at the Taberna de Lagos, and where Brueckner had been drinking. The German was being lairy and showing off when some men came in and one gave Alison a new year hug. 'Chris dragged me out in front of everybody. He grabbed me by the neck, pulled me into the girls toilets and was ramming my head against the wall.'

It took four men to drag Brueckner off, but when two local GNR officers arrived and found Alison sitting on the floor, unable to move from shock and with cuts and bruises, Brueckner had vanished.

She refused to give a statement to police, fearing the ramifications if Brueckner was arrested. 'I stayed there the rest of the night recovering and eventually two friends, a guy and his girlfriend, walked me back to my flat,' she recalled. And that is when the story turned from awful to downright terrifying.

On arrival at her flat on the second floor, she sensed something was strange, particularly when she went into the bathroom and the toilet seat was up. 'I was sure someone was either in there or had been in there,' said Alison. 'I started looking in the cupboards and then thought I'd check under the bed. I peeked under and got the shock of my life. He was hiding under there, lying on his back, staring at me. Can you imagine how that felt? I just froze. I didn't know what he was going to do to me.

'He got out from under the bed, acted like everything was normal, said goodbye to me, walked out and closed the door behind him. I was there all alone, just shaking and shaking. I think he was there waiting to see whether I brought anyone home with me.

'To this day I still wonder what would have happened if I had brought someone back that night. I think, from the previous behaviour, he would have really, really hurt that person and me too.'

Despite the bar attack and break-in, she foolishly agreed to forgive Brueckner and the pair started dating again. While her friends and family were furious he begged for forgiveness, saying he had been 'very drunk' and had lost control. He promised to stop drinking.

But things never really changed and in mid-2005 she found a pair of women's underwear in one of his bags. Upset, she confronted him, leading to another big fight and he ended up driving her home to Lagos. She assumed the relationship was over.

However, Brueckner was not prepared to let her go that easily and began to wait for her outside the restaurant where she worked. 'We had to call the police because he kept trying to get in,' she said. 'He was stalking me constantly.' Things came to a head when he strode into the restaurant and knocked a tray of drinks out of her hand because she had refused to talk to him. The owner called the police who questioned Brueckner, and he was banned from coming into the restaurant.

But this didn't stop him from waiting for her outside begging her to talk to him. On some occasions he got angry and threatened to find her parents and hurt them. 'People had to walk me home each night,' recalled Alison. 'Eventually it stopped but it went on for a long while.'

When he did finally move on, Alison said he had a string of dalliances and relationships with older women. 'There was one lady he used to take out to dinner sometimes, she was a bit older, and he said it was just for company.' He then started dating another 'much older' woman, who was thought to be in her sixties. One could speculate it was the owner of the Old Schoolhouse, who is now living back in Germany.

He told Alison he got paid to walk her dog and clean her home, but she suspects he may have been working in the area as a male prostitute. 'A friend of mine said to me she wondered if he was some sort of gigolo, doing things for money with older women.'

It was an awful chapter in her life and Alison told *the Mirror* she had completely forgotten about Brueckner until 2019 when police knocked on her door over the rape of the pensioner in Praia da Luz in 2005. The crime had allegedly happened not long after they'd broken up, and the police interviewed her three times about his lifestyle and passions. They were particularly interested in their sex life and if he was attracted to older women or children.

Incredibly, they never once mentioned any potential link to the Maddie investigation and Alison only found out that he was a suspect, in June 2020 like everyone else. She said it was 'shocking to discover he was a paedophile', adding 'To imagine I've been with someone who is capable of hurting someone like that is sickening.'

Chapter 25

Chris Diesel

My own insight into Brueckner's personal life came after I was asked to try and find out more about one of only two convictions he had received in Portugal. It came after the Portuguese media revealed that he had been imprisoned in 2006 for the theft of petrol from lorries. Arrested alongside his Austrian friend Michael Tatschl, he had been taken to Portimao Prison to await trial and ended up staying there the rest of the year.

The pair had been caught red-handed in the early hours of April 7, 2006, syphoning diesel from a truck parked up in the port area of the town. I managed to get hold of the official court transcript of their committal hearing in which Tatschl admitted to stealing fuel from at least three trucks that night, amounting to around '250 litres', worth a little over 300 euros back then. They were such prolific thieves that Brueckner had earned the nickname 'Chris Diesel'. Under process number 38/06.4PBPTM, the pair were charged with theft and kept overnight in Portimao Police Station.

The following day, in front of a duty judge at the Family and Youth Court of Portimao, Brueckner and Tatschl were asked a series of questions about their livelihoods and past criminal records, as well as where they lived. Carefully protecting the address of the Yellow House, which they were both sharing at the time, they said they were sleeping in an old blue Bedford van, which they had bought together just two weeks earlier.

They insisted they were new to Portugal (Brueckner said he arrived in March that year) and had only met a month earlier while sleeping near each other in a car park on Meia Praia Beach, in Lagos. They said they had bought the van (number plate AZ-42-47) from a 'pair of Moldovans' in the nearby town of Odiaxere and planned to spend the summer travelling around in it. The van was impounded and, coincidentally, crushed by police in 2009.

Meanwhile, both claimed to have money from back home, while Brueckner said he had a job lined up as a waiter in Lagos starting the following month in May. In his deposition that began at 11.30am on April 8, Brueckner said they were planning to sell the petrol to travellers at the car parks they would be staying at, along the coast.

Through the help of a translator and represented by duty solicitor Sofia Froi, he said he had not been arrested before in Portugal, which was another lie, given his extradition in the 1990s, as well as another offence for 'disobedience' for driving a car without the correct, legal paperwork. He pleaded guilty, but also insisted he was not the ringleader dumping that on Tatschl, claiming it was his idea and he who opened up the fuel tanks.

Judge Antonieta Nascimento was not convinced of their stories and was more interested in their pasts back home. Tatschl admitted that he had been convicted of various offences, including drug dealing and traffic violations, Brueckner admitted he had been convicted of theft and various 'sex crimes'.

One might have expected alarm bells to ring, but he somehow managed to hide the *minutae,* specifically that the offences involved children. He managed to get away with telling the judge that it was a minor sex attack on a youth when he was a teen and that he had served 18 months in prison for it. The official court stenographer recorded it more loosely: 'When he was 17 years old he was convicted in Germany for burglaries and sex crimes.'

Why further detail was not asked for – or added – must be a question for the judge and court typist, but the pair were put back in jail to await a full trial scheduled for the summer.

Brueckner's defence lawyer at the time Serafim Vieira – who has since said he believes Brueckner could be responsible for snatching Maddie – told the Portuguese media in July 2020, 'The question the judge asked him about his previous convictions was disturbing, but he didn't tell the judge it was a paedophile crime and the judge was not obliged to ask for the German police files or investigate it further. The crime was more than ten years earlier and had no bearing on the theft he had admitted to.'

Brueckner and Tatschl applied for bail over the following days with Brueckner claiming he could stay with his German friend, Bernhard Piro, who he listed as a local 'businessman'. A few weeks later, on April 24, 2006, Piro went to the prison to officially log the offer to house the German delinquent at his property in Barrocal. Alongside copies of his passport and residents permit, he confirmed that he knew Brueckner, listed in the process 38/04 4PBPTM, and that he was happy for him to reside in his house until the legal process had come to a conclusion. I'm not convinced his wife Elke was quite so happy.

However, the judge was still not convinced of the pair's story, or trustworthiness and on April 28 refused them bail, claiming they were a 'flight risk'. Instead she remanded them in custody to await trial, which was at first scheduled for July, but then got postponed until mid-December that year.

It must have been a long frustrating eight months in jail for Brueckner and Tatschl who, as I stated in the beginning of the book I would interview many years later when he only had bad things to say about his fellow inmate. Apart from a few visits from friends – Piro among them (he also wrote letters to Piro's 10-year-old son Pablo) – Brueckner spent most of his time working out and watching television. It did, however, give the authorities time to do a social study on the German. I managed to get a copy of the pre-sentence report by sociologist Rita Silva and her coordinator Isa Gomes, but it is thin and lacking detail.

Written for the judge, it explained that Brueckner had 'an experiential path based on the absence of family' and that his development was 'shaped by institutionalisation'. It added that, while he 'usually resides in Germany' – which was incorrect – he had had contact with Portugal since he was 18 and had 'some knowledge and friendships' there. It noted that he had served a year and a half in prison in Germany – without explaining why – and that he had been 'behaving according to the rules' in prison in Portugal and 'benefiting from support and visits from friends'.

Prepared for the IRS social services in Portimao, it noted his age as 30 and described his marital status as single. It also gave his adoptive parents names and offered up two addresses, the one of Piro in Barrocal – even though he was not yet living there – as well as another address in Germany, in Augsburg. This address, Proviantbachstrasse 1, 86153, is an Avis rent-a-car office and a big open space/car park, backing onto a tyre garage called Quick Reifendiscount Augusta.

Running alongside the Proviantbach River, it is a mixed area of industrial workshops and a few blocks of flats. Next door at number 11 is a car repair shop owned by a Klaus Walter, although it was shut every time I tried to call. Hans, the owner of the Quick tyre garage told me that the address given had been a rent-a-car company for as long as he could remember and it had recently been taken over by Avis. 'I definitely remember the name Christian Brueckner but I can't remember why,' he said, 'Or whether he worked around here or not.'

The IRS social report, meanwhile, stated that it involved detailed interviews with Brueckner and prison staff as well as building up 'a dossier' of information on him. Although quite what they gleaned is not clear. It is certainly not in the report that I managed to get hold of. To me it looked like total whitewash and the lack of information may be to do with the 'communication difficulties' that Rita Silva noted, as she had not been allowed to pay for a translator (or had not asked for one). And she explained that much of what was said was 'in English', which was not her mother tongue, nor his.

The key point, as far as I could see, was that Brueckner had 'maintained a defensive position' through the interviews and mostly covered up his history and background. He had clearly wrapped Rita Silva around his little finger, with her noting that he had been brought up in institutions for nine years of his life 'without the presence of parents or family members'. This is far from true.

He admitted this led to criminality and he fled Germany for Portugal as soon as he could. He claimed that his job was working as a mechanic and that he had various friends in the area and that he was looking for an apartment to live in and had some work lined up. Almost all of it untrue. There was very little truth for the judge to go on.

Managing to keep Brueckner inside for the large part of 2006 resulted in a number of positive outcomes. As well as the drastic drop in the number of burglaries in the area and the reduction in reported sexual assaults, the authorities were able to finally charge and sentence him for the crime of motoring 'disobedience' over which they had been chasing him for a number of years.

It concerned the illegal use of a German driving licence in Portugal, after being pulled over in his Jaguar in 2004. 'He had failed to change his licence to a Portuguese one, which you are meant to do after living in the country for six months,' Sandra Felgueiras explained to me. 'It is a crime of disobedience, which is taken seriously here.'

In a couple of documents I was able to get from the Algarve's official judicial headquarters in Faro, it showed that the incredibly simple process 2/04.8FALGS had somehow taken more than two years to complete. This is probably because when he was first pulled over, he had given a fake address to the police in Lagos, meaning they were unable to find him to serve court papers on him.

He had actually given two addresses, one in Germany – Korbinian Platz 7, Munich – an anonymous block of flats in a northern suburb of the city, where there is no suggestion he ever lived, as well Rua Capitao Salgueiro Maia (number 11, left apartment, 3rd floor) in Lagos, Portugal.

Sitting in a scruffy five-floor block above a health clinic and supermarket, it is hardly a des res, but it was opposite a big open area of 100 plus car parking spaces, where presumably he would leave his vans. This is the address he gives in a document that I have a copy of concerning his financial status at the time of his arrest, saying it is his 'girlfriend's house'. In the economic report, he spells his name incorrectly as 'Bruckner' and lists his job as 'a car salesman in Germany'. More lies. He states that he does not own any property, or even his own vehicle (this is a total lie as he owned at least two and probably more) and has no investments or valuables of note.

The truth is he had actually been living just five minutes away at the Yellow House, in Praia da Luz, at the time, but – yet again – he managed to keep that address away from the authorities. The reasons why are now completely clear. There was far too much incriminating stuff to find.

When the court case for driving disobedience was finally heard on October 18, 2006 the judge, Ana Catarina Figueiredo Neto, aided by magistrate Filipa Fonseca, handed him a fine of just 300 euros, but insisted he paid towards the court costs and his defence. Brought up from Portimao Prison for the afternoon session, he was generously given the opportunity of paying three euros a day for 100 days. Quite frankly though, the case did not add up.

I find it extremely odd was that it was deemed necessary to call no less than four witnesses for the prosecution, even including one by video conference from Aveiro, near Lisbon.

So, there were at least eight people present for a court case about a driving licence that was out of date. Really?

I was so perplexed I decided to track down the lawyer who represented Brueckner that day. It was a woman called Florbela Macedo and, by good fortune, she had her services listed on a number of legal websites around Faro. 'I just remember it was to do with his driving licence and that as he was a fiscal resident he needed to change it after six months,' she told me when

I called. 'But I really can't explain why there were so many witnesses for the prosecution. It was a very simple case so it doesn't seem necessary.'

A German translator, Uwe Koller, was also listed as being present for Brueckner, but when I contacted him to ask if he remembered anything about the case or the need for so many witnesses, he went oddly very quiet. The translator – who must have known Brueckner, having also lived in Praia da Luz at the time – clammed up when I phoned him at home. In between long silences, he told me: 'I really cannot help you at all on this matter. But in any case I would never tell you anything said in a case I was involved in.' He refused to confirm whether he knew Brueckner or he'd come across him in any other local court cases.

The last word on the case came two years later, almost a full year after Maddie went missing. In the document I managed to get hold of from the Faro police archives, it stated that police had been unable to collect the money that Brueckner owed for the disobedience crime and they were coming to look for it.

Dated April 2, 2008, police officer José Joaquim da Silva Goncalves, of Portimao police's 'Criminal Investigation Squadron', stated that he had attempted to undertake 'due diligence on the assets of Christian Brueckner', but that he was no longer living at the address he had given. He added: 'Several residents of the block said that he has not lived there for many years and they don't know where he is living now.'

There was no cross-referencing to him being involved in any other specific crime. Once again, it looked like Brueckner had given the authorities the slip.

•••

Staying with cars, there is another fascinating and highly suspicious fact concerning Brueckner's pride and joy Jaguar XJR6 – the day AFTER Maddie vanished, he re-registered it in someone else's name. I probed this bizarre coincidence and in June 2021, just days before this book was finished, I interviewed this rather eccentric person in his native Germany, and asked him why he agreed to have the car put in his name, especially as he was aware of Brueckner's criminality.

Alexander Bischof is a retired telecoms engineer some 20 years Brueckner's senior. He was someone the seasoned criminal trusted and would frequently visit; he even sent him postcards and letters while in prison, he told me.

The British car had been registered to Bischof's name, and address, one day after the toddler vanished. And as the prosecutor Hans Christian Wolters would later confirm, he believes there is some relevance there. 'It's an unusual fact, that's for sure,' he told me.

I spoke to 65-year-old Bischof from his home in Augsburg, near Munich in a bid to understand what happened in May 2007. He couldn't remember if he'd met Brueckner in 2005 or early 2006, but he said it was through a mutual friend called Hubert who had previously sold Brueckner his Jaguar from the nearby village of Aichach.

Brueckner was sleeping in a campervan in a car park close to Bischof's mansion block home in Proviantbachstrasse, where he still lives with his 44-year-old South-East Asian wife Alex. It suddenly hit me that this was the very same street with the Avis office he had given the psychologists in prison for his pre-sentence report in 2006.

'He only lived near me in the sense that he had a good parking place nearby,' explained Bischof, who is also a big Jaguar lover. 'He first parked 30 or 40m from my home, in a parking lot, then he drove around and parked in some nearby woods, which was quieter for him.' I think he meant less conspicuous.

However, in the months after Maddie went missing, when Brueckner left Portugal 'to start a new life', he would spend 'up to two years' coming and going and Bischof even let him spend the odd night in his dingy attic. But his story was a little vague and far from consistent, particularly comparing it to interviews with him in various newspapers over the previous year.

While I believed Brueckner was mostly spending time in Foral in 2007, Bischof told *the Daily Mail* in June 2020 that he had lived with him for 'two or three weeks' in spring 2007, after telling him he was 'between jobs and had no money'. Yet a year later he told me that he 'mostly slept in the Winnebago', which Bischof actually helped him purchase from a computer at his house in the Spring of 2007. He couldn't recall the exact date.

'He said he wanted a new campervan,' Bischof told me. 'He looked for it on the internet in my room and ended up with this huge one, a 1985 dark brown and beige one from the US. I told him he would be better off getting a smaller one from Europe; it would be better for getting the parts, but he said he would be fine and he would be able to live in it. He bought it for 18,000 euros.'

Bischof said Brueckner paid well over the odds for it, in cash, having bought it off a couple who came from outside Augsburg. 'The owners drove it over and I said they could park it outside and Christian went down to pay for it,' he said. 'It was far too much for an old van like that and it was always having problems. I ended up helping him repair it. There was a problem with the electrics, then the headlights, then the blinkers.'

I asked Bischof how Brueckner came to have this huge amount of cash. And given the timing could he have got it from the snatch and sale of Maddie? 'I really don't know,' he said. 'Maybe it was stolen, maybe it was his business with drugs. He certainly had necklaces and watches and he told me he stole them from Portugal. It was one of the reasons I told him he had to go.'

He added he 'was always driving around the country and abroad to Portugal for months at a time ... where he made business buying and selling things.... I know he spent three months in Spain and then he went to Sylt [in northern Germany] two or three times.'

He clearly knew about 'the drugs trade'. Brueckner didn't even try to keep that hidden, recalled Bischof: 'I remember the smell inside his big van.

It reeked of grass. He had all these places where he put it, but the smell was so obvious. I am sure the police would smell it immediately if they stopped him.

'One time I found him inside cleaning the drugs, maybe half a kilo of grass which he had on the table. He was separating the grass from the flowers and the smell was overpowering.'

So, it would have come as no major surprise when he received a postcard from Brueckner in prison in Portugal in the summer of 2006, during the World Cup finals that were taking place back home in Germany. 'He had gone down to have a holiday in Portugal with his girlfriend at the time, who was called Maria, I think,' said Bischof. 'They certainly talked in English and he talked about her a lot. He was very keen on her.

'Then out of the blue I got this postcard from him from jail in Portugal. I think it had a beach on the front and he wrote that he was OK, he had a TV and he was watching the football in prison.'

I asked about their mutual friend Hubert from whom Brueckner had bought the Jaguar, but he said he didn't want to give his surname and that he is 'currently living outside Europe, a long way away'. He then muttered something about the island of Reunion in the Indian Ocean, and Australia. He was deliberately vague. But I kept on asking.

'Well, after Christian bought his Jaguar from Hubert he told me that Christian needed some help. Could I help get him a job in the city, he asked? I said I would see,' he explained.

Later when it came to the unusual move of re-registering the car into his name, Brueckner told him it was 'due to an insurance issue' and that he couldn't keep it registered in Munich, even though it was still in Portugal.

'It had a number plate from Munich and he said he couldn't keep it any longer. His friend [was this Hubert?] could not keep it any longer at his address. He said he needed to get it registered in Augsburg, but because he had no address here he needed to get one in order to get insurance. And I said, "OK, I can give you my address for the number plate and the papers." I figured it would mean he could keep his car to look for work. I was only trying to help him. I had no idea it meant he was driving around doing his business in my name.

'When I look back now I realise he probably had to do something fast. Could it have been Madeleine? I dread to think, but when you are convicted of raping an old woman and molesting young girls, you begin to wonder.'

He confirmed that the German police had interviewed him at length twice. The first time they got in touch in July 2018, he was on holiday with his wife in Tenerife. They didn't tell him what it was about, but when they got home the police came round. 'They looked everywhere, searched every room carefully to see what might be there and asked a lot of questions,' he told me. 'They didn't mention kidnapping or children though, just asked about Christian.

'About eight months later I was taken to the police station in Augsburg where my wife and I gave a full account. It was spring 2019 and then they mentioned Madeleine McCann. Did I remember him talking about her? I said I only remembered her from the newspapers, not from him. It was a big shock.'

Bischof is also alarmed to think that at the time Brueckner was coming in and out of his home, his elderly mother, who has since passed away, was living there. 'She would have been around 75 and she mostly stayed in her room and I hope they had no contact. I tried hard to keep him away from us and I know my mother did not want to be with him. My wife did not like him either. She did not want him in the house. She always said he was no good and refused to sit in the same room as him. When Christian came in to go on the internet she would go to another room.'

I thanked him for his time and he seemed hopeful that Brueckner was on his way to being convicted of snatching Maddie. 'I really hope they can find the right piece of the jigsaw so they can put it to him and he admits to it,' he said. 'It makes me have sleepless nights, the idea of what people like him do. Back in the olden days there was a way to solve it. You got four horses and tied the person to them and pull. Problem gone. For some guys it is the best option.'

Chapter 26

A Friend Confesses

I was deliberating whether to dig deeper into Brueckner's Portuguese prison record when I received a call from Martin Fricker from *the Mirror*. Talk about coincidences. I was sitting on my bed reading a book about Orgiva, the Granada town, which I'd dubbed the 'Glastonbury of southern Europe' and where, coincidentally, my newspaper, *The Olive Press* was born. Written by an expat, Orgiva: A Chancer's Guide to Rural Spain, was about life in Spain's best known alternative community, and we were planning to serialise it in the paper. So when Martin asked, 'Can you get to a place called Orgiva?' I almost tipped my cup of tea over the duvet.

'It's where Brueckner's friend Michael Tatschl lived for many years, the guy he went to prison with,' said Martin excitedly. 'I've tracked him down on Facebook and he would make an excellent interview.'

Despite omitting that his Facebook page actually showed him leaving Orgiva (pronounced Or-heeva) in 2016 – or that his featured image showed him snarling at the camera with his middle finger sticking up – he said it was worth the three-hour drive east into the Sierra Nevada mountains to see what I could find. He promised it would be a lucrative trip with four daily newspapers happy to pay me a day rate to have a dig around. It was also that Eureka moment when two dots itching to be joined were finally united as a concrete certainty: the hippie hangout of Barao de Sao Joao in the Algarve now had a direct crime link to Orgiva, the new age capital of Spain.

I already had a feeling Brueckner would have links to Orgiva, with its little-checked, free-spirited community of international travellers tucked away in a string of hidden valleys in the folds of the southern Sierra Nevada slopes. Called the Alpujarras, it is a region I know well having come across the fledgling Olive Press newspaper there in its first few months, while writing a travel article for *the Mail* on Granada.

An area of stunning natural beauty with fascinating local culture, I had stumbled across Issue 5, while staying at an earthy guesthouse, just outside of Orgiva. Set up by a former energy trader, Jason, who was now living off grid and Mark, a grumpy journalist, who had worked for a few years at the Mercury press agency in Liverpool, it had plenty of attitude. Full of tales of corruption and pleas for the environment, it also turned a spotlight on the drug dealing and criminality the region had started to become known for.

It was a refreshing break from the appalling local English freesheets that spewed dreadful reporting alongside racist op-ed diatribes to their expat faithful from Benidorm to Benalmadena.

I was so impressed I called the pair for a meeting to see if we might work together on a launch of a separate edition of the paper over in my province of Malaga, primarily for the inland expats, centred between Coin, Ronda and Antequera. It was apparent that we shared a lot of beliefs, but had different aspirations and skills, so we agreed that I would set up a stand-alone edition, but we would work as allies.

Having launched my first issue of the Western Olive Press out of Ronda in November 2006, I spent the next year driving backwards and forwards to Orgiva helping them with layout, editing and, ultimately, injecting a dose of commercial acumen that they would certainly need if they were going to survive the coming recession. They may not have been business dynamos, but they certainly knew a lot about the weird mix of expats and Spanish who gravitated towards this inland market town and region.

I quickly learnt about the idiosyncrasies and oddness of Orgiva, and got used to the groups of hippies and punks who whiled away the day sitting by the side of the road, smoking marijuana and drinking from litre bottles of beer and cider, intermittently begging from passersby.

This intriguing make-up started brewing in the 1970s, but accelerated in the 1980s and 1990s as no less than three distinct new age settlements grew up close to the town, one called Beneficio (meaning 'Benefits') with as many as 1,000 residents at certain times of year. Orgiva became famous for Spain's number one hippie bash, the free Dragon Festival – which plays a part in Brueckner's story – and which launched in the traveller settlement of Cigarrones in 1997 and ran for well over a decade. With only a vague start and finish date, usually over a weekend in March, punters often arrive a week before and leave a week later, if at all.

Cigarrones, which straddled the riverbed of the winding Guadalfeo River that passed Orgiva, stretched out over a few kilometres and had a highly transient population, making it hard for local police to keep tabs on it. While largely supportive (at least accepting) of this community with characters such as 'Apache Joe' and 'Grundig', a Spanish hippie who rode around on a donkey, *The Olive Press* also ran its fair share of stories about the criminals, sex offenders and drug dealers that hid out in these nearby hills. The majority of new age residents were not officially registered on the town's padron, nor did they pay taxes, despite sending their children to the local schools. Many also used false names.

I knew that finding Michael Tatschl, or someone who knew him, wouldn't be easy, but at least I had a head start with a photo. Calling a few contacts en route I discovered that he was better known as 'Micha' and that he had returned to live in Austria some years earlier … but he came back most years on holiday. I was told he had a girlfriend, Cynthia or 'Cyn', and used to hang out at the so-called 'Metal Bar' on the edge of the town. Despite the strict lockdown in Spain, the bar somehow managed to stay open, providing an unofficial community drop-in centre for the traveller community that lived in the area.

There was certainly a collection of waifs and strays at the bar and on the terrace outside, many with dogs, when I arrived just before lunchtime. Fortunately most of them were friendly, as was the landlord, who recognised Micha from his Facebook photos, which is not too hard when you have a skull and crossbones tattoo on your neck, your nipples pierced and a girlfriend half your age. The landlord smiled broadly and told me that, despite his appearance, he was actually a muy buen tio, or decent bloke, and was friendly and 'fun to hang out with'. He told me he had lived in the Orgiva area for many years, before heading home to Austria in 2016 or 2017.

Another of the regulars told me he now had a small child and had been back from Austria over Christmas 2019 with Cynthia. We scoured Facebook together and eventually found her page and some pictures of her beside a lake in the Alps with a son of around 18 months old toddling beside her.

After a while I flashed around a few photos of Brueckner and, much to my surprise, most of the gathering crowd recognised him. They recalled him being in town a few times, mostly with Micha, but sometimes on his own, 'with his dogs'. Then the landlord volunteered that Micha had lived with an English girlfriend, an artist called Emma, for a number of years in the nearby village of Tablones. He was certain she was still around, as she had a couple of teenage daughters at the local school. It was an excellent lead.

Excitedly, I headed to Tablones but discovered nobody knew her at all. It was a community of perhaps 500 properties and smallholdings, many of them shacks, spread over about 10km square. It was quite apparent the locals wanted nothing to do with the alternative expat community that mostly lived down near the riverbed in Cigarrones.

Frustrated, and melting in the 38 degree heat, I decided to take a closer look at Micha's photos on Facebook and spotted one of him standing under a pergola of what looked like the porch of a home, that was clearly in southern Spain, with its line of parched hills with two fire breaks as a backdrop. So intent was I in looking for clues, the fact that he was apparently naked standing behind three huge marijuana plants didn't even register!

Vaya suerte, as the Spanish would say – by complete chance I looked up and saw the exact same line of hills in the distance and, crucially, the same fire breaks. It turned out I was standing just 200m away from the plot where he lived for many years and, after walking downhill for a minute, I met someone who knew Emma.

It turned out to be Llewelyn Graves, the grandson of I, Claudius and Goodbye to All That writer Robert Graves, who was living in a commune surrounded by vans. I tried to make conversation, knowing quite a lot about his British-born, Spain-based grandfather, who has a museum in Mallorca, where he wrote the seminal books in the 1930s, as well as his uncle, Tomas, who had written an excellent tome called Tuning Up at Dawn, about the Spanish propensity for noise and fun. Unfortunately Llewelyn was anything but friendly and couldn't wait to get away, but he did point me in the direction of Emma's finca.

She couldn't have been nicer. I was ushered in by her teenage daughter, through the house into the shady back garden porch, where a bottle of cold cider was thrust into my hand. Sitting alongside another local expat Ben, we started chatting about *The Olive Press*.

Eventually, I got round to explaining the reason why I was there. Emma was certainly not surprised when I told her that her ex-boyfriend had been a close friend of Europe's current Public Enemy Number One. She had been keeping up to date with the Maddie case, and was fascinated to know if Brueckner was the guilty man. She had recognised him when his face had appeared on Spanish TV and she recalled how he had visited Micha – pronounced Mika – on a number of occasions, although she didn't really know him.

Although she and Micha had split up in 2016, they were still in regular contact, mainly via text messages, but with the occasional phone call. Intriguingly, he had recently told her about 'a huge reward' he was hoping to get over 'a very big crime case' which he had told her he could not elaborate on. She hadn't put two and two together, but for me it was starting to fall into place.

She said it related to a 'very serious crime' with which he was helping the police. 'He said he really thought he was going to get a big reward for the information he had given them,' said Emma, who had moved to the Alpujarras from the UK two decades earlier. 'He couldn't tell me what it was as he had been told to keep it quiet by the police. 'I guess it is all now starting to make sense.'

She remembered him talking about his friend Christian on a number of occasions, and the pair were certainly kindred spirits as she went on to give me a rundown of Micha's prodigious drug taking and frequent drunkenness. It had nearly led to the break up of his relationship with Cyn, an 'alternativa', whom Emma had known when she lived in Orgiva. Cyn and Micha had got engaged in 2017, with Micha announcing it on Facebook to his 415 friends, I discovered.

However, Cyn, who is also from Austria, had recently told Emma that she all but kicked him out of the home that year after police had intercepted a package of something he had allegedly posted to Austria. Now living near Graz, close to where he grew up, and now with a baby in tow, Micha was doing his best to 'go straight' Emma told me.

It was fairly clear that Micha had long been living life close to the edge. A demi-monde character, who lived off his wits, he had been based, Emma told me, for a number of years in a hard-drinking, drug-taking community in Castell de Ferro, just outside the Alpujarras, which is where they met at a party.

I was desperate to give him a call and was biding my time to ask Emma for his number. After being handed a second bottle of cider I figured the time was right, but she refused. She did, however, agree to call him on my behalf. She understood the importance of the case and, like me, was keen to bring it to a conclusion. Typically, however, her phone died on her, and being an iPhone, it took nearly 20 minutes to come back to life. Time was ticking on, and luckily, with still just 2% battery, Emma decided it would be best to call from my phone, which got me his number after all.

We agreed to put him on loudspeaker and that she would do the initial talking and then introduce me as the editor of *The Olive Press*, which he would know, as we had run a campaign to help one of his friends, who set up the Dragon Festival and was facing prison and heavy fines. We got through immediately and it was clear that he had an excellent rapport with Emma. He also sounded in a good mood, and maintained it even when I was introduced.

We chatted about the paper and the 'Dragon Fest' and I was elated when he happily went on to talk about the time he spent with 'best friend' Christian Brueckner in Portugal, and how he had spent more time with him later in Spain. I told him I knew all about the fuel theft case and had read all the court files. And while it 'was obvious' that he was not the main perpetrator and had merely got caught up with a proper ne-er-do-well, he had spent eight months in prison with Brueckner and obviously got to know him well. So when I said it looked certain that Brueckner was guilty of snatching Maddie, and that Micha must be pleased and relieved to be away from him, I was astounded when he agreed – with both parts.

That is when he made the startling revelation that, he was 'sure Christian snatched Maddie.' Talking in faultless English, with a slight German accent, he continued: 'He was a very sick man, with dark, nasty habits and it was exactly the sort of thing he would have done.' Just then, a baby starting to cry in the background and he asked if we could call again in 20 minutes to give him time to get the baby back to sleep.

It was one of those horrible moments in journalism, when you have finally got your foot in the door, but the chances are it could be scuppered if your subject has time to start having second thoughts. It happens all the time.

After a nerve-wracking 30 minutes, we finally got him back on the phone. Such are the joys of Covid, he may not have spoken to anyone for a week or more, and he was keen to chat.

Over an hour's conversation, Micha told us his story. At 47, he was three years older than Brueckner and had first come across him when he was living on the Algarve in 2003 or 2004. He said they bonded over a love of partying and the alternative scene and were firm 'van lifers' who loved life on the road. Micha revealed how he had indeed ended up parking his own van outside his friend's now-famous Yellow House, overlooking Praia da Luz.

He stayed for some time and eventually moved in, sleeping on the couch, or heading back to his van later for a good night's sleep. In his words, they became 'best friends'.

A free spirit like Brueckner, and speaking the same language, Micha had grown up in the rural area of Murtal in the small town of Knittelfeld, some 50 minutes west of Graz, in Austria. He was a carpenter by trade, but spent many of his years living as a traveller, moving from country to country attending free festivals and taking drugs. He told us he had ended up dealing, which led to a few convictions. He'd confessed as such to the court in Portimao in 2006. But, he said, he was not 'a sick puppy' like Brueckner.

'It started when I ended up staying at his house and camping in my van in the garden,' Micha began. 'We spent a lot of time together and had good fun.' He described Brueckner as 'always very smart and snappy in the way he dressed', sometimes wearing a suit to go out and always with 'good shoes'. 'He liked to walk into town so he could drink and then get home easily later,' he said. 'He did not take drugs at the time as far as I was aware, but he did like to have a drink.'

He occasionally worked as a barman in town and confirmed what Alison had said about a string of girlfriends and that he was 'quite a ladies man', especially attracted to older women. 'He had a German girlfriend who was at least 20 years older than him. I can't remember her name but she lived a few kilometres out of town, he said. 'He would spend time over at her house, looking after her dogs and garden.'

Although Micha was having fun with Brueckner, he soon became aware of his dark side. 'He was definitely quite a strange character,' he said before hesitating. 'How to explain it? Well he was always quite criminal. He liked to brag about the crimes he had done and planned to do. And how he aimed to steal as much money as he could until he reached his dream of having one million euros. Then he said he would stop.'

He discovered that Brueckner was an excellent burglar, who knew how to get into any home on any floor. 'It was easy there in Praia da Luz,' said Micha. 'He was always breaking into apartments in the area and bragging about it to me. He was a very good burglar and would easily climb up to first floor apartments when tourists were out.

'He particularly liked big football games when everyone would be out watching the game in bars. During tournaments, like the European Championships, he had a field day.

'He would climb up to the first floor and steal everything, lots of money, valuables and so many passports. In fact, he had hundreds of passports and lots of Rolexes and other expensive watches. He also had cameras and video cameras and plenty of phones.

'He had a hiding place in the house for them, in the rafters. He kept all the money and many of the passports hidden up there. It was his secret stash and when we were taken to prison, he ordered a friend to go into the house and clear it up and get rid of any evidence of burglaries or robberies.'

It was this decision – perhaps taken rashly – that may ultimately lead to Brueckner's conviction over Maddie. For the man he trusted for this highly sensitive job enlisted a friend or two to help – or told them unwittingly – and between them they stripped the house of all its valuables, including various pen drives and discs and, more importantly, video cameras.

Micha believes the group, which included Germans Helge Busching and Manfred Seyferth, and I later found out another friend, also called Christian, went with the intention of keeping anything valuable and throwing everything else away. They basically 'double-crossed' Brueckner.

But they stumbled on something they didn't expect – a series of sick videos, and in particular, a video camera with a film of him raping a woman. 'That's how I found out he was a genuinely sick bastard,' said Micha. 'It was really unsettling. Horrible. I had only just got out of prison when these guys got in touch asking me what to do.

'They said the video was of this elderly lady who was chained to a wooden post and she was being beaten and raped. There was another video of him attacking a second girl.

'They said, "Hey Micha what should we do with these?" I said: "I really don't know, I don't want to see them" and I think they ended up burning them.'

The thought of the videos still upsets him. And so it came as a huge relief to be able to tell the police about it in 2019. 'I told the police all about that story and I hope they verified it somehow,' he added.

Micha is sure that not only was he capable of snatching Maddie, but that he was involved in other human trafficking too. 'Christian was always on the dark web. He would talk about going on the dark web and always insisted on having good internet in the houses he rented. I don't know exactly what he did, but I suspect it involved drugs and pornography.'

In his only interview on the case, he continued, 'He was always bragging about money and making money. He even talked about selling kids maybe to Morocco ... and it's for that reason that I think he probably sold Maddie to someone. Maybe a sex ring. I didn't really think about it at the time. Just brushed it off as joking. But now I really think he might well have done it.'

With admirable frankness, Micha admitted that he had also 'got sucked into some of his schemes', suggesting it was more than just stealing fuel. Speaking about the night they got arrested for syphoning diesel from lorries, in 2006, he said: 'Taking fuel seemed pretty harmless and we did it for a few months. The cops caught us red-handed though and we got eight-and-a-half months in prison on remand waiting for a trial in Portimao.

'I don't understand why they kept us so long. It was really frustrating. Awful. It's just a small prison, so we got to spend a lot of time together. We were caught on April 7 but we didn't have our actual trial until December 21. We had to wait and wait and wait, right through the heat of the summer. We had been expecting a trial in July or August, but it never happened.'

He said it was in prison that Christian met 'some pretty serious people' and planned to 'start dealing on a larger scale' and with harder drugs, particularly cocaine. 'I heard a lot of conversations about transporting cocaine,' said Micha. 'I didn't want to get involved though and made that clear.'

They were released just before Christmas 2006, although Brueckner paid a heavier price than Micha. 'I ended up with an 1,800 euro fine while Christian said "fuck you" to the judge, who naturally gave him a bigger fine.'

Micha headed back to his family in Knittelfeld, Austria for Christmas but Brueckner stayed locally, initially with his friend Bernhard Piro. Micha didn't return to Portugal until February 2007, when he tracked down Brueckner, who had lost the contract on his rental home and was living between Foral and in his white and yellow VW van.

'He was still living in the Praia da Luz area, which I think confused the police a little as they were not sure where he was living when Maddie vanished. I know where he was. He was living free, camping wild near Praia da Luz and going to raves and selling drugs to the local party crowd. He also stayed at various friends' houses and he had his Jaguar parked up somewhere and was using it from time to time.'

Micha decided not to stick around for long, partly because he hadn't paid his 1,800 euro fine ('I couldn't afford it') and also because he wanted to attend the Dragon Festival in Orgiva that spring.

'We hung around together for a few weeks that February and then I headed back to Spain, where I knew I couldn't get caught and fined. I told him where I would be based and hoped I would see him soon.

'The Dragon was a lot of fun and the next time I saw Christian was in late May or early June that year when he suddenly arrived in Spain out of the blue with this big American campervan, the one with the [children's] swimsuits. The one that has been on the TV.

'He parked it up in Cigarrones down by the river and came looking for me. It was the only reason he had come to Orgiva ... . He knew that I was living there and he knew I had lots of connections to the marijuana world and could help him make money.

'It was the usual Christian. He had an old dog, a big brown and white dog called Charlie. But otherwise he was on his own.

'What was different was that he had quite a bit of money on him. We all wondered where he'd got this big expensive van which he parked up by a group of French travellers, who had a big sound system.

'I remember having a conversation with an English guy who lived there called "Pops" and we both wondered how on Earth could he have had that vehicle? Where did he get the money from? We assumed a big drug deal or something like that. Now I suspect it was Maddie.'

After a few days Christian headed back to Portugal and then to Germany. 'After that he was often coming backwards and forwards to Spain and to Portugal, mostly dealing drugs, and we often saw him there in Orgiva,' said Micha. 'He came in various vans, at least once in the VW van, and he also came many times in his Jaguar too.'

He continued: 'He was normally here transporting hashish, and he always stayed for a few days, which concerns me [with so many children about]. He certainly came back to the Dragon Festival the following year [in 2008] and I think the one after that in 2009.'

Micha told me he thought Brueckner may have been travelling around and committing crimes all over the place. 'I know there have been some sex crimes around the Alpujarras area over the last decade and it wouldn't be surprising if he was involved,' he said gravely. But this is hindsight, and the pair stayed in touch, on and off, for the next few years, before drifting apart 'by 2012 or 2013'.

Indeed, it was only when Micha watched the Netflix documentary in spring 2019 that he realised that it was Christian who 'must have' taken Maddie.

'I knew immediately that he was guilty,' he said. 'The part where the female tourist talked about the man turning up at the holiday apartment while her child played by the front door, the creepy guy with acne and blond hair ... I just knew it was Christian for sure.'

It is a bit unclear what happened next – whether Micha called the police or not – but within weeks he received a knock at his door and four policemen asked him to escort them to the police station. 'It was the first week of April 2019 and there were two Austrian police and two German Police. They wanted to know what my theory was about Christian. And I ended up telling them my story over 14 long hours from 10am to 6pm on the first day and then from 10am until 4pm the next day.

'They were very clear with me from the first minute. They said, "We are investigating Maddie McCann and Christian Brueckner" and I said, "I know what you want. I hope I can help." I really hope what I gave them leads to a conviction.'

'The police told me they are just missing the actual proof, because all his friends know it's him and recognised him. They just need the final piece to the puzzle.'

He wishes that he had gone to the police earlier, when he first heard about the sick videos. He said he didn't because of his own criminal past, which included not paying the fuel theft fine in Portugal, and the fear of being dragged into the case.

'Yes, I do now wish I had gone to the police earlier. It is just I don't like the police. I was quite a criminal back then, involved in quite a few things, while now I'm an angel!

'I dread to think of what other crimes he may have committed since and how I could have prevented them. He was definitely a pervert and all his friends thought that about him. He definitely had some sexual issues, but we didn't think that he liked young children.'

Asked how he would sum up his former friend, and what he thinks will happen next, he expressed surprise that the police had not yet interviewed Brueckner about Maddie, nor searched the home they shared in Praia da Luz.

'I know he did it,' said Micha. 'I was living with him at the time. He was my best friend and he was definitely a pervert and more than capable of snatching a child, for sexual kicks or money I really hope they can finally close this case for the family and find Christian guilty for what he has done. He needs to admit it to the police and close it for good.

'At least I'm sure he's having a terrible time in prison and everyone there will be out to kill him. He won't have a nice life now whatever happens ... and really he doesn't deserve it.'

I asked if we could stay in touch as the case developed. He agreed even though he said the police had told him he 'could not talk to the press'. Talk about closing the stable door after the horse has bolted. Almost inevitably, when I phoned him the next day, he failed to answer.

It was radio silence for over a week, in fact, until he WhatsApped me after the story had run prominently in four British newspapers. Having seen his quotes in the raw, which were followed up in dozens of newspapers around the world, he wasn't happy. He told me he was 'angry' with me and was now 'being hounded' by German media groups and Portuguese TV and had also got quite a backlash on Facebook.

'I don't want to speak anymore. It's not good for my family. Please respect this,' he wrote, adding, 'I already told you too much. Please don't give my number to anyone.'

After promising I wouldn't (I certainly didn't and haven't) and insisting he had done an important job in helping to expose the evil Brueckner, he replied: 'If you want info ask the police! They know everything!' He added an emoji of a man vomiting.

Two months later, in August, I got in touch with him again, having spoken to a few other friends of Brueckner's. I hoped he may have cooled down a little. He made it clear that he would speak to me again, on one condition.

'I'm not happy with your article in the newspapers,' he wrote. 'I told you not to write my name [he actually didn't mention this at all] and don't show photos of me. You did it twice. It fucked up my family connexion, because they don't know my past.

'It would be nice if you could send me some money for all the stress you gave me. Maybe then I would speak to you again.' He added the three monkeys emoji of 'see no evil, hear no evil, say no evil'. Somewhat appropriate, it seemed to me.

As his ex-girlfriend Emma told me some months later: 'He really regretted opening up. He was on a roll and I don't think he realised exactly what he was saying. He was being loose tongued and should have been more careful.'

But she added, 'He also certainly regrets becoming so close to Christian. Basically it suited him at the time. Micha is quite opportunist, narcissistic, self-absorbed, so if things are fine and he's having fun he simply goes with the flow, he will simply not question things and turn a blind eye.'

Sadly, far too many people seemed to have done the same.

Chapter 27

One Word – Guilty

Emma had started dating Micha in 2008, the year Brueckner supposedly confessed to kidnapping Maddie to friends, including Helge Busching and Manfred Seyferth, as well as possibly Micha himself, in Spain. His apparent admission came in Orgiva, at the annual alternative music and drugs mash up, the Dragon Festival.

This curious pair, Busching and Seyferth, claimed they knew Brueckner well from Portugal as well as later in Spain. The two German men – who both have criminal records – said they lived and socialised with Brueckner and knew all about his criminal activity and darker, intimate side. While Seyferth knew him as 'the climber' and even admitted to carrying out burglaries with him in Portugal, it was a statement by Busching to police in 2017 that allegedly led to the current German investigation and 2020 appeal. According to *The Sun*, which tracked Busching down to Corsica, he was 'the first person' to directly denounce Brueckner to police in connection with Maddie's disappearance.

While this is definitely not the case – witnesses actually came forward as far back as 2007 in Portugal and 2013 in Germany – Busching did indeed give a statement to British detectives about Brueckner in Greece in 2017, around the time he got out of prison in Crete in May of that year.

Little is known about 50-year-old Busching, except that he is a shady character – a seasoned traveller who spent a number of years in prison, most recently serving a seven year, five month stretch for human trafficking. I suspect, he is still involved in it.

The chronology of what happened in 2017 is hard to clarify exactly, but as I understand it from a range of Greek, German and British police statements, Busching was released from prison, likely on remand, and somehow struck a deal with the Greek authorities for British detectives to visit him in Greece over the Maddie case.

Indeed, on July 18, 2017, the Directorate of Police Cooperation in central Athens, drafted an official document confirming the 'liaison' between Hellenic Police and the Metropolitan Police. Greek police were more than happy to set up the meeting and noted, pointedly, that Busching had already tried to report his information unsuccessfully to the Portuguese police 'a couple of times' – incredibly, once as long back as 2007 – but had been 'fobbed off'.

In the damning statement, Busching (described by *The Sun* as a 'recycling worker', whatever that means) told British detectives that he had immediately suspected Brueckner of his involvement in the Maddie case as he was in Praia da Luz at the same time in May 2007 ... and moreover, on the night of May 3, was in the close vicinity of the Ocean Club, where the McCanns were staying.

Furthermore – and most damningly – he claimed that Brueckner had actually later confessed to his involvement in the abduction, while they were attending a 'kite fest' in Spain, the following year, in 2008. (He was referring to the Dragon Festival that took place between March 20 and 23 that year.) He told the police that the German, whom he knew only by the name 'Christian', would 'talk in detail of his knowledge' and his connection to Maddie's disappearance.

So sensitive was this information, relayed during interviews in a hotel suited rented by Operation Grange, that the group of detectives, led by DCI Mark Cranwell, had, according to Busching's friend Manfred Seyferth, 'sealed off an entire floor of the hotel and carefully insisted it was swept for bugs'. (If true, it implies that British police perhaps suspected a very sinister high-level involvement in the Maddie case.)

Busching's information, I discovered, was backed up by an internal Greek police report, published by Greek press agency Larissa Press. It stated that he was a 'credible witness' and his information had been 'given voluntarily and without monetary or other consideration'. It added that the information had been 'cross-checked' and that Busching was 'considered a reliable source'.

It is not surprising that this was deemed necessary given his track record as something of a career criminal who had been in custody since 2015 for human trafficking. He had been arrested in 2011 for 'attempting to smuggle' three African migrants in his car from Igoumenitsa, in Greece, to Italy. However, after being charged and given bail, he vanished and did not appear in court until he was arrested again in Thessaloniki in 2015.

He claimed he had returned to Greece on holiday, which is surely unlikely if you know the Greeks have a warrant out for your arrest. He was sent to Chania Prison in Crete, until suddenly (and it is unclear if he needed to stay there to report to a police station weekly) he found himself on a boat back to the mainland to meet the British police in Athens in August 2017. After being grilled in the capital he then moved to the city of Lamia (named after a child-eating monster), an hour north east of Athens.

When Greek newspaper *To Vima* tracked him down to the village of Fthiotida, just outside Lamia, in August 2017, he confirmed his statement to the British police about Maddie, which had, predictably, been leaked.

'Yes, I met members of Scotland Yard and gave important information on the Madeleine case. On the day that she disappeared I was also in the area. I contacted the local police in Portugal back then [2007], but the investigation had moved on.

'Now there is intense interest in what I know and there is definitely something serious happening for them to come and meet me. I am however completely unable to say anything specific about the investigation.' He said he would be 'cooperating' with the British police again in the 'coming days'.

When asked if he believed Maddie was still alive he shrugged his shoulders and said, 'The ten years that have passed since then are many.'

According to Greek media, he was arrested again in 2017, in Corfu, allegedly for people smuggling again, before once again vanishing after getting bail. The Larissa agency told me his last known whereabouts, (before *The Sun* tracked him down in Corsica, France, in 2020), was in the Athens suburb of Agios Panteleimon.

In an excellent scoop, *Sun* photographer Dan Charity got a set of decent pics of him in Corsica, before reporter Nick Pisa managed to snatch a few comments from him. He reiterated that the police and courts had forbidden him from saying anything. When Pisa persevered and asked if Brueckner had ever shown him photos of Maddie, he added, 'Look, I can't talk about any of this. OK? I'm not allowed.' But he did add, 'I hope he stays in jail', and then, 'One word. Guilty.'

Sensationally, I discovered that Busching gave a second, more detailed statement about Brueckner's movement in 2007 and 2008 to British detectives in late 2017. It was taken at Scotland Yard in London under DCI Mark Cranwell. I got a copy of the interviews via the German TV network Spiegel TV and, while heavily redacted, they give a much more detailed profile of Brueckner and his close circle.

Busching confirmed he had travelled to London 'as a witness' and that he was 'ready to support the investigation' in any way needed. He said that he was giving the information on a man 'who I know by the name of Christian' and that now, after conducting further research, as well as looking at photos, he was able to give a further statement.

He said he had first met Brueckner at a bar called Serner Portimao in Portimao, sometime between 2003 and 2005. He said he had been invited back to Brueckner's house late that night, somewhere outside the Algarve resort but he couldn't remember exactly where. He said he had 'tried to find it on Google Maps' without luck, but remembered it as a 'detached white house with a red-tiled roof' with a car parking area behind it (presumably the Yellow House).

He went on to stress that he had 'never been a friend' of Brueckner's and had only been introduced via an acquaintance called 'Michael' (surname redacted, but almost certainly Michael 'Micha' Tatschl), who he, in turn, described as 'an accomplice of mine'.

He also talked about his friend 'Manfred Seyforth' [sic], whom he had met in a place called 'Jaluma' in 2001. 'He is, like myself, a traveller,' said Busching. 'We have travelled around together in Europe now and then since we got to know each other in 2001/2002.'

Finally – and potentially of critical importance – he said he would provide information about 'another man', who was 'the owner of a business, in Portugal'. However all the other information has been redacted by the

German police.

He went on to list a series of places he had spent time with Brueckner in Portugal and Spain, which he felt were relevant to the investigation. In particular he mentions Orgiva and its 'hippie commune', as well as the yearly 'Dragon Fest' that takes place in March. 'Hippies and travellers from the whole of Europe travelled there to take part in it.'

Across the border in Portugal he said he could mention 'numerous places', but the most important 'is Santa Clara'. I started getting excited.

'Santa Clara is located roughly 100km north of the Algarve, where there is a dam,' he said. 'There is a large German community there and – similar to Orgiva – many of them are hippies/travellers.'

He said he often stayed there, pitching up in his caravan, before adding: 'Santa Clara is where the Rebel Farm is located. I lived there for a long time in a trailer. I don't know the exact address. I only know how to get there.' It is then, during the interview at Scotland Yard that he shows DCI Mark (Cranwell, I assume) where it is approximately on Google Maps, before finding him Rebel Farm's website.

Annoyingly, the next few paragraphs are redacted out before Busching mentions his meetings with Brueckner in Orgiva over the following years. There is a lot missing, but it ends, 'Two weeks later I saw Christian for a short while for the last time. He came to Orgiva to buy hashish, which he wanted to bring to Germany. He left on the same day and I have never seen him since.'

There is no exact date of this meeting but it must be between 2008 and 2010, because Busching confirmed to police that he himself had lived in Orgiva for a number of years and didn't leave until 2010. 'I finally left in 2010 and went to Austria, then to Italy and finally to Greece,' he stated.

The rest was largely irrelevant to the case, as he whined about his 'unfair' arrest for people-smuggling: 'Yes, I am a small-time criminal, but not a people-smuggler. Picking up hitchhikers; that was not trafficking.' He claimed he had finally served his sentence in Crete and was freed on April 12, 2017, although he admitted he was on remand until 2021. He also failed to mention that he was actually involved in a second people-smuggling case in Corfu, for which he is still apparently facing justice.

The parts of his statement I could read had given me a couple more useful leads and confirmed some of Brueckner's key movements.

The most obvious place to visit now was Santa Clara and the ominous sounding Rebel Farm.

Chapter 28

Rebel Farm

During a second serious lockdown in Spain, in mid-January 2021, I somehow took a three-day trip to Santa Clara, in the rugged depopulated Alentejo region of southern Portugal. This large, dry area, which literally means 'Beyond the Tagus' river, is one of Europe's poorest. Due to thin soils and little rainfall, as well as a problem of communications and investment, the inland Alentejo region has suffered mass depopulation since the 1970s. This in turn has led to a weakened local workforce and gene pool, which has led to high suicide rates in the region, by far the highest in the Iberian peninsula and among the highest in Europe.

The most recent official EU stats in 2013 show the suicide rate is 21.4 per 100,000, compared to just 9.5 in Lisbon or 5.8 in northern Portugal. The district of Odemira, in which the village of Santa Clara lies, held the dubious honour of being the suicide capital of Portugal some decades back. This resulted in a series of in-depth studies and visits from sociologists from around Europe, according to an administrator at the local village hall.

On the face of it, the region is anything but unattractive, with large tracts of open unspoilt countryside, low pollution and terrific weather.

Certainly the village of Santa Clara-A-Velha and its nearby reservoir is a scenic spot. A typically charming village with a population of just 900, it boasts the sixteenth-century church Santa Clara de Assis, and its surrounding area, with its orange groves, fig and olive trees, has become something of a paradise for Northern European immigrants. A fertile area, thanks to its river, Mina, which winds its way out of the nearby reservoir to meet the sea at Vila Nova de Milfontes, it is easy to pitch up close to the reservoir and live off the land, growing vegetables and picking the seasonal fruit.

Largely undiscovered by tourists, this sleepy place around 100km inland is the perfect location for hippies and van lifers who are able to live undisturbed, as many of them do. It is for this reason that many of the southern Alentejo villages and towns can count on up to 50% of their residents being from abroad. Santa Clara is no exception and officially around 30% of the locals are Northern European, mostly German, while unofficially it might well be as high as half. 'The problem is that many of them fail to register with the local authorities, yet use our facilities and send their kids to the local schools,' complained the town hall administrator. 'They live in vans or on isolated farms, often many of them together, and it is hard to get a true figure of how many are here.' She cited two outlying hamlets in particular, Corte Brique and Corte Pereiro, as key offenders.

The main problem with residents not being registered is that regional and European funding is based on population numbers, so if a town or region has 20% missing from its census, it will get 20% less revenue. And then there is the 'problem of illegality', explained the Santa Clara employee, with drugs being the main issue. 'There was a big raid in Corte Pereiro that picked up quite a few big drug dealers recently,' she said. 'But there are plenty more still out there.'

With that I headed north a few clicks to track down the appropriately-named Rebel Farm, which sits the other side of the Barragem de Santa Clara Reservoir and the hamlet of Luzianes-Gare, with a population of around 400 people.

There were few clues online, nor an official website, and incredibly, no newspaper or TV network had written a word about the place, or indeed, mentioned Busching's claims. Fortunately it did have a Facebook page, where the majority of its posts were about motorbikes, mostly Harley-Davidsons, and there were a few photos of tattoos, ostensibly linked to the farm's owner, whose name appeared to be 'Cheyenne'.

The Facebook page described it as a 'Bed & Breakfast' that offered 'tattoos & piercing' alongside 'horse riding'. There were seemingly worse places to stay, and its catchline certainly stood out: 'Choppers, friends & good people ONLY! Junkies, crusties and other useless bastards are NOT welcome!!!'

I hoped I was not among the latter, although I suspected there was a good chance the owner would consider journalists 'useless bastards'. Taking note of the capital letters for 'NOT welcome' and the three exclamation marks at the end, I decided to call my journalist friend Martin Brunt, the best-connected crime reporter on British TV, to see if he had heard of the place. I knew if anyone had heard of Rebel Farm it would be Martin. He had done lots of reports on the Maddie case for *Sky News* over the years and spent many months in Portugal digging into the case.

'Sure, that's the Hells Angel guy, Jon. Be very careful,' he warned predictably. 'A strange place and a strange man. We took the drive up there a couple of months ago. A lovely spot, but the guy's a nutter. He nearly beat us up. It was really scary. You definitely need to take care.'

Screech! I slammed on the handbrake and pulled over onto a verge. 'Really?' I spluttered.

He went on to explain how he had been given the tip off by a German contact at *Spiegel TV* a few weeks earlier, after one of its journalists had tried – and failed – to get anything out of the German owner of Rebel Farm.

Manfred Seyferth had also later told police that not only had he, Busching and Brueckner spent some time at the farm, but the sick videos 'stolen' from the Yellow House had supposedly ended up at the farm. 'Perhaps they came in a vehicle that was sold to the owner, or perhaps the owner or someone else there bought them,' Martin mused. 'I've heard a variety of stories.'

He agreed that the whole thing was vague and totally unsubstantiated, and he hadn't seen the actual statement from Busching … but as *Sky News* had been doing a special ten-minute report on the case in the run up to Christmas 2020, he and his producer felt it would be an idea to give it a try. He said it had been something of a mission to find the farm and when they got there they found the owner in a foul mood and with no intention of answering questions.

'He was riled from the very off and came charging out of the gate to have a go at us,' said Martin. 'I really thought he was going to punch me. He was apparently most furious with the cameraman, who he had spotted filming outside before we knocked on the gate.

'When he calmed down a little, he joked that we must have been expecting trouble as we had turned our car around for a quick getaway. He found it disrespectful, even though it was clearly quite sensible. So my advice Jon is tread very carefully.'

Warnings didn't come much clearer. In my years as a journalist I've been chased down the road by fascist skinheads and doorstepped suspected murderers, but here I was, on my own in a foreign country, in a remote area, with no neighbours to hear my screams. And I mean no one as Rebel Farm sat on its own in the middle of nowhere, some 3km from the nearest village and 400m to the nearest property.

I called my wife to tell her exactly where I was going, and I stopped in the local village of Luzianes-Gare for directions and to ask a few gentle questions. Absolutely no one wanted to comment on the farm or its owner, although someone working at the town hall told me that the police had to be directed there on two separate occasions in 2019. She said detectives from the PJ gave nothing away other than it concerned 'something abroad' and they were looking for a particular vehicle.

She pointed me in the direction of a dirt track, which had a small wooden sign pointing to 'Rebel Farm'. It was the first of five or six similar signs that guided me into the beautiful rolling hills that make up the Alentejo outback. I passed a tractor loaded up with logs, and a one-tooth farmer with his cows, before arriving at the isolated ranch.

Its gate was shut and there were a fair few cars around, including a white transit van with 'Rebel Farm' painted on the side. Making sure I parked my car facing towards the gate and being careful not to take any photos, I took a deep breath and went to ring the bell. Except there wasn't one.

The bell was actually a real bell hanging outside the gate, but given it was a fairly big place and I could hear the muffled sounds of what sounded like Lynyrd Skynyrd's *Free Bird*, I figured there was no chance it would be heard. I gave it a couple of clangs but nothing happened, so I walked around the side and shouted 'Hey, Cheyenne' a few times, until the music stopped and a stocky man, about 55 to 60, strutted out of a garage/workshop at the side. Wearing jeans and a leather jacket and with a beanie hat pulled low over his forehead, he looked every bit your classic biker.

Luckily, he appeared to be in a good mood. I smiled cheerfully and asked if he was the owner. 'Yes, that's me,' he replied. 'What do you want?'

I launched into the usual spiel about my research into Maddie and said I had driven all the way from Ronda in Spain to speak to him. It was a fortunate opening gambit, as his eyes lit up and he told me he knew the Ronda area well and used to live there in 'an abandoned castle', but refused to tell me exactly where.

I explained that I had read an official police document (an interview with Busching) that had mentioned Rebel Farm and hoped he had not been inundated with journalists. I added that the claims of Helge Busching could well be 'complete rubbish'.

It was at this point I noticed the tattoo under his eye, which normally signifies some sort of violent activity or death. And I think he saw me gulp. He told me he 'never talked to journalists' and that the last TV crew that came (clearly Martin Brunt's) had to be 'chased off the property'.

Sensing he was in the mood for some banter, I persevered regardless, sympathising with his obvious lack of guests due to lockdown, and also that he had been dragged into the Maddie case, apparently without warning. He said he wasn't bothered about the Covid situation, and was happy not to be going out or seeing people. He added that he didn't need tourists at his B&B as he had enough money from other work. He said he was just finishing renovating and repairing an old Harley-Davidson, adding it had been a healthy earner, and, in fact, he needed to get back and finish it.

I said I only needed five minutes and to ask a couple of questions and, quick as a fox, he asked 'how many?' I said, 'six or seven tops', to which he replied, 'Well you can have three, so get a move on.' I hadn't actually prepared anything, as I was expecting to be chased off the property, so I had to wing it. Pretending to find a list in my notebook I bought a few precious seconds and then asked when and why the police had visited his farm and what were they looking for?

While aware this was actually three questions in one, he hadn't noticed and went on to confirm that yes, they had visited the farm on a couple of occasions over 'the last year or two'. He added that they were 'looking for a van' which they didn't find.

'They turned up unannounced and searched the whole place and grounds, but they didn't find anything,' he said. 'The van they were looking for, a Bedford van, was definitely not here and, I can tell you for sure, it never was here. They found my caravan at the back, but nothing else.'

I asked about Busching's claims that he was somehow involved in the case and asked if he had brought the videos to the farm. (He didn't need me to elaborate on the videos: he knew they had been mentioned in connection with his farm in a police statement, and Martin Brunt had already tried to question him about them.)

'It's complete rubbish, I have no idea why he said all that,' said Cheyenne. 'He's making it up. He [Brueckner] definitely didn't stay here. In fact, I don't remember him at all. OK, yes, he might have come to one of our weekend parties back in the day, but there would have been dozens, hundreds of people here so it would be easy to come in and out without being noticed.

'Anyway, I can tell you I am not into raping old women or killing children. It's definitely not my thing. And the groups I know, and anyone in prison who does things like that, gets dealt with in certain ways.'

I didn't need to ask what he meant by that, but instead picked him up on the prison line. What did he know about prisons? Had he spent much time inside? 'Well I wasn't in for anything sick like that,' he said. It didn't feel sensible to push further.

I moved onto the area in general and what his take was on the amount of hippies and van lifers who had settled in southern Portugal.

'There are too many of them,' he said. 'And, put it this way, if anyone comes in here with heroin or strong drugs they will find themselves thrown out very fast. I am not into junkies and crusties. I never had them at my parties.

'They are all down the road in places like Monchique and Corte Pereires. All those so-called "pizza party" nights. You buy a ticket for a pizza and then go and take and do what you want. You need to go and investigate those. There is a lot more crusty than actual pizza crust at those nights. And more than meets the eye. It's not my thing.'

By now we were getting on famously and he went on to explain that he had settled down in Portugal 'many years ago', having lived in Spain for a while, and had a long-term German partner, whom I later discovered was called Ulrike. While I could find no link to anyone of that name on social media or online, the town hall later confirmed that the property was in her name.

Either way, Cheyenne clearly didn't wish to talk about her, so instead I complimented him on his English, which he said he had picked up in Croydon back in the 1970s, when he lived in London in his youth. He said it had been a great three or four years of his life and he had been immersed in the heavy rock heyday of legendary bands Uriah Heep and Deep Purple. It had been a heady time to be in the capital and he said a fair few of those original hippies ended up moving to Spain and Portugal.

'Many of them turned up in the original Bedford vans, which is why there were so many around here,' he explained. 'They were mostly good people, not like the drug-taking crusty idiots you find today.'

All in all, he seemed genuine and honest. Certainly less suspect than Helge Busching, who to me seemed very shady.

Before parting company with Cheyenne I asked him what he made of the Maddie case and his opinion on Brueckner. His reply was surprising. He shrugged his shoulders and, almost as an aside, revealed he had actually had a unique insight into the case when he had received a visit from Brueckner's eccentric German lawyer, Friedrich Fulscher, a few months before.

'He came here as part of his research and to build up his case,' he said. 'And he was a decent guy. In fact, he showed a lot of courtesy, unlike those TV journalists. He explained the whole case to me and went over the ridiculous claims of Helge and insisted I was not in any way a suspect. He said

Helge was just some dodgy druggie, not to be trusted.

'Ultimately he said the case doesn't add up and he is convinced he can prove that his client was not involved in any way and he will get him off. How he is going to do that though, I have no idea.'

...

The case against Brueckner and his links to Rebel Farm strengthened a few weeks later, when Manfred Seyferth backed up Busching's claims that they had been staying there (or at least near there) in 2006 – and that they may have left (or sold) the rape videos and cameras in the area.

It came during an interview with Seyferth by the *Discovery Channel* during their three-part documentary, *Prime Suspect*.

The eccentric German drifter gave the programme a lot more detail on Brueckner's criminal behaviour and the 'dozens of things' he stole in Praia da Luz, which meant his house was full of electrical devices, vats of stolen diesel and other valuables. And so when he heard that Brueckner had been sent to prison for fuel theft in April 2006, he and Busching decided to break in and steal it all.

He said they had hatched the plan while staying in Santa Clara at a place run by '*the Bandidos*', an infamous motorcycle gang with various criminal links in Portugal, presumably referring to Rebel Farm.

'My colleague [Busching] and I were in the mountains in Santa Clara at a place that belonged to the Bandidos. And after two or three weeks my colleague had the idea that we could look inside Christian's home because he was in prison ... and we could see if there was anything we could take.

'We drove off at night to the home and found it open. The back door open, the front door open. Everything was ripped apart and in a mess. I thought that was the police. They had done it. That is what they do when they are looking for stuff.'

But it surely hadn't been the police, as he and Busching had found a gun and various other items including the video cameras, all of which detectives would have hopefully seized. 'There were just a few electronic devices. That was it ... and there was only 20 litres of fuel,' he said. 'It was all empty. Nothing was left. I took a pistol I found and he took a camera – the famous camera – and we went back to the place in the mountains.'

He later told Sandra Felgueiras at RTP that they had bundled everything in an Opel Corsa that was in the grounds of Brueckner's house and returned to Rebel Farm. When they got there, he claimed Busching turned on the video camera and found the series of 'terrible' torture videos with Brueckner in them, clearly filmed in his home. Despite Seyferth telling him to 'throw the films away', which Micha Tatschl had also insisted, Busching later told police that he had left them in his motorhome, which he had then sold. To whom, he did not say.

Despite a number of attempts to speak to Cheyenne by phone in early 2021, I was unable to speak to him. He never picked up.

Chapter 29

Convicted

It would take something of a Houdini escape act to get Christian Brueckner off the hook. A two-times convicted paedophile, living in Praia da Luz at the time Maddie went missing ... a man frequently on the dark web, who talked about selling children to Morocco and bragged about being able to hide them in his RV. A bona fide sexual predator, with a criminal record since the age of 15, currently being probed over many more crimes, at least three of them in Portugal. Oh, and a man, who frequently burgled tourist accommodation in the Ocean Club block where the McCanns were staying.

It sounds like an open and shut case, but what concerns me is that much of the anecdotal evidence of Brueckner's alleged involvement in the disappearance of Maddie seems to come from two witnesses who themselves have long track records in crime.

However, it was Helge Busching and Manfred Seyferth's evidence that recently helped to convict Brueckner of the rape of an American pensioner in Praia da Luz, in 2005, 18 months before Maddie went missing. It was this conviction in 2019 (he appealed but it was ratified in autumn 2020), which resulted in a seven-year prison sentence that took the pressure off German detectives having to quickly find the evidence to charge Brueckner. As he will stay in prison for at least four years, they have time to gather enough evidence.

Busching and Seyferth had been summoned to give evidence at the court case in December 2019 after they claimed to have seen a video of similar attacks filmed by Brueckner himself. They told the court in Braunschweig (also known as Brunswick) that they had found the video in his rented Yellow House when he and Michael Tatschl were awaiting trial for fuel theft in 2006.

Seyferth – who admitted to working as a burglar with Brueckner, as well as stealing diesel from lorries with him – told the court that the explicit home movie, found on a video camera at the house, showed an elderly woman getting beaten with an object 'that could have been a scimitar or perhaps even a type of ruler', before being tied up and raped.

After the rape, he claimed the attacker took off his grey mask to reveal himself, and to Seyferth's shock it was Brueckner. 'He literally sat on the bed and pulled the mask off his face,' he said in a witness statement.

According to official documents, Brueckner had entered American pensioner Diana Menkes' house, Casa Jacaranda, in Praia da Luz at about 10.30pm on September 2, 2005, through a patio door. He dragged her through the house, before tying her down and beating her on the breasts, stomach and backside, with a 30cm-long object. He then tied her up before carefully setting up the video camera to film himself raping her.

In what was clearly an organised and well-planned attack, he hung a rug up at a window behind, which he kept in place with books, to prevent anyone from being able to look in. Continuing with his torture, he then forced the victim, who was naked, tied and gagged, to stand up for around 15 minutes during which he beat her repeatedly with the thin, bendy object, which he had brought along for the purpose. Finally he raped her.

As Seyferth later told *Spiegel TV:* 'CB was speaking the whole time, even as he mounted the camera in a fixed position. Then with the stick or ruler in his hand he clipped her on the breasts, so tra la la. Then, what else? Oh yeah, she was ordered to suck him off. You could half see that.'

Finally, the filming completed, he led her to the kitchen where he forced her to hand over money, around 90 euros, as well as her laptop.

She was then led to the bathroom where she was told to sit down and 'stay calm' for ten minutes before raising the alarm. He left on foot.

In evidence given by the victim, who moved back to America, and has since died, she said she had been 'home alone' when the patio door was slid open and she was grabbed by the stocky man, who dragged her by her hair into a bedroom. She said he spoke English with a foreign accent and went on to describe her ordeal as a 'long and planned procedure'. She described him as a real professional, who would have done it before and would do it again. She felt he 'enjoyed torturing' her.

The heinous crime was investigated by the Portuguese PJ from nearby Portimao and Lagos, but was closed the following year, with no key leads, despite the close proximity of Brueckner's home – just over 900m away – as well as his previous convictions in Germany. He had also come into contact with the local force a number of times that year surrounding his appalling treatment of his ex-girlfriend Alison.

However, his road to prosecution only began by complete chance in 2017 after Busching told police about the videos he had found at the German's house in 2006. As noted, his information was supposedly given to police after the ten-year anniversary of Maddie's disappearance, in May 2017 when the two men had met in a bar in Germany and a news report on the tenth anniversary flashed up on a TV screen in the pub.

But the bar-room confession could easily have been in Greece, where Busching had recently got out of prison, or in Portugal, where Brueckner was mostly living at the time.

Supposedly, the pair had been drinking and reminiscing about the times they had spent together in Portugal and Spain, when the subject of Maddie had come up and Brueckner had admitted his involvement again (the first time had allegedly been at the Dragon Festival in 2008) and given more details. *The Sun* reported that Brueckner told his friend he had indeed 'snatched her' although this is surely guesswork.

He was also reportedly said to have got out a mobile phone on which he had also kept a video of himself raping other women. (When the news of Diana Menkes' rape came out, Busching assumed an older woman he had seen in the video was her. However, as I will explain later, it was, alarmingly, another victim.) Could Brueckner have actually been set up by Busching and police into making the confession and showing off the video? Was it a clever sting operation? It is not yet clear.

Either way, in early 2018, with Brueckner locked up in prison in Germany for child sex abuse, the BKA started doing a cold case review of other potential crimes that he could have been involved in – aside from Maddie. It was only then that they stumbled across the rape in 2005 in Portugal, when they knew he was living on the Algarve. They discovered it had never been solved so they asked Portuguese police for the victim's testimony and any other evidence they still had on file. By amazing fortune – unlike in a similar case the previous year involving an Irish victim (more of which later) – a box of evidence had been kept, completely by accident, at Faro Police headquarters.

German police officially requested it in March 2018 and discovered that among a package of eight items – including bloodied sheets and the rope used to tie the victim up – was some key forensic evidence, including a hair from the attacker on the bedsheet. Incredibly, when the hair was sent off for analysis at a lab for DNA, it came back with a match: Christian Brueckner. It was an amazing breakthrough and in August 2019 Brueckner was charged, before finally being put on trial at Braunschweig Court in December that year.

•••

Diana Menkes was approaching her 85th birthday when, out of nowhere, a detective from Germany phoned her at her home in Pasadena, California. It came as a shock when the softly spoken policeman from Braunschweig started to gently probe her on what must have been the most harrowing event of her long and purposeful life, which sadly ended in March 2021, I discovered.

A former graduate of English and journalism at America's prestigious Stanford University, in San Francisco, she had gone on to travel the world as well as hold down a demanding career as a periodical journalist, mostly in Washington DC. Her 16 years at the American capital's respected Smithsonian Institute saw her edit countless books and museum catalogues, as well as the journal Isis and manage the Archives of the American Art Journal.

She married an Austrian rocket scientist, physicist Josh Menkes, whom she met while working at the Jet Propulsion Laboratory, where she edited their titles, and the pair picked up a love of travel, which took them around the world, frequently working in exotic places, including Tokyo and the Middle East.

'She was a born traveller and had an amazing life,' her nephew Michael

161

Foulger, told me from his home in Pasadena in June 2021. 'Right from the off she had the travel bug and did things far from normal in her era. There were so many adventures, around Africa, India and the Middle East. And even after her husband died she frequently still travelled on her own, perhaps a bit naively,' he added.

It was maybe inevitable that she and Josh would end up making a permanent move abroad, with Europe being the most logical place for their jobs. 'We expected them to end up in somewhere like Paris or Madrid, but they ended up on the Algarve in 1986,' continued Michael. 'They loved the warmth and the ocean, the swimming and snorkelling in the sea.'

It was a charmed existence. Even after Josh died suddenly in 1988, Diana vowed to stay on in Portugal. She had a flat and some good friends in London, where she would frequently take breaks, but Praia da Luz became her long-term home. She knew the area and its locals well and loved the laidback way of life.

That was until 2005 when an evil rapist crept into her beachside villa and brutally raped her, on camera, for well over an hour. It was an ordeal that was to confirm Christian Brueckner as one of Europe's most sickening, heartless criminals.

'It was a horrible attack, which definitely had an effect on her,' recalled her nephew. 'She dwelled on it a bit, but she did not want it to ruin her life – she carried on as best she could. She only really talked to my mum about it. She wanted to move on.' Bravely, she did just that and continued to travel, spending her 80th birthday in Laos.

And when the time came, she was more than happy to help convict Brueckner added Michael, who told me he was still 'in the middle' of sorting out all the arrangements for her will and probate when I tracked him down.

'When she got the first phone call from Germany, they told her they had found some critical forensic evidence and wanted to try and convict him. She agreed to help and a few weeks later a DI [Detective Inspector] came over to visit her and talked the whole thing through.

'She started telling me some things about the case and I began to read up on it. I later found some documents and was amazed by what she went through. And when the chance came to prosecute she didn't back off. She was a brave woman right until the end.'

When the case went to trial, she was able to give evidence on a video link from the US due to her geography and age.

With her evidence, the testimonies of Seyferth and Busching as well as the DNA match of his hair, it was a fairly straightforward conviction. However, the geographical evidence of Brueckner's proximity to the villa is also tantalising, as there was an easy escape route up a footpath through unlit fields. Less than 1km from his rental home, it was a footpath he knew well as he regularly walked along it when he took his dog down to the beach. In court, Brueckner admitted exactly that and confirmed he knew the villa well for that reason. But he said he had never been in the home, nor had he ever met Diana Menkes.

Bettina Thoenes, a reporter for the *Braunschweiger Zeitung* newspaper, which followed the trial said Brueckner gave a good impression in court as he was eloquent, well prepared – often quoting from legal text books – and had an 'intelligent appearance'. He said he 'couldn't imagine how one of his hairs could be found on her bedsheets' and insisted it 'must have got there another way'. He said the most likely reason was that it was taken into the house by a cat as he 'regularly stroked and fed a friendly cat near the villa, and it is possible this cat took the hair into the crime scene.' He added it was 'also possible that one of his hairs may have been transferred onto the victim through coincidental and unconscious contact with her, such as in a shop or pub.'

He tried hard to pick apart Diana's description of him, insisting his eyes were blue, not dark, and that he had never been 'strongly built', nor ever weighed more than 75kg. He also said he spoke excellent English, in particular because of the work he had done for an 'English newspaper', and because he had spent many years talking to English customers in various pubs he worked in, and he had many English-speaking friends. His lawyer also cast aspersions on her testimony and memory, hinting she may have had a form of dementia.

Brueckner said he believed the culprit was probably an Eastern European construction worker, 'of whom there are many on the Algarve'.

Finally he claimed he had been in a stable relationship at the time (a total lie) and had no need to undertake such crimes. 'I had a normal relationship [with a girlfriend] with no acts of violence or sadistic/masochistic practices,' he said. Alison, of course, might beg to differ. The judge certainly did, finding him guilty and sentencing him to seven years in prison. Given he was currently finishing a 21-month sentence for drug dealing at Kiel Prison, he would merely stay where he was for much longer. He was actually moved to Oldenburg prison, known as the 'Alcatraz of Germany', in mid-2021.

An appeal made on a technicality by his lawyer to the EU's Court of Appeal in Brussels was thrown out at the end November 2020, meaning he will now not be considered for parole until 2024 or 2025.

•••

Not only did his incarceration take considerable pressure off the BKA from charging him with snatching Maddie, it also led to the police to re-open another horrific rape case against a young Irish woman called Hazel Behan in June 2004.

In the vicious attack, a hooded attacker had climbed up to her first-floor apartment and filmed the long, protracted rape, before fleeing. Yes, read that again; CLIMBED UP and FILMED the sex assault.

Behan was just two weeks from her twenty first birthday when the attack happened in Praia da Rocha, just 30 minutes from Praia da Luz, and near where Brueckner had lived for a number of years in the 1990s. She had been working as a holiday rep when the rapist appeared in her flat at the Condominio Clube, Praia da Rocha III at 1 am, wearing tights, some sort of leotard and with a mask over his face. He had taken off his shoes and left them on the balcony outside.

After actually calling her name, he raised a 12-inch long machete and dragged her into the kitchen/dining area. He ordered her not to scream, then gagged her with a cloth, before tying her up, beating and raping her repeatedly.

The man, who Behan estimated was about 6ft tall and had 'piercing blue eyes', spoke English with a German accent, but could be 'Belgian, German or Dutch'. He had also clearly been planning the attack as he knew her name and had arrived with a bag full of tools, including chains and whips, as well as scissors to cut her nightclothes off. He also had a video camera, which he set up on a tripod after he had tied her to the kitchen breakfast counter.

Waiving her right to anonymity, and having followed the Maddie case and read about Brueckner's conviction for the rape of Diana Menkes, Behan told *The Guardian*: 'It seemed to me he had worked everything out, he had a plan and was very deliberate.

'He consistently cleaned his hands, and repeatedly changed condoms. This went on, I guess, for around four or five hours. When he was finished, he took me down from the counter, but I could not stand up because of the ropes digging into the backs of my legs. He wanted me to perform a certain act on him which I just couldn't, I was gagging.

'He got angry and ordered me into the bathroom and he picked up the machete. I was convinced he was going to kill me, and I threatened to scream and said I would not go in there.

'My hands were still tied behind my back and he leaned me over a small bench and put a sheet over my head. I thought that was it, my life was over. But underneath the sheet I watched as he backed out of the door, put on his shoes and ran away down the street.'

Chillingly, in the weeks running up to the attack, Behan noticed that someone had crept into her room. 'At first I thought I was just being paranoid,' she told the newspaper. 'But bits of money went missing, and things had been moved around.

'I now know my attacker had entered the room and been stalking me in the period leading up to the attack. I now wish I had followed my instinct and told someone in a position of responsibility.

'My mind was blown when I read how he had attacked a woman in 2005, both the tactics and the methods he used, the tools he had with him, how well he had planned it out,' she said.

She is certain her attacker was Brueckner. Although he wore a mask, she could see he 'had blond eyebrows' and those piercing blue eyes. She also recalled a mark on the top of his right thigh, 'either a pull in the tights, a birthmark or a tattoo'. While this is a contentious issue (with his lawyer insisting he has no birthmark or tattoo there), German media reported that Brueckner did have a birthmark on his upper right thigh. In any case, read again. It could have been a 'pull in the tights'.

It is what happened after the attack that is perhaps even more alarming.

After calling police, almost certainly from the same PJ department led by Amaral and Pereira, an enormous platoon of officers, understood to have been up to 30, showed up. They took the attractive foreigner back to her apartment where she was asked to strip off and stand naked in a 'star jump-like stance' while they took photos of her. 'That was one of the most humiliating aspects of the whole ordeal,' she said.

She was taken to the local hospital where a gynaecologist examined her, but she doesn't know if any forensic evidence was taken.

No attempt was made to examine her wounds for evidence and when she returned to the apartment several days later with her mum, she found one of her nails on the bed that must have come off while she was trying to defend herself. 'So I am not very confident that they examined the room closely,' she said.

What is also odd, and relevant today, is that she was asked to keep the attack quiet and not talk to the media as it would put tourists off from coming. 'Then I read about the poor American woman and the possible link that was being made between her attack and the person who abducted Madeleine, and I was so full of anger,' said Hazel. 'I knew in my gut it was the right thing to do to speak out.'

Predictably, given it was Portugal, her rape had led to no conviction and the case was dropped the following year.

'I think if the police had done their job investigating what happened to me, if this is indeed the same man that attacked the American and abducted Madeleine, they might have prevented the attack on her, and Madeleine would now be at home with her parents.'

Now in her late thirties and living in Ireland with her husband and two children, Hazel gave a statement to the Met Police, who informed her they were taking her case seriously and would be contacting Portuguese police. At the end of July 2020, after considerable global media pressure, Portuguese police finally retrieved the archived files, which were being held just around the corner at Portimao Court.

The 110-page case file includes details of evidence collected by police from the scene of the attack. Among these were the scissors used to cut off her clothes, her underwear, fingernails and a shirt on which blood was found. The items were tested for DNA, according to a report in the file, while swabs were also taken during her medical examination.

However, surprise, surprise, everything was destroyed in March 2007 on orders from the judge, because it had been kept in 'adverse preservation conditions'. Adverse? In what way? The rest of the evidence was destroyed in 2009. On what grounds evidence needed to be destroyed after just five years in such a nasty rape case I have no idea. Space is not a premium on the Algarve and it was not exactly taking up a huge container. But the police clearly did not believe that the attack was worth remembering.

They concluded it had been an isolated case, and the attacker's modus operandi had 'not been witnessed in other cases'. Yet just a year later, nearby, an elderly woman was attacked in a very similar way AND filmed by a northern European. It was surely investigated by the same police department. Why hadn't they looked for any similar cases, with such a modus operandi? Or indeed blonde foreign men, speaking English?

The police appear to have either given up or deliberately ignored both cases, lamenting that finding the attacker in the Behan attack was difficult as there were 'thousands of people from several nationalities' in the resort at the time, as the Euro 2004 football tournament was taking place. As his friend Micha told me, Brueckner was most certainly around that month. He had robbed lots of holiday apartments that month.

While Portuguese police confirmed they were reopening the case in September 2020 (perhaps due to strong foreign pressure), it was announced that the German BKA were also opening an investigation into the rape. However, despite early optimism that it might lead to the case being solved, it emerged in November 2020 that there was no obvious DNA link to Brueckner in the apartment. Of course most of the evidence had already been destroyed let's not forget and Brueckner appears to always carefully plan his sex crimes.

However, in December 2020, German prosecutor Hans Christian Wolters was more optimistic when he insisted that he foresaw new convictions against Brueckner in 2021. 'Whether and when charges will be brought in these cases cannot be predicted at present,' said the BKA chief. But he added: 'I am also very confident with the investigation into Madeleine's disappearance but due to the scope of the case, the other proceedings (such as Behan's) can be expected to conclude earlier.' I would ask him about these a few months later

Chapter 30

An Evil Psychopath

When Manfred Seyferth was interviewed again by Portuguese, British and American media between Christmas 2020 and January 2021, he was adamant Brueckner was a 'bad man' who would be convicted of other sex crimes in Portugal. He described him as a dangerous paedophile with serious sexual problems and said this with certainty having lived in a caravan in the garden of the Yellow House in Praia da Luz, 'in 2007', although I am pretty certain Brueckner was no longer living there then. Perhaps he meant 2006.

The 65 year old said he had first met Brueckner when he had run out of fuel and he had sold him a stolen canister. 'He wasn't my type of person,' he told the *Discovery Channel* documentary from outside his caravan parked in Ancona port, in Italy . He said Brueckner was 'wearing a tie' and 'went around like a head waiter with an arrogant way about him.' While he said he 'didn't like him' and he was a 'catastrophe', he still ended up spending time with him and breaking into homes with him.

He claimed that he had last seen him at the Dragon Festival, in Orgiva, in March 2008 when he had turned up in his big winnebago 'with a young girl, who looked about 15.' He told *The Sun*: 'I didn't like it one bit so I had nothing to do with him [at the festival]. That's why I think he may have something to do with Maddie. He broke in and saw her and because he likes young girls – he's got lots of convictions – he took her.'

Seyferth also confirmed that, like Helge Busching, he had also been grilled by police in Greece, in March 2018, over his links to Brueckner, specifically what he knew about the other rape of Diana Menkes and the rape videos he has seen. Two detectives had visited him in Lamia, where he was living with Busching, who was out of prison having served his sentence for people smuggling.

The police asked Seyferth to come with them to Thessaloniki to make an official statement. 'A guy from the LKA [Braunschweig Police] came to see me in Lamia, but he didn't ask about Madeleine, he just wanted to know about the rapes,' he told Sandra Felgueiras on *Sexta as 9*. 'I told them everything I could about the elderly woman and the teenage girl [in the videos] and off I left.'

After the Diana Menkes court case in Braunchsweig, the police approached Seyferth again. They were interested in the people Brueckner socialised with, in particular a pair of Russians siblings. They actually told him it was in relation to a 'murder case' and he was then taken by car on a four-hour drive to Frankfurt.

'I don't know why it was in Frankfurt, but they were specifically interested in these two Russians, who lived in Spain,' he told Felgueiras. 'They were keen to know if I knew them and said it was over a murder case, involving Christian Brueckner and it could involve these two Russian brothers.'

Seyferth insisted he was unable to help them and finally they let him go. When asked about the Russian connection to the Maddie case, prosecutor Hans Christian Wolters told the RTP programme he was not keen to elaborate. While he did eventually confirm to Felgueiras that the German police were 'looking for these Russians', he would only say the pair had been in contact with Brueckner at the time that Madeleine disappeared, and nothing more. I assume they know this from his phone records.

Drifter Seyferth claims to have known Brueckner well, despite insisting in every interview that he didn't like him. United by their criminal leanings, Seyferth described Brueckner as a 'great burglar'. Indeed, the first time he met him, Brueckner told him he was fit and strong as his job was 'climbing facades' in order to break into hotels and apartments.

'We called him "The Climber" because of his skills,' Seyferth told *The Sun*. 'He was athletic and strong and an expert at getting into apartments and hotel rooms. I saw him many times climb up to first and second-floor apartments and break in. He would take watches, passports, money and anything electronic that he could sell.'

He told the *Discovery Channel*: 'He would take anything that would make him money, anything that would bring in a few marks.' And then he added, perhaps as a Freudian slip, that Brueckner went out 'every night' WITH an accomplice to commit crimes. 'They went out every night, like animals, to do something,' he said. 'They earnt very good money.'

Whether he was talking about Helge Busching, Michael Tatschl or someone else, we can only speculate. Seyferth admitted he also worked with him but insisted they were petty crimes. 'Yes, I stole some diesel and some solar panels [with him]. I'm a thief but I don't do anything else – not like Christian who is sick,' he said.

'Christian is a bad, bad man. He is an evil psychopath. He is obsessed with small children and I didn't like it,' said Seyferth. He referred to one of the videos he claimed he had seen of Brueckner raping and molesting a teenage girl, around 15 or 16 – the age which Seyferth said 'was usual for his girlfriends'. He had tied her to a post inside his property. He said the police had shown him photos (possibly stills from the film) of the interior of what was either the Yellow House or the Old Schoolhouse that may have come from this video.

The girl was strung up to the support beam – which can be seen in the photo of his house released by German police in the 2020 appeal. He said she was begging for help while he sexually abused her. Describing it as 'pure torture' and in 'no way voluntary', he said she threw up during the ordeal and Brueckner responded with "Oh man, my lovely carpet! Don't throw up on my lovely carpet!" Seyferth said he didn't watch any more.

'He is evil because of the things I saw on the video with the old woman and the girl,' he said.

In terms of the items they found at the Yellow House, we have to assume that he and Busching kept them all, aside from the video camera and films. Did they take his money, as well as his other valuables and perhaps the passports he had stolen? Or did someone else take them? It is not known how much, if anything, they gave back to Brueckner, although Seyferth admitted they had seen Brueckner after he came out of prison and they certainly saw him again the following year at the Dragon Festival in Spain, suggesting their relationship was not too strained.

In terms of evidence that could be used against Brueckner, it is unclear if the videos have been handed into the German prosecutors or not, although Wolters has firmly denied he has them. There is a high probability that they were among a huge stash of over 8,000 videos and photos Brueckner later buried on CDs and memory sticks at an old box factory property he owned in Germany (more of which later).

Regarding the gun (could this be the same one that Christian apparently wielded a few times while living in Foral?), Seyferth claims they threw it away in a 'nearby reservoir'. Why he and Busching did this is unclear and he refused to be drawn on which reservoir, or further details, saying they simply 'panicked'.

Could this have been the lake beside the Barragem da Bravura dam, a desolate spot, a 35 to 40-minute drive inland from Praia da Luz?

It seems the most likely location, being the nearest to Praia da Luz, and, coincidentally it has twice been pinpointed as the place where Maddie's body may have been dumped.

Chapter 31

Part of the Jigsaw

Occupying an area 4km wide and with a perimeter of 40km, the Barragem da Bravura dam and the Albufeira da Barragem de Odiaxere reservoir, are a short hop from the Old Schoolhouse in Bensafrim that Brueckner spent time at with his older girlfriend, as well as his other popular haunt of Foral, where he lived with Nicole Fehlinger. There are only a handful of isolated dwellings dotted around the dam and the reservoir, but this area has been mentioned various times regarding the Maddie case, unsurprising given it is just a 23km drive from Praia da Luz.

The most recent story regarded an employee of the Ocean Club, who allegedly found a letter in the front doorway of Apartment 5A, from where Maddie vanished, pinpointing the reservoir as being her 'final resting place'. A handyman spotted it on the first anniversary of her disappearance in May 2008 and immediately gave the note to the local police. He later revealed that the letter had been headed 'Madeleine Beth McCann', with a description underneath of how she had been allegedly dumped in the Barragem da Bravura reservoir.

He told *The Mirror*: 'It was raining that night so it was soaking wet when I found it. It clearly said Madeleine's name at the top. It was written in Portuguese. I spoke to the other staff about it and they said to hand it in to the Portuguese police. I gave it to them, but I have no idea what they did about it.' Referring to the isolated reservoir he said, 'It would be the perfect place to hide a body.'

Yet despite the specifics of the letter, police are not believed to have ever properly scoured the lake with divers. While they did send sniffer dogs to search the fringes of the lake and nearby woodland, I don't believe a full search of the lake ever took place.

Furthermore, I don't believe they ever interviewed any of the various hippies and travellers, who lived beside the lake in 2008. As Kit Thackeray, a Brit who has lived next to the reservoir for more than 30 years, said, 'There were Germans living in campers all around here in the early 2000s. Of course they could be anywhere now.'

The same reservoir cropped up again in relation to Maddie when a letter was sent to Dutch newspaper *De Telegraaf* earlier in June 2007, just weeks after she'd gone missing. Dutch police said at the time they were taking the contents of the letter 'very seriously' with the author claiming Maddie had been buried under rocks in deserted scrubland in an area near Odiaxere, the nearest village to the lake.

De Telegraaf reported that they had been sent a map on two A4 pages containing a cross and a question mark indicating a spot which was the 'probable finding place' of Madeleine. This was 'north of the road under branches and rocks, around six to seven metres off the road.' Tests were carried out on the letter and the envelope and as soon as the results came through they were sent to the Portuguese detectives investigating the disappearance. A group of seven Portuguese police officers later visited Arao, a small hamlet north of Odiaxere, where they reportedly spent over an hour looking in nearby fields.

Dutch police confirmed they were taking it seriously as a similar letter had been sent to the same newspaper the previous June, following the disappearance of two girls, Stacy Lemmens, 7, and 10-year-old Nathalie Mahy, from the Belgian city of Liege. The author claimed to know where the girls' bodies were buried, and they were found two weeks later in a storm drain a short distance from the location identified.

A convicted child rapist, Abdallah Ait Oud, was eventually arrested for the murders, but intriguingly, the DNA of a mystery third person was also found on the bodies. That person has never been established.

Dutch detective Sita Koenders said of the Maddie letter: 'We carried out forensic investigations on the letter straight away and ... we are awaiting instructions from the Portuguese and will start an inquiry into finding the author if that is required.'

In Portugal, Chief Inspector Olegario da Souza said 'everything necessary' was being done to confirm the allegation. 'The information indicated an area 15km from the place of the disappearance of the child,' he said.

But it does not appear that the Portuguese police did much actual searching. As far as I could see they spent a few hours scouring the area with sniffer dogs, but didn't properly probe the edge of the reservoir about 3km away. Nor, it should be assumed, did they search a smaller lake by a garden centre, called Corte Veleda, less than 2km away.

Police dogs did allegedly take a close look around the Barragem do Arade reservoir, which was an easy 20-minute cross-country drive from Fehlinger's house in Foral. Nothing was found.

There has been a fair amount of interest in the string of reservoirs that form a belt around the inland of the Algarve region. There are five in total, within approximately an hour's drive of Praia da Luz, also including the Barragem de Funcho, the Barragem de Odelouca and the previously-visited Barragem de Santa Clara. All of them were popular pitching-up spots for hippies and van lifers in 2007. Each one had (mostly unofficial) sites in which to park up vans and caravans and effectively live totally unsupervised for most of the year. Although this has mostly now changed, I have been told.

Back in the mid 2000s however, they were part of the Drifters' Map of southern Europe, which attracted hippies mainly from Northern Europe who lived freely and untaxed outside of Europe's supposedly organised tax and social security system. Even in 2021, these settlements still exist near Orgiva, and there are plenty more in Portugal. I also know of half a dozen in Andalucia.

Brueckner was one of the van lifers who moved about at will between these settlements in southern Portugal and Spain, selling drugs to much of the footloose population. His former friends Michael Tatschl, Manfred Seyferth and Helge Busching also spent varying amounts of time living amid these drifting communities. But there is another individual who ALSO spent considerable time socialising with Brueckner and allegedly spent a long time living by one of these lakes.

His name is also Christian, I can reveal, and he was a long-time close friend of Brueckner', whom he may have known from his youth in Germany. The blond expat, who lived in Portugal for around two decades – possibly even longer than Brueckner – vanished two or three years ago and now lives in the Far East, I have discovered.

I had first been made aware of this mystery German by Micha Tatschl in June 2020 during our long phone interview. He described the Christians as very close and said they spent a lot of time together at Brueckner's friend's home by a reservoir, 'about a half an hour drive' from Praia da Luz. This made it most likely to be Barragem da Bravura. He said the man was of a similar age to Brueckner and his full name was 'Christian Post or Christian Bost'.

Micha said Brueckner talked about Christian often and visited him regularly, although what they got up to he had 'no idea'.

'He would frequently go off to see a number of people,' he told me. 'This would include his German mechanic friend, where he got his VW van, as well as this other friend Christian, who lived about half an hour away by a lake. He was his other best friend, as far as I was concerned.'

It was a little convoluted and unclear, but we must assume the first friend is Bernhard Piro, who had agreed to put Brueckner up when he got out of prison in December 2006, and who had bought his VW at some point. The second friend has never been identified, nor exactly where he lives, but police in Messines confirmed they had been looking for a fellow blond man in connection to Brueckner's sex crimes in 2017 and would like to establish his name.

One might assume locating him would be a priority for the Portuguese, as well as German police and indeed I discovered efforts have been made quietly behind the scenes.

According to Bernhard Piro, it become a priority in 2019, when German detectives were finally able to track the second Christian down to Vietnam, a notorious location for sex offenders and child sex trafficking. Could this be the mystery businessman, whose name was given to German police by Helga Busching, then redacted in documents seen by the German media? Could this also be an accomplice who might have been with Brueckner on the night Maddie went missing? And could he be the same blond friend who was out with him at a festival in Messines in 2017 (of which more later)?

I can reveal that Christian Post, to use his correct name, moved to Vietnam in 2017 or 2018 and has since moved across the border into Cambodia. 'He first went back to Germany and then on to Asia,' Piro told me at his breakers yard, in Barrocal in January 2021. 'I knew he had gone as he was finding it very difficult to live here. Making money as an expat is not easy and he was struggling. It was late 2017 and he said it was time to go.'

The next time he heard about Christian's whereabouts the police were looking for him. 'They eventually tracked him down to Vietnam, the detectives told me when they visited me the second time,' said Piro. 'They did it via his contacts in Germany. I mean, the police have some pretty good tools to find people, don't they?'

He said detectives hadn't revealed any more information, but that it had clearly been 'important' to find Post. He believes that if anyone knew the movements and behaviour of Brueckner it would have been Post. 'The pair of them were very good friends,' he told me. 'They had known each other for years and had a close understanding of each other.'

Piro first met Post, who was an electrician by trade, in the early 2000s. Heralding from the north of Germany ('somewhere around Hamburg'), he immersed himself into expat life on the Algarve. 'He did lots of odd jobs and fixed TVs, stuff like that,' explained Piro. 'And he was a very good musician, a pianist mostly. Christian (Brueckner) told me he was amazing on the piano and I think he often played at restaurants and bars at weekends.'

Piro was first introduced to Post when he was asked to fix one of his cars that had been parked outside Post's home, 'somewhere north of Lagos, around Odiaxere'. My ears pricked up, as it was around this area that an anonymous person had claimed to *De Telegraaf* newspaper Maddie had been buried.

I was keen to try and pinpoint exactly where he lived, but Piro couldn't remember any more, even when I got Google Maps up on my phone. 'It was a long time ago. I just followed him back to his home, where he lived with his girlfriend, a German-speaking girl,' recalled Piro. 'I only met him a few times after that and fixed a few of his vehicles. We were not friends.'

I asked if he thought Christian Post could he have been one of Brueckner's accomplices. Could he have been involved in Brueckner's crimes? 'I really have no idea what involvement he might have had,' he insisted. 'He seemed pretty normal to me.'

That said, he confirmed that Post was one of two or three people Brueckner had enlisted to help him clear out his Yellow House on being arrested for fuel theft in April 2006. 'There were a few of us who went over to help and Christian Post was definitely one of them.

'Christian Brueckner asked me to go over and collect a few of his vehicles [presumably including his Jaguar, a Mercedes S-Class, an Opel Station Wagon and a small VW panel van] and I didn't go into the house. I just went into the garden to get the cars. But I know he definitely called Christian Post to go in too, so he would have seen what was inside.

'As for the other two, the two who allegedly burgled the place. I did not know them and I don't know if Christian called them or not or why they went in there. I have no idea about Christian's friendship with them, or who they really are.'

I tried to get hold of Post in South East Asia without any luck. I wanted to put to him the claims that he might have been involved in some of Brueckner's crimes... at the very least helping to cover them up.

However, I discovered that a journalist at *Der Spiegel* magazine in Germany, had somehow managed to locate him via a Skype interview on June 9, 2020, just a week after Brueckner was first named as prime suspect in the Maddie case. Naming him as 'Christian P', reporter Hubert Gude tracked Post down to the town of Kampot in Cambodia. He described him as a 53-year-old 'musician and IT technician', who had got to know Brueckner after a gig in a music bar on the Algarve in 2005.

Post told Gude that he had visited the Yellow House in Praia da Luz on various occasions and had visited him in prison in 2006. He also helped to move some items out of the house following his arrest, which suggested he had helped to cover up some of his crimes.

'I met Christian from time to time,' he told Gude. 'He fixed my car and I helped him with his TV.'

He described Brueckner as a 'messy person' and revealed that he clearly made a lot of money out of thefts and burglaries, and on one visit saw 'around 30 to 50 passports' stacked up in three piles at his house.

When he asked him why he had so many, Brueckner said they had been acquired during break-ins in the nearby resorts. 'He told us he went on tour from time to time and climbed up facades in the process,' he said, clearly suggesting that the thefts were merely a side show to his main reason for breaking in: sexual deviance.

He went on to reveal that on visiting him in prison soon after his arrest, Brueckner had complained about the food and lack of alcohol and had effectively ordered him to send him a box of oranges laced with vodka. 'But I didn't want to do that, which made him really angry,' said Post.

What he was prepared to do, however, was help him move some of his belongings – including a few boxes – out of his house, while he was inside. Why he had agreed to do this, knowing the kind of man Brueckner is and, presumably, that clearing out the house might help him cover up numerous crimes, is open to conjecture.

He told *Der Spiegel* exactly what he found. 'There was a series of disgusting CDs. More than 100 of them. Dirty movies with animal porn, stuff like that,' he said, claiming that he had thrown all of it away. This went down badly with Brueckner, who had been 'very angry' with his friend on his release from prison in December 2006. So angry that Post says he refused to see him again, which I don't actually believe.

When I eventually got hold of Gude to find out more and ask for his help in contacting Post, he said he would try but doubted he would 'want to talk to me'. But he did tell me to phone him back the next day to give him

Pic 28 and 29: Two pictures of Nicole Fehlinger from RTP's *Sexta as 9* TV show and below (Pic 30) the villa Casa Magali, which she was 'accused of robbing' with ex-boyfriend Brueckner

Pic 31: The Granada village where Brueckner parked up for the Dragon Festival in 2007, the festival itself (Pic 32) and his best friend Micha (Pic 33) left, who he went to prison with in Portugal in 2006

Pic 34: Brueckner's friend and occasional accomplice Manfred Seyferth in a TV interview and (Pic 35) Rebel Farm where he allegedly 'took' the rape videos he stole from the Yellow House

175

Pic 36 The house that Brueckner grew up at in Bergtheim, in Germany, and (Pic 37) the entrance to its celler where he was said to have been locked in as punishment

Pic 38: Nicole's father Dieter Fehlinger with author Jon Clarke

Pic 39: One of the warehouses at Brueckner's rented German Box Factory and (pic 40) his writing on the wall about his ex-girlfriend in a second warehouse (pic 41) where he kept many vehicles including the blue Twingo

Pic 42: Renault Twingo, riddled with bullets, that Brueckner used to move things to the Box Factory, while (right, Pic 43) a surgical scissors found by the author underneath the spare tyre in boot. Meanwhile an apparent shallow grave (Pic 44) in a side annexe, and the same annexe (Pic 45) with mattresses, womens sunglasses and beers

Hiermit kündige ich, Christian Brücke 38118 meine Mitgliedschaft im GV nächstmöglichen Termin.

● Außerdem kündige ich den Pachtvertrag Zeitpunkt.

2.4.16 Chat Be

Pic 46: Author Jon Clarke outside Brueckner's kiosk in Braunschweig, (Pic 47) his landlord Juergen Krumstroh at the allotment he rented nearby, and his official signed leaving note (Pic 48)

177

Pic 49: Author Jon Clarke with prosecutor Hans Christian Wolters in Braunschweig, while (Pic 50) interviewing Brueckner's best friend Bjorn with Rob Hyde (left) in park

Pic 51: Pensioner rape victim Diana Menkes, suspected Irish victim Hazel Behan (Pic 52) and suspected victim Joana Cipriano (Pic 53) who vanished near to Praia da Luz in 2004

Pic 54: Official Missing Persons file photo of Lina Valz, the Messines slide (Pic 55) where Brueckner was arrested in 2017 and PC Vanessa Viera (Pic 56), who accosted him

Pic 57: Artist sketch of so-called 'Tannerman' seen carrying a child near Ocean Club on night Maddie went missing, (Pic 58) an FBI-trained artist mugshot of possibly same 'creepy' guy also seen lurking around the Ocean Club, and (Pic 59) a 1999 Portuguese police mugshot of Brueckner with mouth firmly kept shut in all photos

TEL + 34 902 300 213

time to dig out his notes on the interview to see if there was more he could help me with.

It turned out to be very useful and he confirmed that Post was meant to deliver the boxes from the Yellow House to the Piros house in Barrocal. 'But Christian told me he refused to take them all as he knew that the Piros had a young son and he "should not see stuff like that" so he threw them away,' he explained from his office in Hamburg. 'He also claimed that he wasn't really a friend of Christian Brueckner. They only visited each other on a couple of occasions and they simply gave each other a hand fixing things.'

Post had also told Gude that Brueckner 'planned to be a millionaire by 40', which is exactly what Micha had told me.

Gude had also managed to document for the first time the disturbing derelict box factory Brueckner owned in Saxony, which we'll visit later, as well as his drug dealing arrest in Sylt. He was also the first to name an ex-girlfriend who accused him of sexually assaulting her 5-year-old daughter in Braunschweig in June 2013. Again, more of which later.

Gude had excellent access to the case, which led to him speaking to a number of people connected to Brueckner over the years. This included a friend from Praia da Luz, who said she had met him when he sold boat trips in the port of Lagos, and two young women from Munich, who met him while on a summer holiday in the Algarve in 2003, and who described him as a 'bon vivant' who sold them oranges.

The two women told Gude they had stayed in touch with him over the following years by email – which he would sign off as 'Little Cloud' (Wolkchen) – and that Brueckner actually visited them in September 2003 in Munich en route to Augsburg. They revealed that 'Chris', as they called him, had liked to gamble and while they were in the Algarve had taken them to a casino, presumably the one in Praia da Rocha, near Portimao, where he had a membership card and where Nicole Fehlinger allegedly worked from time to time. Also coincidentally, where rape victim Hazel Behan was living in 2004.

So good were Gude's sources, I was certain he had managed to access the BKA file in Braunschweig. When, towards the end of the article, entitled The File Christian B (Die Akte Christian B), he quoted a large chunk of information based on Busching's claims, I knew he must have been fed the information from BKA detectives.

Quoting him as 'Helge Lars B', he revealed that he had first got in touch with British police about Brueckner's involvement in the Maddie case in August 2017 from a Greek prison. He said he had gone on to speak to German police a few months later, also from prison, and was then let out.

Gude reported on their fuel theft and how he and 'an accomplice' [Seyferth] had broken into the Yellow House while he was in prison, and found it 'full of stolen goods, cameras, clothing, laptops'. Intriguingly he also reported that they also found a pair of swimming goggles, 'which strangely enough were painted gray [sic] on the inside'.

But crucially, Gude reported, the pair had stolen not one, but TWO video cameras and 'a total of about 20 tapes with them'.

These tapes had been mistakenly reported as featuring the rape of Diana Menkes, but the two films that Busching and Seyferth saw are the rapes of two other women. If Busching is telling the truth, and has been reported correctly by Gude, the other 18 tapes may well contain the actual proof the German police have that Madeleine McCann is dead. 'I'm certain that's what Busching said that in one of his statements,' Gude told me later. 'He said there were a lot of tapes, around 20, I believe.

'And the Menkes rape is not on them,' said Gude. 'The ones that Seyferth and Helge saw were of another older lady [in her fifties] and a younger teenager. They were able to describe them graphically to police and prosecutors certainly believed them. The problem was finding the tapes. They said they had left them in a vehicle … at the Rebel Farm in Santa Clara, but police apparently could not find them.'

Given the courts convicted Brueckner of the rape of Diana Menkes in 2018, based in a large part on the evidence given by Seyferth and Busching, the authorities in Germany must be taking this pair seriously. "The judge certainly believed them," prosecutor Hans Christian Wolters later told me.

Gude then went on to report something almost apocryphal, something that has been backed up what I had been told from various friends of Brueckner. It was during the Dragon Festival in Orgiva, in Spain, in 2008, that he first admitted to 'having had something to do with the disappearance of Madeleine McCann.'

It had taken me a long time to speak to Hubert Gude, who finally got back to me by email saying he would 'try his best' to contact Christian Post in Cambodia with my contact details. 'If he wants to talk to you, he will send you an email,' he wrote. I heard nothing. When I did finally speak to Gude by phone in March 2021, he confirmed that he had spoken to Post via a Skype interview in Cambodia and 'he must certainly still be there as he couldn't get out due to Covid.' He then opened up about his theories on the case and on other information he had discovered on various trips to Portugal to interview certain key witnesses around Germany such as Nicole Fehlinger's father Dieter.

He didn't wish to comment on where he had got the official police testimony from, but he had clearly got a big dossier of documents. There was one key thing missing from Gude's in-depth article though: he had got nothing from Bernhard Piro. Despite managing to locate his breakers yard in Barrocal well before any other journalist (again suggesting he had seen the case file), he had got the cold shoulder from the taciturn mechanic, a key witness in the case. Piro would only tell him that Brueckner was 'here from time to time', adding: 'I don't want to say anything more about Christian.'

Piro had fended off dozens of journalists on numerous occasions, but I felt he was beginning to trust me not to sell him out for a one-off story or knee-jerk headline. He had clearly brushed off Gude, and when I went to visit him for a third time, in March 2021, he was still smarting that Sandra Felgueiras had hinted on Portuguese TV that he might have been involved in the case and could have been an accomplice of Brueckner's. He obviously felt the need to set the record straight; I just needed to be patient, as he chose his words carefully and frequently refused to answer my questions at all.

While he insisted he hadn't been interested in the Maddie case and 'never read newspapers', his wife Elke had been following it since 2007 and he got fed all the latest twists and turns from her. Understandably, he didn't remember all that much from 2006 or 2007, but this time he told me more about his interviews with the police after they uncovered his connection to Brueckner.

As we know, they had discovered – and impounded – Brueckner's infamous yellow and white VW campervan, which Piro had bought off him. When Piro was asked to come to the police station for questioning about its former owner, he said, 'I had no idea it was about Maddie. I told them what I could but insisted I didn't remember much. They didn't tell me what it was about and I really didn't have a clue.

'They then came back about a year later, this time with two BKA agents and a liaison officer from the embassy in Lisbon. There were the same questions although a bit more detailed and it went on for a fair bit longer, maybe an hour and a half to two hours.

'It was only at the end when they asked me specifically if I could try and recall what he was doing when Maddie McCann went missing in May 2007, that I realised why they were after him.

'They hardly tell you anything, but I knew they were onto something big. They were very professional and had a clear purpose of where they were going with the investigation. A sense that they were sure of it. I don't know what they found in the van, but I hope there was something of use.

'I just hope I have been able to provide a part of the jigsaw that helps to piece together what happened to poor Maddie.'

I probed him a little on why he had allowed such a dangerous criminal into his home. 'Obviously I really regret that I let him into our lives,' he said. 'And if I had known what he had done before I wouldn't have allowed it. All the shit he has brought on us has been awful. I guess I am just a good person and just wanted to help Christian.'

He believed that ultimately he was one of the few people that the German could turn to in a time of crisis. When he contacted him from prison, he was in tears, explained Piro. 'He said nobody was coming to visit him and he was all on his own. He begged me to visit and I just felt sorry for him. It was my first time in prison and I remember it was a really odd experience. All those guards, having to put all my things in a locker.'

This was April 2006 and Bernhard had, by then, known Brueckner for over a decade, since he first arrived in Portugal in 1995. Even though he knew he had been back to Germany to serve the rest of a prison sentence, Bernhard had no idea what it was for and assumed it was for something minor. He said he had always been personable and appeared above board and he had seen him many times since he came back from Germany at the start of the decade.

He admitted the pair had done various deals on cars and vans and Christian had brought him a fair bit of work. 'He just seemed like a nice enough lad and I didn't think the fuel theft thing was anything serious. I felt sorry for him and, after visiting him, I agreed to put in an official offer for him to stay with us,' he explains.

But it wasn't until nearly Christmas in 2006 that he finally got a knock on the door from Brueckner asking to stay having just got out of prison. 'He came to stay with us for a short time. A few days, a week or two, not longer than that. He was soon on his way,' said Piro. 'I really don't remember too much.'

They kept in touch however, and he definitely saw him again in 2007, probably on 'various occasions', largely because he spent most of that year living ten minutes away in Foral with Nicole Fehlinger. Bernhard had known her for years, having first met her through her ex-husband Mathias, although he claimed he didn't know her well.

He couldn't even remember – or didn't want to confirm – that it might have been at a party at his home when Brueckner had met Nicole. His wife, Elke, who worked for the IAPRS and regularly crossed paths with Nicole, later confirmed it. But Piro did say that they were 'together a lot' after that, although he didn't want to discuss their relationship.

One thing he was happy to talk about was when Brueckner visited him in Barrocal to show off his huge new motorhome. 'I don't remember exactly when it was, but it was so big he didn't attempt to drive it up my lane. He parked at the bottom on the main road and walked up and insisted I came down to look at it.

'It was a big one and he was pretty proud of it. It certainly must have been big as we have had trucks coming up our lane delivering vehicles and if they can get up and he couldn't then it must have been.

'I have no idea how he got the money to buy it. Perhaps I should have asked.'

Looking back, Piro knows he was naive to have trusted the fellow German. 'It is fairly clear Christian got about a lot. He was driving around Portugal a lot and I think he was probably selling drugs, maybe more,' he said. 'I think he is probably a classic sociopath. Charming and friendly when he wants to be, but deep down very dark and dangerous. I'm just a nice person who likes to help people and I fell into his trap. Obviously I regret that now.

Chapter 32

A Suspect Since 2013

Over the summer and autumn of 2020, I looked into countless accusations against Christian Brueckner. His connection to the disappearance of Maddie had become one of the biggest stories of the year, garnering thousands of column inches a week. There was a media frenzy over the story, predictably perhaps in the UK, but also in Germany and Portugal, and more surprisingly in Spain and America, and even Australia, where the Nine network dedicated an hour to the case on its flagship 60 Minutes programme.

Brueckner was being linked to new unsolved crimes by the week and was becoming Public Enemy Number One, at least for parents, around mainland Europe. There was growing alarm over the ease at which he had been able to drive around Western Europe, largely unchecked, for so long. By my calculations he had made the journey from Germany to Portugal, via Spain and France, dozens if not hundreds of times from 1995 to 2017.

There was also understandable concern over how he had been able to leave Germany in April 2016 when, as I will explain, he had just been convicted of the abuse of a 5-year-old girl. And again in 2018, when he was let out of prison due to a clerical error, while awaiting trial for drug dealing and rape, having been extradited from Portugal. It was only by sheer luck that he was apprehended quickly after he moved, slipping so easily over two or three borders and ending up in Italy.

In total, he was linked to over a dozen missing children around Europe and was also accused of being involved in various rapes and other sex crimes. Police forces in at least four countries are still trying to establish if he could have been involved in many more local crimes.

But while the media reported that his name had first been brought to the attention of police in Germany in connection to Maddie in 2017, when he allegedly told a friend in a bar that she was 'dead' and he knew what had happened, it later emerged that German police had suspected Brueckner as long back as 2013. However, they ended up making a fatal error, one seemingly quite out of character for Germany, which is known for its ruthless efficiency.

Brueckner's name had actually been thrown into the ring in October 2013, after the McCanns had appeared on the German equivalent to the UK's Crimewatch, *Aktenzeichen XY ... Ungelost*, with new information and photofits of two new men. The two-hour ZDF programme, presented by Rudi

Cerne, was watched by 7.26 million people (its highest viewing figures for 15 years, proving quite how fascinating this case is all over Europe, even six years on). The men spoke German, or Dutch, and they were seen lurking around the McCanns' apartment on the night Maddie went missing. The pair have – to this day – not been located or eliminated from police enquiries.

'If you know anything, please please be brave and get in contact. We need your help' Kate McCann pleaded to German viewers, while Gerry stressed: 'We miss her every day, but there is no evidence that Madeleine is dead.'

The appeal came two days after a similar appeal on Crimewatch in the UK, and after Scotland Yard had changed tack in the investigation, its detectives switching their interest to a mystery man (the so-called 'Smithman') seen carrying a child on the night in 2007 as well as two strange men hanging around the resort. The revelations had come about after a two-year cold case review under Operation Grange, launched in May 2011, had led to the interviews of a staggering 442 people in 30 different countries. Within two years, police had drawn up a list of 41 potential suspects and in 2013 were still pursuing an incredible 2,797 lines of inquiry out of an original 4,920.

Detectives were focusing their attention on a dark-haired man carrying a child with blonde hair, possibly wearing pyjamas, towards the beach. The man, aged between 20 and 40, was spotted by an Irish family, the Smiths – hence the name 'Smithman' – who were walking back to their holiday apartment that night.

Incredibly, while an e-fit of the individual had been created for private detectives hired by the McCanns in 2008, the image had only been made public, on German and British TV, in October 2013 during the new inquiry. Police said they were also looking into who was behind a 'sharp rise' in burglaries in the area in 2007, as well as a group of bogus charity workers who had been approaching individuals in the resort, during door-to-door 'collections'.

Crucially, e-fits of two fair-haired men said to have been seen 'lurking around' the apartment and believed to be German, were also released that week. One of them had allegedly been seen twice by the same witness on two separate occasions. He was described as being about 30 to 35 years old, thin, with short hair and spots on his face and wearing a black leather jacket. Brueckner was 31 at the time, with adult acne and was known to wear a leather jacket, specifically by neighbours in Foral in 2007

Police also announced that during one particular break-in, in the same week Maddie went missing, a man had entered a flat where young children were sleeping. In this sinister incident, the intruder came through the patio door, had a good look around – including into a cot where a baby was sleeping – and then left without taking anything. The alarm was raised by one of two other children, who had spotted him while pretending to sleep.

The release of the e-fits led to a huge response from the public, with a number of people providing the name of one individual. That name was never released. In total, 700 calls were made to Crimewatch that week, and over

20 emails were sent. Detective Inspector Andy Redwood, who was leading the inquiry, felt the new 'timeline' and the suspects seen lurking around the apartment held the key to discovering what happened to Maddie. He said he was 'extremely pleased' with the response to the programme adding that her disappearance 'had all the hallmarks of a pre-planned abduction that would have undoubtedly involved reconnaissance.'

The appeal had a similar response in Germany with the McCanns' televised appeal resulting in 500 tip offs with some intriguing names being thrown into the ring. Among those was Brueckner, who had apparently been fingered by 'several' of the callers, one of whom claiming that in 2007 he had been working for a swimming pool company based near Praia da Luz. Could this have been the ex-husband of Michaela's pool company?

The key witness had contacted Wiesbaden Police Station via an official contact formula on the XY website, on November 1, 2013, Germany TV station Spiegel reported (one must assume this was discovered by journalist Hubert Gude). Having listed the reasons he believed Brueckner was involved, the contact, who claimed to be one of his former friends, said he should be brought in for questioning immediately.

At the time, Brueckner had been primarily based back in Germany, as far as I could ascertain, although he was taking regular trips to Portugal and Spain. As we will see, he had a base (two, in fact) in the northern German city of Braunschweig, where he had been running a kiosk selling sweets and snacks next to a primary school, as well as a third, as-yet-undiscovered box factory, further north.

German police were certainly fully aware of him by then, as he already had a dozen convictions to his name, including two child sex offences. So when the name was handed over to the BKA police headquarters following the XY programme they rightly decided to take a closer look at him. When they sent a letter to their counterparts in Braunschweig to start probing him on November 1, they were probably expecting some sense of urgency.

However, incredibly, the regional headquarters of the BKA did little more than send a clerical letter asking him to come in for routine questioning 'over the Madeleine case'.

The letter, which I have a copy of, was addressed to his kiosk, at 33 Altstadtring, a busy ring road that runs around central Braunschweig.

Dated November 4, 2013, it was headed 'Summons as a witness'. I assume it must have been delivered by hand, as the date he was ordered to appear at the city's police headquarters was just two days later on Wednesday, November 6, at 1pm.

Addressing him as 'Herr Christian Stefan Brueckner', it announced that the investigation concerned 'Events relating to the crime scene of missing Madeleine McCann (in Portugal)', adding 'Need for preliminary investigation of Christian. B. Request sent November 1, 2013.' It said that he would be required to give his exact movements and timings 'from midnight on May 1, 2007 until midnight on May 31, 2007'. He would need to advise them if he was unable to attend.

Police at Braunschweig Police headquarters have not yet produced evidence of Brueckner appearing that day in November 2013, or indeed, what he might have said. Clearly the letter would have given him at least two days to cover up his tracks and hide any evidence that might have connected him to the crime.

When confronted on this matter by German newspaper *Der Spiegel*, former head of Braunschweig Police, Ulf Kuch admitted sending the letter and alerting Brueckner to the reason behind it was 'a huge mistake'. The former boss, who has since written a book on links between immigration and crime after retiring from the force, claimed he did not know about the summons despite his role at the time as supervisor for the officer who issued the notice.

Another policeman spelt out to *Der Spiegel* that such a high-profile case would normally have required investigators to gather more evidence before approaching a suspect directly. 'This should not have happened and in no way complies with common procedure in such a delicate case,' he said.

Christian Hoppe, an investigator for the BKA, claimed, however, that there had been a complete lack of concrete evidence to merit a follow up. 'The information we had then was not sufficient for an investigation, and certainly not for an arrest,' he said in June 2020.

According to Bjorn R, a friend of Brueckner's at the time, he found the letter hilarious. He told *the Mirror* that Brueckner mocked detectives about interviewing him and bragged that they had 'zero evidence' on his links to the Maddie case.

'He laughed about the summons,' Bjorn told journalist Patrick Hill. 'He was just waving this piece of paper about. It was like a little trophy to him. After a couple of weeks we started winding him up about it saying, "Maddie's downstairs in the cellar. Come on Christian get Maddie out of the cellar." He'd smirk and laugh and then say, "Leave me alone, leave me alone. Just because I was in Portugal for 12 years, they send me this. Just because I was living there at the time and also in that timeframe I was close by. Just because I was living out of a van."

'He kept going on about it and waving the paper around saying, "I have nothing to do with this, they are trying to get me." It was like he had rehearsed what he was saying. He said that he went to answer the summons and he told police that he had nothing to do with it. I asked him, "But why say that as you're only a witness?" He just said, "Let's have a party!"

'He told me, "They asked me a load of questions and I answered them." Then he said: "They've got nothing on me. They can't get me."

Bjorn, who I would later meet in June 2021, now wishes he had done more to look into him at the time. He also feels that the police in Germany made a mistake by not moving faster to catch him. 'The police didn't take it seriously enough at the time. The cops in Braunschweig have messed up badly. Now I feel sick to my stomach when I think about him.'

He told *Spiegel TV* that Brueckner's social group all suspected he could have been involved in the Maddie case. 'He became more talkative after a drink and he would talk about his time in Portugal and how he had stolen quite a lot of stuff, like cameras, things like that,' said Bjorn. 'He told me that on some evenings he would break into places wearing a snorkelling mask so he wouldn't be recognised.'

Another former friend told *the Mirror* Brueckner joked about sex crimes that had taken place in Portugal, and had laughed when he recalled how he had broken into an apartment of British teenagers, naked, and masturbated over them until they woke. The friend was speaking as police uncovered another home Brueckner had lived in on and off, in Hanover from late 2007 to early 2009. He told *the Mirror*: 'We never thought his crimes involved children – he was a kleptomaniac. We just thought he stole everything in sight. He told me what he got up to when he lived in Portugal. He said he had been surviving by breaking into hotel rooms, stealing cameras and laptops.

'But the strangest thing he ever told me was about breaking into a room where four teenagers from Britain were sleeping on the sofa and floor. He said he was naked and had left his clothes outside and he was masturbating. When one woke up and tried to wake the others up he panicked and ran out. He said he ran naked through the town. He told it like a funny story.'

For me, the most telling part was that he 'left his clothes outside'. A pattern was beginning to develop.

The former friend, who had met Brueckner at his kiosk in 2013, said he didn't know for certain where it had happened – but he believes it was in Praia da Luz or Lagos. 'We used to drink in a back room. He talked about his crimes and was kind of proud about it,' he said.

He also boasted about the alleged theft of 100,000 euros from the Portuguese couple in Praia da Gale (which makes it even more galling that Portuguese police dropped that case when so much evidence pointed to Brueckner and Nicole Fehlinger: Elke Piro would also tell me that Brueckner admitted the theft to her). He told his friend it had been one of his most successful hauls and that he had 'bought various properties' with his share of the money. Some of it went to buy a house in Bavaria, where he lived as a child, some went to hire the kiosk and some of it went into the purchase of 'a disused factory, somewhere in East Germany.

'It was all thefts, burglaries and drugs he talked about,' continued Bjorn. 'He even claimed the palm trees in his garden were stolen. There was not one day when he didn't steal something ... . But he didn't talk about children.'

...

Brueckner had a habit of living in, or next to, small wooden houses on hired green spaces, where Germans grow vegetables or just relax – a bit like allotments. Dubbed 'allotment homes' by the British press, it has been discovered that he built a cellar in one and extended the cellar in the other. One allegedly was found to contain a child's toy bucket.

His first allotment home was a short drive away from an apartment block Brueckner was registered at while living in Hanover. Neighbours claimed he had been living off grid there in late 2007, and possibly a year or two later – and he talked about planning his return to southern Europe. (Interestingly, another neighbour who used to row with Brueckner over his dogs fouling on his property claims he lived there much later than that.) He slept in a VW Transporter that he parked next to a hut on the plot. 'I remember his van and his dogs,' Wolfgang Kossack, 73, told the *Daily Mail*, estimating his arrival at some point in 2007 and his departure approximately a year later. I suspect it was more likely 2008 to 2009.

'No one knew he was there and he never did any gardening,' said Kossack. 'He did not plant anything or try to grow anything. He just sat around drinking beer.' He said the small wooden structure next to the van was used to keep tools, but it also had a kitchen and underneath it was a cellar that was only unearthed when the building was demolished in 2008. The retired electrician said he remembered Brueckner (who had apparently borrowed the home from a man he had met at a music festival) often came with a younger girlfriend, and he had two dogs with him. The big one must have been Charlie and the smaller one he remembered distinctly was called Frau Muller.

Kossack said he only realised the allotment's link to Brueckner in July 2020 when, during a two-day search, more than 100 officers carted away dozens of blue bags of potential evidence, much of it allegedly rubble from a basement that Brueckner was thought to have dug. It also included the toy bucket. Samples of mud and soil were sent away for evidence. It was not immediately certain what police were looking for, but a few weeks later, the BKA confirmed it was for 'digital storage devices'. They didn't reveal if they found any.

Brueckner appears to have lived around Hanover until early 2009, when he started to spend more time at the dilapidated box factory he had bought. But he certainly returned to Hanover plenty of times after then, as he had at least two convictions in the city, one for forging documents in 2010 and another for theft in 2013.

He was living mostly in nearby Braunschweig between 2012 and 2015. He had moved there to take over the rental of the kiosk and an attached apartment by the city's western ring road. It was happy days for the predatory paedophile as neighbours recalled how he regularly allowed children to play on the till 'for fun', lavished them with free gifts and let them go into the storeroom at the back.

In between leaving the shop for weeks on end to take trips to Portugal and Spain, he would openly discuss and sometimes joke about being involved in the Maddie case with friends and staff. Lenta Johlitz who worked for him, recalled how he 'totally lost it' during one conversation about Maddie one evening with friends.

'He wanted us to stop talking about it,' the 34-year-old told *Bild* newspaper. In fact, he shouted out, "The child is dead now and that's a good thing", and then he added: "You can make a body disappear quickly. Pigs also eat human flesh."'

Johlitz later reiterated the conversation to ITV News saying he had got 'very aggressive, nervous and agitated' during the conversation. 'He said very loudly, "the child is dead" and "after all these years you wouldn't find such a corpse anyway."'

A former caretaker at the nearby primary school, Grundschule Hohestieg, which is just 100m away, feared that Brueckner may have regularly groomed children at his kiosk. Peter Erdmann, 64, who worked at the school, said, 'The kids would come to school holding toy ponies and teddy bears. I used to ask them where they got them from, and they told me, "Christian at the kiosk gave it to us."

'He told me he had a box full of gifts in the kiosk and he used to give the kids the presents when they walked past in the morning. At the time, I did not think anything of it. I used to go and see Christian in the kiosk, and he always came across as friendly. He would give me shots of Jagermeister. It turns my stomach now to think of his intentions and I wish I had raised what was going on with my bosses at the time.' Later, I would visit this kiosk, which also had a small bar, and discover that, surprise surprise, it had a cellar.

Another former neighbour, who lived next door, insisted he was definitely a dangerous man, who treated women very badly. The man, Norbert M, who didn't wish to give his full name, said one former girlfriend of Brueckner's (almost certainly Kosovan Nakscije Miftari, who is reported to have started dating him in the summer of 2014, when she was only 17, but, as I will later explain, I believe she may have met him in December 2012, when she was just 15) had told him he would regularly abuse and 'even strangle her'.

'She was a very small woman, puny,' he told German TV network *RTL*. 'She told me Brueckner hit her and strangled her and I saw strangle marks on her neck.' He said it 'should be a priority' for police to find her, particularly as she 'was a minor' at the time.

Norbert, whose family owned the kiosk, took over the franchise and apartment when Brueckner left in 2015, leaving it in 'a disgusting condition'. 'There was rubbish everywhere,' he told *the Sunday Mirror*. 'The floors and bottom of the walls were black and there was vomit and insects everywhere. Pest control had to disinfect everything.

'There were broken windows. The bedroom was wrecked. Everything was damaged. He was an animal. He held parties all night and neighbours complained to police. Who knows if the children got involved? It wouldn't surprise me.'

He said Brueckner allowed children as young as nine to work for him in the shop and also claimed that two dogs died there when he left them alone without food and water on a six-week trip to Portugal.

'I couldn't tell you what made Brueckner tick, but things went downhill quickly when he took over the kiosk,' said Norbert. 'At first he was pretty friendly, but he ended up owing a lot of people money. Hardly surprising. Very little was sold in there and there was hardly anything on the shelves.' Towards the end, he was alienating the neighbours with alcohol and drug-fuelled parties. 'And he definitely got more and more aggressive,' added Norbert.

Another problem was the type of people that started to hang around the kiosk, with neighbours growing increasingly concerned. They were right to have been as one of those youngsters, Robert M, went on to commit a particularly nasty sex crime on a small girl in the same block a few years later. The 8 year old was 'brutally' raped by Robert M in the attic of the same building in February 2019, after 'luring the girl' inside while she was walking home from school. *Bild* newspaper, which reported the vicious sex assault, even suggested that Brueckner and Robert M might have worked together on other similar crimes.

An alarming postscript to this period, and potentially relevant to the investigation, came from Norbert, whom I would later attempt to track down. Brueckner returned some time later with acquaintances who threatened him with a knife as the German demanded to take various items from the flat, which didn't actually belong to him. These included an air-conditioning unit and, perhaps most suspiciously, a freezer. What was so important about taking a freezer at knife point? We can only guess.

•••

The second allotment home Brueckner had was a one-bedroom property that sits in the Allotment Club Kennelblick just a 1.5km walk south of his kiosk to the south of the city. Sandwiched between the A 391 and the 39 Autobahn motorway, as well as the main train line in and out of the city, he took over the lease on October 1, 2013, before handing it back on April 2, 2016. Later, I would visit this home.

One of around 150 small plots, each with a small house built on them, it was described by a former friend as a 'shed with a bed' but it also had a small cellar underneath it, which Brueckner decided to renovate and expand. According to neighbour, Manfred Richter, he excavated the ground under the house carrying out piles of rocks and rubble by hand, creating a 3m deep, 6m wide cellar.

'He started in the morning and worked until evening and it took him two months to complete,' recalled the pensioner. 'He ended up putting planks of wood over the hole [in an attempt to hide it] but the work still got him in trouble with the allotment bosses.'

While it is not known if anything was ever done about it, or if he was fined, he would be regularly seen at the allotment at weekends, sometimes with his young girlfriend, thought to be teenage Miftari. The pair would spend most of their time drinking beer and listening to music.

Other neighbours said he treated his girlfriend 'like a slave' and one former friend, who visited the allotment, told *the Mirror* about a sinister plan he had for the plot and the cellar.

'There was a hole in the floor inside the allotment house and one day he told me he wanted to put see-through Perspex glass over it. I said to him, "What the hell for? Just so you can look down into a dirty old cellar?" Now I think maybe he wanted to build a Fritzl-style cellar like the guy in Austria who kept his daughter down there.'

It was an alarming thought and one that clearly crossed the mind of the current owner Sabine Sellig, who was so concerned that Brueckner might have kept children or women in the basement that she has stopped sleeping there. The tour guide revealed that she 'no longer felt comfortable' staying at the small house, that she had spent a lot of money renovating since buying off Brueckner.

'I worry that I could be sleeping on top of the body of Madeleine Mc-Cann,' she told *the Daily Mail*. She called the police and asked them to search the house and dig the ground to check. As we went to press, that still hadn't happened.

...

Around the same time as Brueckner was digging out a cellar, a sinister online chat between him and a fellow paedophile had allegedly taken place. In the alarming Skype conversation from September 29, 2013 Brueckner even talked about 'catching and trapping' a 'small girl' and filming the abuse.

The conversation was found on a computer seized at his house in July 2014, while police investigated and later prosecuted him for child pornography. While it is possible that he was being set up by an undercover police officer, the chat could be almost chapter and verse in the planning and seizure of Maddie, as well as German 5-year-old Inga Gehricke, whom he had already been linked with (and of which more later).

Using his often-used alias 'Holger' and his Facebook handle '*wahnsinnderholger*' (which translates roughly as 'the madness of Holger' or 'Crazy Holger'), Brueckner couldn't have been more explicit about his desires. It was later catalogued during an internal police memo, which was sent to the Central Criminal Service headquarters, in Stendal, while detectives were probing Brueckner over Inga's disappearance.

Talking to someone called '*Panikspatz86*' ('Panic Sparrow'), Brueckner enquires about the making of new child abuse films and discusses the risks involved in it. Below is a transcript in full (as best as I was able to translate), with some of it redacted by German police.

You will need to make your minds up, but for me, it seems the pair have known each other for some time, as they are intimate and honest with each other. One stand out element of the conversation is the reply by *Panikspatz86* of simply 'mm' in reply to Brueckner's statement that it is vital to hide all the evidence and leave no trail. Did he mean 'Maddie McCann' when he wrote 'mm'? This is a huge point of contention and possibly a massive clue regarding his involvement in the case. Surely the answer would be 'yes' or 'I agree' to Brueckner's question, and I am reliably told by German speakers that the phrase 'hm' or 'hmm' would be most commonly used if he wanted to convey the meaning of being thoughtful.

The grotesque line about 'deepthroating' lasting too long – which must refer to choking someone, potentially to death, during fellatio – is another big clue. One must assume the BKA police in Germany have other conversations seized from Brueckner's electronic devices and are being extremely careful about what they are releasing and to whom.

It should also be hoped detectives were able to track down the person behind the alias *Panikspatz86*, unless of course he is a detective or private investigator trying to entrap Brueckner. I was unable to find anyone definitive using this alias and the only possibility was a man in Brandenburg, who appeared to have a lot of friends who were prostitutes. The transcript was somehow acquired by *Spiegel TV* although the *Discovery Plus Channel* also got hold of it.

Skype Chat Message (September 29, 2013) between Christian Brueckner and friend:

P: *hi*

CB: *how's it going? :)*

P: *pretty good*
P: *and you?*

CB: *pretty good??? Things bad with me, I just want to fuck a little girl already [the words 'to fuck a little girl' are my estimation as this is from a screenshot]*

P: *yeah, who doesn't want that*

CB: *do you have new films?*

P: *no unfortunately not yet. I haven't had time this week [again, my estimation]*

CB: *ok, sending such films around is real dangerous*

P: *true*

CB: *I would film lots of short films. Hehe.*

P: *Oh yeah, do that*

CB: *I will document*
CB: *If so then I will film lots of short films ... hehe*

P: *oh yeah, do that*

CB: *I will document exactly how she is tormented.*

P: *Cool*

CB: *yeah, well, we'll see. Don't just talk, but do! hehe*

P: *:)*

CB: *Capture something small and use it for days. [This almost certainly refers to a child, but his lawyer could argue it refers to something else.] That would be...*

P: *Though that is not dangerous*

CB: *ah, when the traces left behind are destroyed ...*

P: *mm*

CB: *if for example the deepthroat lasted too long...:)*

P: *has that... you...? [text missing]*

CB: *ok, such messages are really dangerous [words are unclear, but it looks like it says this]*

P: *true*

As German crime profiler Mark T Hoffman said in *Discovery's Prime Suspect*, the chat is 'truly shocking'. 'Christian B is clearly talking about abducting children and using them,' he insisted. 'It is not just a fantasy, that is clear. He wants to act out his fantasies.'

'If he is guilty of the Madeleine McCann case he will certainly feel more assured he can get away with this and do it again.'

Chapter 33

The German Maddie and Horrific Home Evidence

Sabine Sellig's plea to dig up her allotment in Braunschweig is surely sensible having read the alarming Skype chat between Brueckner and his online friend from 2013. Brueckner had also been living on and off at her allotment at the time of the mysterious disappearance of Inga Gehricke on May 2, 2015. Dubbed the 'German Maddie' it is another baffling case with very few clues.

It is hardly surprising that Brueckner is among the main suspects as 5-year-old Inga's case has often been compared to Maddie's, given that no trace has been found of either girl, and no charges have been brought in either. Similarities are certainly intriguing with blonde-haired Inga going missing almost exactly eight years to the day of Maddie's disappearance.

She vanished from a stretch of woodland by the church-run assisted-living facility, Diakoniewerk Wilhemshof, for people with mental health, alcohol, drug or sexual addition problems, near the village of Uchtspringe, between 6.30pm and 6.45pm. Initially, police assumed she had got lost in the forest while trying to gather wood for an evening barbecue, but it soon became apparent that she had been snatched, with at least one witness hearing her screams.

It turned into a week-long manhunt – the largest missing persons search in German history – but Stendal Police with tracker dogs and helicopters were entirely unsuccessful. Despite over 1,000 helpers, including firefighters, involved in the search, they were stumped, and police said that Inga must have been kidnapped. Police chief Reimar Klockziem told reporters Inga's disappearance was 'inexplicable and unbelievable'. He added, 'It's as if she has been beamed off the earth.' The same could be said of Maddie... and, indeed, Joana.

Celebrated German crime profiler Axel Petermann later ruled that there was 'no recognisable motive, no crime scene, no traces of a crime, and no body'. The only clues they had were from a local hunter, who claimed he heard a scream coming from a girl at around the time, and a local farmer who saw a dark blue van driving away from the forested area, close to the Wilhelmshof facility. It has never been formally identified. The sniffer dogs also allegedly picked up scent beside a main road that linked Berlin with

Hanover. They led the police officers along the A9 motorway in the direction of Berlin, to the Klein Marzehns junction, reported *Der Spiegel*.

Brueckner became a suspect some two months later when detectives in Braunschweig started considering the Inga case and forwarded information to their counterparts in Stendal saying he 'could be a person of interest'. On July 23, detectives opened a case file and started to probe him locally, which threw up a number of interesting links.

The first showed that Brueckner had been in the area and was involved in a car accident the day before Inga went missing – a busy Bank Holiday Friday – apparently driving a blue Mercedes Vito van. The minor accident took place at Raststatte Lappwald services near Helmstedt, on the A2 motorway, 24km from Brueckner's allotment. The blue Vito, registered to his friend (who may have been with him), bumped into another car.

The accident report is one of many currently kept on Brueckner in case file Romisch 593 (Roman 593), at the Department of Public Prosecution in Stendal. According to *Der Spiegel*, it includes a huge dossier on the dangerous paedophile, including the aforementioned 2013 Skype chat. Among the files is an investigation into his links to an employee of the Diakoniehaus woodlands centre charity (next door to where Inga went missing), who is believed to have known Brueckner since his early years as an offender.

Suggesting Inga's disappearance could have been an 'inside job', planned by the two men, perhaps with others involved, the employee in question was said to have 'acted strangely' in the days after she vanished. 'The accused man had a narcissistic personality disorder and highly conspicuous sexual behaviour and had already been sentenced to seven years in prison in 1996 for serious sexual abuse,' reported *Der Spiegel*. 'Since then he has been in Uchtspringe (Diakoniewerk) for therapy and was only released in June with a positive prognosis.'

My ears pricked up as I had read on the excellent online crime portal Websleuths that Brueckner had allegedly also undertaken therapy in the same facility. I took a closer look and discovered that in 2019, while being held in prison in Kiel, Brueckner reportedly sent a letter to the Diakoniewerk centre. Could this have been to a member of staff or a fellow sex offender that he knew from before? Could it have been the man alleged to be involved in the Inga case?

Diakonie is the social welfare organisation of Germany's Protestant churches; a charity that helps people or children in need of care. Brueckner was adopted via Diakonie as a child and was returned to a Diakonie-run orphanage as a teenager when his cruel and unloving adoptive parents could no longer cope. Could this letter have been to one of these childhood friends? Was the recipient a worker, or a patient? Was Brueckner trying to exact revenge on the charity, which he felt was responsible for his unhappy childhood? I sent an email to the team at the centre and tried to call to find out a bit more, with no luck. So until the police release further information on the letter or Brueckner confirms who it was sent to, we must keep guessing.

One German newspaper claimed the letter was for Silvio Schulz, a dangerous sex offender, who was handed a life sentence in July 2016 for killing two young children close to where Brueckner was living at the time. Schulz, who is in his mid-thirties, had abducted one 6-year-old boy, Elias, from a Potsdam playground in July 2015 before strangling the screaming child to death and burying his body in an allotment similar to the one Brueckner rented in Braunschweig. In October the same year, he kidnapped 4-year-old Bosnian migrant Mohamed Januzi from the crowded and chaotic area outside Berlin's Lageso refugee centre. Police said he admitted to abducting and abusing Mohamed before strangling him to death with a belt.

Detectives found masks, gags and S&M accessories at his home, as well as newspaper cuttings of abducted or killed children, to which he had added handwritten notes such as 'young girl knife'. Officers also found 1,564 DNA samples at the house, most of which matched people involved in the case. One blonde hair could not be accounted for and police believe it may belong to Inga, but this has not been confirmed. Could it be Brueckner's?

The court heard Schulz was constantly on the lookout for children to kidnap and – like Brueckner – took and kept many photos of potential victims. When he was arrested, police found a 'kidnap kit' in his car which contained chloroform, sleeping pills, cable straps, thumb cuffs, a stun gun, latex skull masks, gags and various strangulation devices.

While Schulz had an alibi on the night Inga went missing – allegedly working as a security guard, over an hour away – he did live in a small village of Kaltenborn, Brandenburg, only a 90-minute drive from Uchtspringe.

After pressure from Inga's parents, in autumn 2020 the case was reopened. It came after the lawyer for Inga's family, Petra Kullmei, slammed Stendal Police who had closed the case after just four weeks, insisting it was 'lacking ambition'. It is not known if anything new has been found, but prosecutor Thomas Kramer told *FOCUS* magazine that they had 'no concrete evidence' that Brueckner was in the immediate vicinity of the crime scene on the actual day of her disappearance.

And he added his links to the crime had already been investigated 'comprehensively and intensively'. I tried myself and finally got an official reply from the Prosecutor in Stendal saying that 'after additional research' into Christian B's links to Inga, they have 'no new facts' and there are 'no indications' that he was in the vicinity or 'knew anyone at the nearby psychiatric hospital'.

However, the probe into Brueckner's links to Inga was to lead to what is very likely a key discovery in the Maddie case. During their research, detectives discovered that Brueckner had a third property in the Saxony region, a disused box factory where he stored thousands of videos, which included child pornography and bestiality as well as films in which he featured.

Just under 100km from Stendal, this creepy five-acre smallholding, in the village of Neuwegersleben, which I would visit in June 2021 and make a shocking discovery, had been the subject of an intense six-day police hunt over missing Inga starting on January 16, 2016. According to an ex-girlfriend of Brueckner's, he had bought the former factory via an auction in 2008 or

2009. In an exclusive interview for the Prime Suspect documentary, the girl-friend who only gave her name as 'M' said he had 'big plans' for the derelict facility.

Still living in the Lower Saxony area, she recalled how she had met him via an 'over thirties' night in her local town, which I assume was Braun-schweig or Hanover. While he was 32 and she was 52 they hit it off and dated for four months in 2009. He told her that he had 'got stuck living there' as his car had broken down and he 'couldn't move on' so she agreed to let him move into her apartment, while he also hoped she would help him do up the factory.

'As I was graduate of engineering he thought I'd make some drawings,' she said. 'He wanted to rebuild everything. It was all in ruins … . The area was huge. If you wanted to hide something you'd certainly be able to find places.'

While over 100 officers found no connection to missing Inga during the week-long search (nor Brueckner, who l later discovered had been in the factory HIDING from the police), they did find a number of intriguing vehicles, many without number plates, including a huge 30-year-old Tiffin Allegro Bay RV, which was almost certainly the one Brueckner had driven down to Portugal with around the time Maddie went missing in 2007.

Conveniently, 'M' still had photographs of the campervan, actually tak-en in the grounds, alongside pictures of Brueckner and his dog Charlie. But it was what police found in the grounds and inside the motorhome: a set of children's clothes, among which were a series of girls' swimming costumes, that was so damning.

While pictures of the children's clothes and swimsuits were carefully photographed and documented (they are still in the file at Stendal Police Station), German police only released pictures and information on them in 2020.

Detectives also stumbled across the burial site of one of Brueckner's dogs … and under it, in a Lidl carrier bag, an alarming hoard of child sex abuse images and videos. The stash had been found entirely by accident when a policeman kicked over the ashes of an apparent bonfire and spotted a bone from a dog. I believe this is Brueckner's beloved Charlie, who had died in his Braunschweig apartment in 2014 and he had been brought here to bury.

It was a spine-chilling find with more than 8,000 videos and photos on a series of, at least eight USB memory sticks, dozens of CDs and other storage devices. Most damning of all was the fact that Brueckner himself appeared in at least 100 of them, police revealed.

While police refused to give me a total breakdown of all of them, it emerged from German media that most of the images or videos contained sexual abuse of babies and young children, while some files showed sexual assaults on dogs.

'Around 100 files were recordings of Brueckner, partly naked or wear-ing black hold-up stockings, pleasuring himself with an anal plug or with the spherical head of a tow-bar and a workbench as well as fishing floats,' reported *Spiegel TV*. In some of these videos he was said to have worn disguises, including one as a clown. It made the leotard, allegedly worn in the rape of Hazel Behan, just that little bit more believable.

The vast majority of what was found has not yet been documented fully and released by the German police. Indeed, according to prosecutor Wolters, in January 2021, officers in the sex crimes unit were 'only allowed to process so much at any one time', confirming they might still be going through them. It still seems like a long time and made me wonder if they still had all the files. As Wolters told me bizarrely, I would have to ask Saxony police.

What I can reveal, however, is that detectives also unearthed other extremely damning evidence that links Brueckner closer to crimes on the Algarve. It came in the form of a number of SIM cards that were found at the box factory site. Among them, in particular, was one phone number for a British man whose holiday apartment in Praia da Luz had been robbed around the time that Maddie went missing, I was told by impeccably well-connected journalist Hubert Gude.

'I don't remember where exactly this tourist was staying,' Gude told me. 'But it is a very damning link between Brueckner and break-ins on the Algarve. 'I believe police found this extremely relevant to the investigation today.'

Chapter 34

A Catalogue of Abuse

Some of the material police found at the Lower Saxony box factory in January 2016 was on discs that came from a Casio Exilim EX-Z850 compact camera. The actual device (reference number 5031912A) had been seized by detectives at Brueckner's Braunschweig kiosk address two years earlier in 2014. It was taken when they had raided his home on February 7 that year while they were investigating him for child abuse.

It came after a girlfriend reported him for making lewd advances and allegedly filming her 5-year-old daughter in sexual poses on June 16, 2013.

The Exilim camera had a total of 391 child pornography pictures on it, while 68 further videos were found on a separate 'Tom Tom' card showing the rape and abuse of minors, not believed to be by him. It also allegedly had a number of photos taken of children in playgrounds in Portugal, which would have close relevance with another crime I investigated around a play park in the Algarve (more of which later).

The camera and its contents became the main evidence against Brueckner during two trials in 2016 and 2017, in which his ex-girlfriend, known only as Anja P, accused him of assaulting her daughter, *Der Spiegel* reported.

Despite the severity of these accusations, he had, somehow, managed to slip away from Germany to Portugal after an initial hearing on February 16, 2016, at Braunschweig Lower Court. It is unclear exactly how this happened, but he did admit his guilt when he was extradited back to Germany a year later on appeal from the prosecutors and was handed a 15-month jail sentence at Hanover Crown Court.

I managed to get hold of the ten-page judgment from Braunschweig Criminal Court, from September 2017, which was prepared to justify his immediate imprisonment on his return after extradition. Aside from a detailed catalogue of the abuse of Anja P's daughter, it also revealed that many of the other photographs Brueckner had stored were of children under the age of 14 being abused by adults, while others involved children being forced to perform sex acts. Police said the majority of the videos had been downloaded from the internet and stored on the camera's memory cards.

The judgment adds that he had also kept several lewd photos of another girlfriend – not Anja P – having sex with him. Police also found a Reck P6E gas pistol with eight rounds of ammunition – it is illegal to possess this without a licence under German law.

Regarding the daughter of Anja P, the abuse took place at his apartment and in a public park in Braunschweig, just three months before Brueckner became a suspect in the disappearance of Maddie in 2013. He had taken dozens of pictures of the abused girl and saved them, like a trophy, on his camera with the intent to 'later arouse himself sexually'. Five of them were taken in the local park on March 16, 2013.

'The camera was found in the living room of his apartment and there was no doubt the camera belonged to Christian B,' prosecutor Wolters later told me. 'He had spent the morning looking after the daughter … and on the camera there is one pic of him looking up a slide from below with his erect penis in the foreground. He also took pictures of her sitting on the grass with her legs spread wide, while he pushes her knickers to the side and touches her vagina.'

As well as abusing the child, Brueckner also regularly beat up her mother, as Anja P revealed in an interview with *Der Spiegel*.

She had met Brueckner on an internet site called '*Chat2000*' and initially found him charming and 'a real lover of animals and children'. The woman, who cannot be fully identified for legal reasons, claimed he would frequently launch into violent attacks after she moved into his kiosk apartment. 'He hit me when he was drunk or in a foul mood,' she said. 'He was very aggressive.' So clearly his behaviour with women had not changed at all.

She eventually plucked up the courage to report him to the police in July 2014. While it is not known if she had seen or heard about his summons over Maddie the previous November, she provided a detailed written statement to help prosecutors. 'I believe he abused my daughter on at least three occasions, but the police only charged him for the one occasion because they had actual photos of the abuse,' she said.

An initial court hearing took place on March 1, 2015, in which she described him as an 'extremely possessive and violent man' who kept a constant eye on her. 'I was not allowed to do anything, he did everything,' she told *Der Spiegel*. 'I had to stay at home. He could come and go as he pleased. And when he came home drunk, I was hit. There was no reason for it.'

She said she believed Brueckner, whom she dated for nine months, was capable of anything, including snatching Maddie. She certainly believed that he abused other youngsters in the area because a number of parents were in the habit of entrusting him with their children, particularly 'those on welfare'.

The detailed judgment from the later emergency court session on September 27, 2017, also noted that at the time of his arrest in July 2014, Brueckner was on parole for a drugs offence he had committed in Niebull, a small German town near the Danish border. The offence involved the 'dealing of large quantities of narcotics' for which he was handed a 21-month prison sentence. The court heard how he had bought at least ten kilograms of marijuana from someone called 'Julia' in Oranienburg in the summer of 2007 and spring of 2008. There were a total of at least ten separate transactions and he spent at least 32,000 euros, earning well over 40,000 euros, the court heard. He was sentenced by Niebull District Court on October 6, 2011 and initially given a suspended sentence as the judge believed the conviction 'would serve as a warning to not commit any more criminal offences in the future.'

How wrong could that judge be? Had he not seen his criminal record? However, after the later conviction in 2014, the suspended sentence was revoked and he was ordered to serve the full term. Furthermore, while he was being investigated over the child abuse charge, he was caught stealing diesel from a truck in May 2015. He was then arrested for drink driving in September the same year and, two months later, assaulted a different girlfriend at a bus stop in Braunschweig. We must assume that this was teenage Nakscije Miftari.

While this younger girlfriend, also known as Nadia, has never gone public about their relationship, she has been helping police in the Maddie investigation and her family have spoken out about the abuse and beatings she allegedly suffered at his hands. A diminutive blonde – whose photo wearing a red dress (which I have evidence to show was taken when she was just 15) was beamed around the world alongside a smart-looking Brueckner – she had 'naively' got involved with him after meeting him at a nightclub in Braunschweig.

Speaking to MailOnline, her older sister Azra Miftari revealed that Nakscije was vulnerable and had been put under the care of a social worker. She said her sister had had a violent, turbulent 18-month relationship with Brueckner, who 'hit her regularly'.

'It was horrible for her,' she said. 'But she was young and naive. We told her he was too old for her but she didn't care.'

She revealed that detectives from the BKA had interviewed the entire close-knit family and had specifically asked them not to speak to the media. It is not clear why, but, as Hubert Gude told me, Nakscije found child pornography on Brueckner's computer and may have actually called in police to seize it.

Could it be that she found photos or videos of Maddie? Could this be the evidence that makes the German police so certain that she is dead? When I looked for Nakscije at the beginning of 2021, I was told by her sister she was still lying low, allegedly in a safe house, presumably hoping Brueckner will never get out of prison. Despite clearly having a social media profile on Facebook, Instagram and Tik Tok, she wasn't interested in communicating. At least with journalists.

Chapter 35

Protection in Portugal?

Christian Brueckner had done what he always did best when things got heavy: he fled south to Portugal or Spain. With things heating up in Germany, he knew the southern European nations had far more lapse levels of policing … and maybe, just maybe he had some high-level protection in Portugal. It was early April 2016 just as the initial trial over his abuse of Anja P's 5-year-old daughter was ending that he had somehow done a bunk. Whether it was due to an administrative error, or he was awaiting for his sentence to be ratified at the higher Hanover Criminal Court, I was unable to discover. Perhaps he escaped a prison van?

But while there was unequivocal evidence that he was guilty – and he had even admitted to the crime – he was somehow out on the streets that April and able to move around. His exact movements are unclear, but by the time the authorities realised it was a mistake and issued a warrant for his arrest on June 20 he was long gone. And quite sensibly, with police probing him over missing Inga Gehricke, as well as the recent discovery of thousands of photos and videos at his box factory.

He was certainly aware of the week-long search of the factory earlier that year – although there is no evidence he was arrested at the time. He must have feared detectives would find his damning personal stash of child pornography buried under his dog.

On top of that, after the conviction in the Anja P case, the suspended sentence over drug dealing in Niebull was now null and void and he would have to serve the time. I discovered he was also just months from being convicted of GBH of his ex-girlfriend Nakscije in Braunschweig, for which he was eventually fined a mere 500 euros, in absentia, on February 27, 2017.

He had been arrested during the daylight beating at a bus stop in what was described as a 'particularly vicious attack' which left Nakscije in hospital.

With nearly 20 convictions to his name in Germany, including driving illegally, selling drugs and child abuse, the police were clearly on his case and he was living by the skin of his teeth in his native country.

No such a problem in lapse old southern Portugal.

However, even he knew that pitching up at his old stomping grounds of Praia da Luz or Lagos would not be a great idea. There were too many old expats who might remember his violent behaviour with ex-girlfriends, his strange movements at night and, maybe even that he was around on the very night that Maddie went missing. Much better to head inland to sleepy Foral, and what better place to pitch up than Villa Bianca, which was still owned by his old acquaintance Lia Silva. After all, the hospitality had always been good, the neighbours were mostly welcoming and the services were practically free.

And so, quite unbelievably, soon after Easter in 2016, Brueckner was living again at the very same property he had shared with Nicole Fehlinger between 2007 and 2008.

What was it about this scruffy corner property in the tiny inland village that appealed to him so much? Familiarity, of course – when it comes to criminals, this is a key factor. But it was also close to a number of people he trusted, such as mechanic Bernhard Piro, who he actually stayed with again for a couple of weeks, as well as folk he probably continued to sell drugs to, and most likely swapped and sold pornography to.

There were possibly a few of his former accomplices around, such as Christian Post, while the likes of Manfred Seyferth, Michael Tatschl and Helge Busching could also have been living nearby at the time. And let's not forget that it was close to a myriad of coastal resorts that he knew well, where he had many vivid memories, and where he could be in and out in a matter of minutes on back roads, should he wish to commit crimes.

It was much safer to live closer to the laidback towns of Silves and Sao Bartolomeu de Messines, both sleepy places with populations of around 10,000, popular with families who worked on the nearby Algarve, but wanted a quieter, cheaper life inland.

Quite how he was so easily absorbed back into the crumbling pink villa in Foral is anyone's guess, but he seems to have found some like-minded expats, who had created a fair few of their own problems in the community.

The tenants in question were fellow German and Austrian couple, Oliver and Karin Stenard, long-term expats, who moved like nomads up and down the Algarve with dozens of animals as part of their family. Oliver told Portugal's TV network RTP that Brueckner had moved in with them for three months in 2016, while the villa's owner Lia told me she believes it was for much longer.

Brueckner was employed as a 'gardener and handyman' and was tasked with looking after the Stenards' animals – described by Lia as 'a zoo', which included a flock of sheep, pigs and dozens of dogs. Quite why they needed to pay someone to do that when they didn't have regular jobs themselves, is up for conjecture. But given Brueckner's alleged penchant for zoophilia, it might explain why the couple would later claim on the TV show *Sexta as 9* that they believed he was 'abusing' their animals. Indeed, Karin even said she saw him becoming 'amorous' with one sheep called Wolfie and caught him chasing it around the garden one evening.

The relationship with Brueckner inevitably broke down and he and Oliver got into a fight that ended up with both receiving medical attention.

Police and an ambulance were called and, according to Lia, Brueckner ended up 'needing stitches' and Oliver had a broken nose.

She said it started after Brueckner had insulted Oliver's wife. 'He made some sort of sexual suggestions to Karin and Oliver told me that he simply wasn't going to put up with that,' Lia told me.

She had actually watched the fight, which resulted in 'blood all over the place', as she was by then living back in the apartment next to the villa. 'They were really going for it, punching each other and screaming … . I couldn't be bothered to go out and stop them. They could have killed themselves as far as I cared.

'Neither of them wanted to press charges. I think there are probably good reasons why,' she added tellingly. 'I don't know exactly what Christian was doing there. He and Oliver basically lazed around for most of the day as far as I could gather. Karin went off and did some work at bars on the coast and then in the Alps over the winter, but Oliver did fairly little.'

When I'd first spoken to Lia the previous summer, she claimed she hardly remembered Brueckner and she had been fairly selective in her memories on two subsequent visits. But by January 2021, Lia was happy to reveal how Brueckner had indeed come back to stay at the villa, that she had bought in 1998 and named after her daughter Bianca.

'Little did I know he was the same guy. It hadn't really clicked until after the journalists had all gone that I suddenly remembered it was him in the fight,' she said. 'Yes, I did see him when Oliver was living here. He was here for a little while, living in the house. He certainly was not living in a car or van then.'

Once again though, she clammed up and declined to tell me any more about him, claiming she had 'too much' to do in the house and was unable to talk any longer. It was clear she was beginning to worry about what she was telling me, as by then she was aware that I was writing a book. But she did add that she believed the fight was at some point in early 2017, despite Oliver and Karin claiming it was on September 22, 2016.

'Either way I certainly do not remember the police coming around to look for Christian. They were always round here trying to deal with Oliver and the problems he caused walking his dogs in the nearby streets, but not Christian,' she said. 'Obviously they should have been looking for him instead.'

This was all rather dispiriting, particularly given Brueckner's history in Portugal and that, as it turned out, there was a Europol extradition warrant out for his arrest from the beginning of September 2016. He had actually been sought in Germany since June 20 that year.

We certainly shouldn't blame the local GNR force in nearby Messines, for its badly understaffed team had to deal with a remarkably large number of crimes and wanted criminals on an almost daily basis, I found out. But it emerges that their failure to check Brueckner's credentials – if at all – after Karin called them following the fight with Oliver led to him dodging a European Arrest Warrant, yet again. And so incredibly, Brueckner remained a free man, and continued to get odd jobs around the Algarve area to support himself.

According to a detailed court report prepared on his final return to Germany in 2017, he had been working as a 'gardener' and even a 'caretaker' as well as 'at a stables'. I have been unable to find out exactly where these businesses were located and I am horrified to think that he might have been a caretaker at a school, creche or language academy.

Either way, he was still living at large in the area in June 2017, when he allegedly exposed himself to a group of young children in a park in nearby Messines.

Chapter 36

Caught Red Handed

It was already long past their bedtime and the group of excitable children were starting to get manic. Aged between eight and twelve, they had been enjoying a later than normal evening out at their local playground, as their parents enjoyed one of the town's most popular annual fiestas. Now a firm fixture on the Sao Bartolomeu de Messines calendar, the Festa do Caracol, or snail festival, at the Jardim Municipal was as much a celebration of the start of summer as the region's local cuisine. Taking place in mid-June, as the heat of the Iberian Peninsula cranks the mercury into the forties, it was very much a family event that most of the town would have been attending, plus thousands from the wider region.

With a mixture of stalls and events, as well as live music on a main stage, the three-day bash was meant to end by midnight, but had drifted on well into the early hours. By then in its fifth year, it was well known among the expat community. The Brits and Germans particularly loved the Batucada drummers, the kick-boxing demonstration and the traditional Portuguese music, known as *Fado*. They also loved the variety of ways they could try eating snails, which were not just a delicacy of France, but many parts of the Iberian Peninsula too.

It was June 10, a Saturday, the best night of all, and everyone was well lubricated by 10pm when an already drunk Christian Brueckner rolled up with a blond friend – whom I believe may have been fellow German Christian Post. They gravitated towards one of a trio of municipal bars and got stuck in on the local brews.

Brueckner was likely in a good mood, happy to be away from the complications of life in Germany, and was soon dragging his friend over to chat up various local girls. The pair were also seen chatting to a couple of local expats whom they knew from nearby Foral; Brueckner was also seen rolling up and smoking a joint.

Brueckner knew Messines well, as I discovered when I spent an afternoon digging into the events of June 10, which were to become the start of the end game for the prolific paedophile.

It turned out he had been a regular visitor to Messines and, in particular, the municipal town square where the event was taking place.

In one corner of the square, beside a paddling pool, was a children's play park with a slide, a climbing frame and a number of swings (see photo section). And, conveniently, you could park right next to it in a line of parking spaces facing the playground just 5m away.

Back then, there was not even a fence around the children's play area and a paedophile could snatch a toddler and drive away almost instantly. Degenerate Brueckner might have been thinking the very same thought, for he would frequently park up for an hour and watch the playground. 'He often stopped off here for an afternoon beer,' revealed the owner of the Colegio Bar, which sits on Rua Ten-Cel Jorge Vargas Mogo, just across the road.

After I agreed not to publish his name, he opened up about his regular client, who kept himself to himself, but was always polite and friendly. I was visiting on a busy afternoon, in between lockdowns, in autumn 2020 and around two dozen local farmers and workmen were downing beers. Friendly to a man, they each took a good look at the photos I had of Brueckner on my mobile phone and at least three or four recognised him from the bar, although none could give any real insight, apart from the bar owner.

'I remember him well as he was always alone, always polite and never stayed that long,' he told me. Indeed, he would park up his van beside the playground and then sit at one of a handful of tables that his staff would set up on the pavement on perpendicular Rua Dr. António da Costa. 'From here he would have been just ten metres from the park and could see all the kids playing, as well as their mothers chatting nearby as he had his beer and smoked a cigarette or two,' continued the owner. 'There was definitely something odd about him.'

While I cannot be certain that he sat here and planned the grooming of any of the children, he was apparently always alone and mostly on his phone, but what was to allegedly happen late on that Saturday night in 2017 proved that he posed a serious danger to youngsters.

The phone call came in to Messines GNR police station at 2.15am from local policewoman Vanessa Viera, who was actually off duty having a night out with a couple of friends and her own 5-year-old daughter. Despite being on her third or fourth glass of wine she had managed to pacify a group of fathers from strangling a drunk German, whom they had accosted stumbling around the playground with his flies undone.

'His name was Christian Brueckner and he had been playing with himself under the slide,' Viera explained to me, in her backroom office of the crumbling old police HQ in the heart of Messines. 'And it took all my powers of persuasion and strength to hold the fathers off him. They wanted to kill him.'

Diminutive Viera (see photo section) has both an intimate first-hand knowledge of the McCann case, as well as the strange mix of bizarre people who have long gravitated towards the Algarve region. In 2007 when Maddie went missing, she had been sent to guard the entrance to the Ocean Club apartment of the missing toddler's parents.

Spending nearly two weeks in the coastal resort of Praia da Luz that month, she was tasked with keeping an ever-growing army of journalists at bay, as well as ensuring the PJ detectives could go about their duty unfettered. She also had to ensure the distraught family could get as much space and freedom as possible.

'I definitely got to see first hand the tragedy and trauma that the poor family went through,' she told me. 'It was awful. I could really see their pain and the suffering.'

Never for one second believing they could be behind the disappearance, she was as shocked as everyone when they had been made official suspects a few months later. She was particularly critical of the investigation by the PJ (like various police I spoke to in the lesser GNR force during research for this book); she also later realised that she had probably had a couple of brushes with Brueckner in subsequent years.

The first came when she had been involved in the hunt for the missing teenager Lina Valz, in nearby Foral, in September 2008, and the second was when she had to investigate the fight between Brueckner and compatriot Oliver Stenard in 2016.

So perhaps there was some deep, subliminal need to ensure that this dangerous man did not get away for a fourth time in June 2017.

She had been relaxing after a stressful week. 'We had been out for many hours and the crowd was already starting to dwindle,' she recalled. 'There may have only been a few hundred people left and most of them were pretty drunk.

'A few of my friends had their kids playing in the nearby park, while I had my daughter beside me, like I did at all times. Suddenly two of the kids came running over and said there was a man with his trousers down under the slide.

'The dads rushed straight over and found this guy crouched under the slide. As they ran over he got up and started doing his flies up. They were really angry and grabbed him and started pushing him around. They were all set to beat him up, when I somehow got between them and him, pushing the dads off.

'I told him I was a policewoman and asked his name. He told me "Christian", but didn't give a surname and didn't give me any address in Portugal. He told me he was visiting some friends in Portugal. He looked drunk, but his clothes looked fine and he was not smelly.

'I asked for his passport, which he said he didn't have. I insisted he must have some sort of ID on him. I said, "What about a driving licence?" and to my surprise, he replied, "Yes" and took it out. It was from Germany, but it had his full name and date of birth. I took a note of it and then phoned in my colleague, who was on duty at the local station, while keeping the licence.

'All the while I had to keep the dads off him. They kept asking him what he was doing, calling him a "sick bastard". I had to somehow hold him with one hand and push them away with my other arm. It was stressful.

'I then asked him what he was doing with his trousers down. He said he "needed to go for a pee pee" and I said, "Why there in the children's park when there is a public toilet just by the square and also various bars?" He replied, "I was desperate, I really needed to go."

'The dads didn't believe him and one actually ran over to the slide area and shone the torch of his phone around to look for anything wet, any evidence of it. There was nothing, no liquid and he shouted over, "It's dry, totally dry." His reply was simply a shrug and he mumbled something I didn't understand.'

After more than a decade in the force, she knew something wasn't right and she refused to give up. She asked how he had got to the festival, who he was with and where he was staying.

'He was evasive but he said he had come by car, but when I asked where his car was, he said he couldn't tell me. He "didn't have it anymore" and he didn't have any keys. It was strange.'

She knew instinctively that he was not a typical tourist and, in any case, she definitely recognised him from the area. 'He looked so familiar and I knew I had seen him before. It was then I realised he hadn't come alone and I recalled seeing him and his friend at one of the bars in the square.' She added that two of the other parents also remembered he had been chatting to another tall blond man.

'I asked him where his friend was and he just smiled and wouldn't say anything. He wouldn't tell us where he was staying either. We searched all around for his friend, but it was clear he had completely vanished. He must have taken the car or van.'

A few minutes later her police colleagues arrived. They handcuffed him and took him over to their patrol vehicle, where they radioed in his details to police headquarters in Lisbon. Unsurprisingly there was a fair amount of excitement when they discovered he was a wanted man back in Germany.

'They told me there was a warrant for his arrest and they bundled him in the car and took him off to be held in the cells overnight,' explained Vanessa.

He was taken to Messines station before being transferred to nearby Silves Police Station, and on Monday June 12 he was taken to Evora, where he was put before a judge for a brief extradition hearing.

While that was the end of Vanessa Viera's dealings with Brueckner, she is pretty certain that he has a number of like-minded friends in the area and, also, 'very likely' an accomplice. She has a rather dim view, in fact, of her hometown and the region in general.

'There are so many strange people going through the Messines area every month,' she told me. 'Put it this way, there is no way I would ever let my daughter out of my sight.'

Messines is indeed something of a crossroads. Just half an hour inland from the busy tourist resorts of the Algarve, it sits right next to both the IC1 highway, as well as the IP1/A2 Autovia do Sul toll motorway north to Lisbon. And it is also just 10 to 15 minutes to the busy A22 motorway that straddles the entire Algarve from just a few kilometres north of Praia da Luz, all the way to the Spanish border.

'It attracts a strange crowd', she said. 'It's a town of movement, drifters, who come and go. People on drugs, doing criminal stuff. Lots of foreigners.

You see them late at night, stumbling around, like zombies, off their heads. They suddenly appear. It is actually a little frightening.'

Her view of Foral wasn't any rosier: 'I've had to go there various times for disturbances and problems. It's a small village yet there are always issues there. It's a strange place.'

She even actually referred to Villa Bianca itself, as she was aware of the strange house and its itinerant lodgers. 'I think you can tell Lia to look for better tenants in future,' said Vanessa. 'She certainly picks them.' She declined to say anthing more.

Chapter 38

A Schoolboy Error

Looking back at Brueckner's 2017 crime record today, I can see that he was transferred north to Evora, where after a brief extradition hearing at the provincial court he was kept for two weeks at Evora Prison. Despite being captive and available for police to grill him over the alleged child sex offences in Messines (he wasn't actually sent back to Germany until June 22), there was seemingly very little interest in that.

It was the second time that he would be extradited from Portugal, where Brueckner certainly appeared to have a guardian angel. I managed to get a copy of the official charge sheet from Messines GNR Police Station and discovered the address he gave to police on his arrest was indeed back in Germany: his kiosk in Braunschweig, where he hadn't actually lived since early 2015.

He avoided listing any address in Portugal, where he had actually been based for well over a year, some of the time in Foral, a few months in Aljezur and, according to a good source, in Alcochete, near Lisbon, where he had rented a garage/lock up.

The arrest report, written up by duty officer Catia Filipa Sobreira, at 4am on June 11, noted his date of birth, address, as well as his parents Fritz and Brigitte Brueckner. It noted him as 'single' and that his driving licence (number B200000UCE11) had been issued in Germany on November 14, 2001 and that he had got his first licence on March 21, 1995, four months after his eighteenth birthday.

While the form described him as a 'suspect', there was very little detail on the actual crime he had allegedly committed that night in Messines. Under the 'Description' section of the form, Sobreira had mostly laid down the timings of how the GNR had been brought in to arrest Brueckner. It noted the station had received a call at 2.15am and that Brueckner was being held by a group of local people (including her colleague Vanessa Viera) after being accused of being an 'exhibitionist' and 'exposing his genitals to a group of children'. Undersigned by her colleague Vitor Bruno da Silva, who had been with her at the arrest, she noted they had called up Brueckner's name on the central database and quickly found out about the European Arrest Warrant.

Yet, disgracefully, and unbelievably, the case was hardly investigated and was dropped within a couple of months. It was only reopened again in November 2020 after German police had actually opened a separate case to look into the crime, as well as considerable pressure from a number of parents of the children who had been the victims.

One of them, Nelia Bras, gave a moving interview alongside her daughter, now 12, to Prime Suspect. She said she had been sitting at a table about 10m from the park when her daughter 'suddenly came running over' terrified of a man. The girl, who was eight at the time, told the documentary, 'I was with my friends in this playground when under the slide, where there was a hut, I suddenly saw this man with his trousers down by his knees.'

In the distressing report, in which both she and her mother were fighting back tears, she continued, 'He looked dangerous and I did not feel safe.'

While Brueckner has still not been charged with the crime, the parents are hopeful that they might finally get justice. 'I feel so relieved now that nothing else happened,' added mother Nelia. 'Knowing he is such a dangerous man who can do such bad things to people and children. It still makes me afraid and I really hope he gets punished for it.'

•••

On October 9, 2017, the High Court of Braunschweig finally issued its verdict on Brueckner. It ruled that he must finally serve, in full, his 15-month sentence at Wolfenbuttal Prison in Lower Saxony, for 'creating and owning a large amount of child pornography', found at his home in March 2015.

And with a 21-month suspended drugs sentence from Niebull Court now also coming active, due to his persistent re-offending, one might have expected the German authorities to have ensured he didn't leave prison again … at least for a few years! Particularly as the country's crack BKA detectives were now on his tail for a number of sex crimes, including the rape of 72-year-old Diana Menkes in Praia da Luz, not to mention the potential snatch of both Inga and Maddie.

But this is where the German authorities inexplicably take leave of their senses and put themselves in the same ballpark as the Keystone Cops down south. Despite a long list of alleged offences, and a court case now beckoning for the vicious 1995 Menkes rape the prison door inexplicably swings open.

It is almost as if the courts had forgotten the huge stash of child pornography found hidden at the box factory – over 8,000 files in size –the previous January in 2016. The German authorities must have known how dangerous he was and that the likelihood of him reoffending was high.

I managed to get a full copy of his court records dating back to the 1990s. It made for colourful reading, no less so for the huge number of convictions he had acquired by 2017. Altogether, there were 15 noted in the document, starting from his first arrest on March 20, 1992, at just 15 years old. Convicted at Wurzburg District Court, on May 4, 1992, he was found guilty of three offences of stealing cars, as well as driving without a licence, for which he was sent to a young offenders institution. As noted earlier, it didn't have the desired effect as just two months later on July 11, 1992, he was found guilty again, this time on three counts of theft. The list went on, including burglaries, drug offences and most alarmingly the sexual assault of various children, as has been covered in earlier chapters. Yet, inexplicably, on August 31, 2018, less than a year into his 15-month sentence, and before his 21-month drug conviction had begun, he was let out of prison.

The regional authorities in Schleswig-Holstein, where he was being held in Kiel Prison, have now ordered an urgent investigation into why he was allowed out. And quite right. The answer is still not fully clear, except that by good fortune he was picked up again and quickly – just four weeks later in Italy.

The mistaken release was due to a legal loophole and communication breakdown between the German and Portuguese authorities (proof that the streamlined Schengen zone concept doesn't always work). It occurred when just days before his expected release on August 31, the German authorities raced, but failed, to keep him in prison by invoking the 21-month suspended sentence for drug dealing from Niebull.

While it should be simple, it was actually an incredibly complicated five-page document, which I have seen. In a bizarre legal headache, according to EU rules, prosecutors in Germany were required to ask the judiciary in Portugal for its consent to extradite him for the separate drugs offence. And because the Niebull conviction had not been mentioned when an arrest warrant went out in 2016, nor was it mentioned at his extradition hearing in 2017, they would have to go through the entire process again. A paperwork nightmare that inevitably failed to complete in time, because on August 31, the prison doors at Wolfenbuttel slammed open and Brueckner stepped out.

It is not known where he went first, but he certainly visited Braunschweig which was just ten minutes away and Hanover not much further. He knew plenty of people in the local area to visit, including his close friend Bjorn. What is certain is he did not hang around in Germany for long and he may have crossed up to six borders around Europe, including Holland, Switzerland and probably France, before ending up in Italy.

He was finally picked up on September 27, 2018 in Milan, after some amazing fortune. It emerged he had been caught after he had brazenly gone to the German consulate on September 19, claiming he needed a new passport after being robbed on a train from Switzerland.

It was something of a schoolboy error for Brueckner, who must have surely suspected his name would have been logged onto a central computer at the consulate saying he was wanted.

Perhaps he believed he was bulletproof having just walked out of prison with the drugs offence apparently cancelled. He may not have known what was going on behind the scenes.

Either way, an alert for his arrest flashed up on the consulate computer and staff straight away called in the local Milanese police, who agreed to set up an elaborate sting operation. This involved a fake appointment for Brueckner to come back to the embassy nine days later to pick up his new passport, by which time an International Arrest Warrant was in place.

'We agreed on a time with the consulate and set our trap on September 28,' Lieutenant Andrea Papa told *the Mirror*. 'We had a description of him as blond and tall and we waited out of sight near the entrance. When we arrested him we could see the surprise on his face – he was really worried,' continued the senior detective from the city's elite murder squad. 'He was in jeans, trainers and a military jacket. He had no phone or money, just a Bible and a business card with his lawyer's number.' Papa said he looked like a homeless man and described him as 'pathetic' and 'smelly'.

'We actually felt sorry for him and gave him a bottle of water,' he said. 'At first he didn't want to come with us but then he saw there were six of us so he didn't resist.'

Why he had a Bible is anyone's guess. Was he trying to convey an image of a God-fearing man? Maybe he had converted in the past, possibly in prison? I have heard that Brueckner had a breakdown around the time he lived at the allotment home in Braunschweig. Could that have led to him finding faith? Apparently, his German lawyer Friedrich Fulscher once told the press that he was not there to help Brueckner find redemption…

Initially, the Italian police had no idea of the severity and quantity of the crimes Brueckner was being sought for, including his connection to Maddie. 'When we heard the news about the McCann case we were very struck, more surprised than he was when he was arrested,' said Papa. 'We were actually shocked to the very core knowing the sort of things this man may have done.'

Chapter 39

His Links to Other Missing Children

As I neared the end of this book in June 2021, Christian Brueckner was being probed over at least five missing children including Inga Gehricke and Peggy Knobloch (a 9-year-old German girl who disappeared in 2001: her body was found 15 years later), as well as up to half a dozen rapes, with the Hazel Bevan case in Portimao reopened at the beginning of August 2020. During his time on the run, it seems very likely that he committed other crimes on the Algarve and probably nearby in southern Spain.

In addition, he may have committed crimes in Belgium, Holland and Denmark, as well as Italy; while in Germany police have recently reopened the file on 6-year-old German boy Rene Hasse who vanished from a beach on the Algarve in 1996, just 40km from Praia da Luz. His father, Andreas Hasse, revealed that BKA detectives had been in touch for the first time in 20 years to reveal they were re-investigating the case.

It's a haunting story. The boy from Elsdorf was on holiday with his family in Aljezur, on the rockier, wilder west coast of Portugal, where Brueckner frequently took girlfriends for days out and would also park up his van for weeks at a time, friends told me. He was also certainly living in the area on June 21, 1996, when the schoolboy vanished allegedly running towards the sea. While the authorities ruled that Rene had drowned, they have never found his body, which makes it more suspicious.

He had been running ahead of his mother and stepfather during a walk on the beach when, after losing sight of him, they never saw him again, just found his clothes lying on the beach. This is surely very suspicious and very unlikely. Did nobody watch him undress alone? Run into the sea alone? Drown alone? While his parents begrudgingly accepted he drowned, they insisted it was strange that he would have wandered into the sea by himself. They also claimed that his footprints 'stopped in the middle of the sand', not by the shore, suggesting he might have been abducted. More cold water was poured on the drowning theory when an expert found tide and current conditions made a swimming accident unlikely that day.

His father believes it was 'very possible' that Brueckner could have snatched his son. 'Rene was also a very careful child, he would not have easily clambered into the Atlantic alone,' he told a local German newspaper.

Brueckner has also been linked to the brutal murder of a teenager in

215

Belgium. Police there are trying to establish whether he was involved in the death of Carola Titze, who was 16 when she was killed. Carola's mutilated body was found in sand dunes in De Haan, in Belgium, where she was on holiday with her family. In the days before she was killed, she had been to a disco with a mystery blond German man, who has never been located.

Police in Belgium reopened the case in 2020, due to the possible links to Brueckner. The former judge, who investigated the case for decades but was forced to oversee its closure in 2016, told a newspaper that Brueckner's face certainly fitted. 'The description of this German matches,' said Paul Gevaert. 'The fact that he stayed so long in Portugal would explain why we never found him.'

Meanwhile in the Netherlands, the unexplained disappearance of 7-year-old Jair Soares in 1995 is also being revisited by police there.

The Portuguese child was last seen on a beach on August 4, just south of Amsterdam. However, I am pretty certain that by then Brueckner was living on the Algarve, having fled Germany in March of that year, after getting his driving licence.

What is much more likely is a fourth, little-reported, crime for which he is now being probed in Portugal. That crime is a sinister sex attack on a 10-year-old German girl on a beach in Portugal, just ONE MONTH before Maddie vanished. The incident took place on Salema Beach on April 7, 2007, at 3.30pm when a naked stranger masturbated in front of Joanna Eilts before her family chased him away.

The Eilts had been on holiday in the tiny village of Salema, just 12km from Praia da Luz, when the assault took place. The girl had been clambering over rocks around the headland that led to the beach, Praia da Boca do Rio, where I know Brueckner frequently parked up his VW Westfalia van in early 2007 having got out of prison in December 2006.

She had been playing in a rock pool with some other children when the naked stranger approached her and asked her name in English, before grabbing her by the arm and pulling her onto the sand where he started to play with himself. When he realised that she was German, he started to talk to her in German, as he carried on masturbating. By amazing fortune Joanna's older brother had been playing nearby and having heard her cries ran off to warn the parents.

They ran over and spotted the pervert immediately, at which point he ran over some rocks and up a cliff to get away, I'm sure back to the car park at Boca do Rio Beach, via one of a series of paths. He was naked and was wearing just a backpack (perhaps with a video camera in it?) and had a bandage around his arm.

It was broad daylight and they had a very good look at him, they told police in nearby Vila do Bispo, where they reported the attack. So well had they seen him that they promised police 'if we cross paths with him, we would easily be able to identify him'.

Just over 13 years later both Joanna, now in her twenties, and her mother, Annette, were able to do so to the German BKA, who have now reopened the case. While the family do not want to talk to the press about the case, I was told by prosecutor Hans Christian Wolters, they are happy to press charges.

I managed to unearth a copy of the original report thanks to Sandra Felgueiras, who had tracked it down. Signed by the victim's mother, two days after the attack, she described the assailant as white, with tanned skin and short blond hair. She said he was 20 to 30 years old (Brueckner was 30 at the time, but looked younger) and about 1.80m to 1.85m in height.

She also said he had several marks (or scars) on his body and had, she estimated, four wonky teeth, with his top jaw protruding his bottom jaw (something he would fix that autumn when he flew from Lisbon to Germany for expensive maxillofacial surgery).

The report was filed at the GNR police station in Vila do Bispo, and was sent up to Lagos Court, before being passed back to a detective to probe a few days later.

However, somewhat predictably, the cabo (captain), whose name was Antonio, had archived it in just 24 hours on Saturday April 14, 2007, without even visiting the area, which was just TEN minutes away by car.

His reasoning was that, 'Going by the description the individual is not a resident of Vila do Bispo and is almost certainly a foreigner. As there is nothing more to report and there is no possibility of carrying out any due diligence at the moment, the inquiry is closed.'

Absolutely shocking and coming just 19 days before Maddie went missing. Could he simply not be bothered to go out and try and locate the foreigner, who would have surely stood out? He had been naked, after all. Or was there something more sinister at play?

Had he actually bothered to visit the car park at Boca do Rio Beach, or the next one along, Praia das Cabanas Velhas, by Barrancao village, where Brueckner also frequently stayed, there is a good chance someone might have recognised the excellent description. The four teeth sticking out, the short blond hair, the marks on the body and the apparent cut on one arm that had been bandaged. Then there was his age and the fact he was German who spoke English. Oh, and his height. He was described as being about 1.83m, or 6ft tall. Brueckner's exact height.

It is not known if the Keystone Cops led by Goncalo Amaral ever investigated any potential links to the crime in Salema and Maddie's. Had they, they might have realised there was a German man, who spoke English, with short blond hair, six feet in height and 30 years old, living just 800m outside Praia da Luz. He'd only been there for six or seven years.

Or perhaps they did know Brueckner lived there!

To this day I am convinced that Brueckner was protected by the Portuguese police and maybe others. Amaral – who made enough money from his book to buy a new house and now lives in Olivais, near Lisbon, driving a Jaguar, no less – continues to frustrate the inquiry by making strange claims about Brueckner, his appearance and his vehicles. He has long claimed that German police simply picked the 'perfect criminal' to suit the crime and that he is merely a 'scapegoat'.

Criminologist Dr Graham Hill, formerly of Surrey Police, who investigated the case in 2007, recently said the fact the police missed, or deliberately ignored clues, raises a lot of 'unanswered and difficult' questions. 'How long have the Portuguese police known about this guy?' he asked last year. 'In what context did he come into the investigation? And if he did get eliminated from the investigation, how did they do that?'

Meanwhile, former British detective Mark Williams-Thomas, who exposed the crimes of infamous paedophile Jimmy Savile, and is currently making a documentary on the Maddie case, said the information released in 2020 reveals 'more incompetence' of the initial investigation. 'In 1999 Christian Brueckner came to the attention of the Portuguese police, having committed a sexual offence against a child. Yet, eight years later he was not considered a suspect. It is now clear police failed to trace, interview and eliminate a local child sex offender.

'Had they done so, Brueckner would have been flagged up as a significant person of interest and potential forensic evidence obtained from his campervan.'

Was this all deliberate? Given the amount of alarming coincidences in the case so far, it does seem likely, and possible that it is linked to a wider cover up. Let's not forget Casa Pia.

Either way, by 2013, all records of the Salema beach assault had been erased from the police archives in Lagos, and it was very lucky that Sandra Felgueiras was able to find an old copy. As the seasoned Portuguese journalist later told me: 'It is so, so shocking. I mean how on Earth did Portugal let a dangerous paedophile live for two decades in our country and escape so many alleged crimes without even investigating him?'

It is also fascinating to note that just one week before the Salema assault, Brueckner had been photographed and filmed by a trio of Germans he picked up while they were hitchhiking between Portugal and Germany. The photos show fresh-faced Brueckner with short blond hair, clearly tanned, while on the drive from Malaga Port – where he picked them up – to Almeria, some 290km away.

He had answered an appeal from the trio who were undertaking a challenge set by a German radio station called Der Trip Deines Lebens, or Trip of a Lifetime, in which they had to get a caravan back from Portugal to Saxony, in Germany, by hitching it to trucks and vans, by drivers without payment.

In what could have been a dry run for his journey with Maddie five weeks later, he told the three he was a car dealer and he had borrowed the VW van from a friend in order to help them. He said he had driven all the way from the Algarve to help (although there have been suggestions he could have just arrived on a ferry from Morocco, and equally that he could have been at the Dragon Festival in nearby Granada, which had finished two weeks before). He happily drove almost the entire length of the Andalucia coastline to Vera, in a journey that took around three hours.

Asking them to call him the 'Happy Hobby Hippy' as he liked hanging out with hippies, he discussed his Jaguar car and was extremely chatty and friendly. The trio, a DJ and two competition winners, later spoke to the *Daily Mail,* and showed them their exclusive video (the only one I have seen) of Brueckner, flashing V-signs and even talking to the camera. Take a close look and he does indeed appear to have an overhang of teeth from the top jaw, making him seem a little gormless.

It emerged that the three were interviewed by German police in 2019, giving detectives as much information as they could on his behaviour and movements at the time. What is extremely interesting – apart from his appearance – is the state of the van, which had been parked up at Piro's junkyard in Barrocal, while he was in prison the previous year. It was in a very poor state with rusty bodywork, stained seats and wires dangling from the dashboard. The trio actually made a note of this and were extremely concerned to think that just a month later he might have used it to snatch and transport Madeleine McCann.

Chapter 40

Who Were His Accomplices?

While police in three countries continue to probe Brueckner's links to the Maddie case, I believe a lot of evidence suggests he was working with an accomplice at the time. Aside from the obvious length (30 minutes) and location (close to the Ocean Club) of the phone call he received the night Maddie went missing, there is a good deal of information to suggest that he worked with a string of small-time local criminals. But could he have also been working for a larger number of accomplices, and may he have made considerable amounts of money from snatching her?

I believe he had links to various dangerous paedophiles, two of whom had close connections to the Algarve in the years he lived there, and one he probably knew from back home in Wurzburg.

I discovered he used a Facebook profile of a dog (with the name *Holger Wahnsinn* - the same as his Skype chat name coincidentally) to protect his identity online. Maybe this was a way to communicate with fellow paedophiles, and also meet perverts who indulged in bestiality (as Brueckner also allegedly had sex with some of his pets). I believe he shared photos and videos of abuse on paedophile exchange networks and swapped tips on capturing and abusing children, as illustrated in his Skype chat in 2013, where he talked about 'trapping something small'.

One investigator who worked on the case, Dave Edgar, believes it is very likely Maddie was snatched by a child prostitution gang that could have been protected. The retired detective inspector, who worked for the McCanns for a number of years, told *the Mirror*: 'There was a very narrow window of opportunity for them to get away with Madeleine. So it does point to it being planned and some level of surveillance, perhaps of the apartment. If the motive was gang-related child prostitution, there might have been more than one person involved.'

Police are probing claims that Brueckner may have been spotted with another man and a 'white van' close to the McCanns' apartment on May 2 or 3. The pair were seen by tourists Derek Flack and his wife. Derek said they were 'standing at the corner of the path watching in the direction of the apartment that Madeleine would later disappear from.' He described both men as Caucasian, dark skinned, medium stature, 1.70 to 1.75m tall, and about 25 to 35 years old.

The evidence given by sisters Jayne Jensen and Annie Wiltshire also described two blond men in their thirties standing on a ground-floor balcony near Apartment 5A on the night Maddie went missing. They told police the men, both tanned and in Bermuda shorts, were outside the patio doors of an empty apartment looking out over the resort's swimming pool and restaurant area. 'They had a view of the whole Ocean Club and the McCanns' apartment,' said Wiltshire. 'It has haunted me ever since.' Her sister later told the Netflix documentary that she felt the men were 'wrongly placed', but thought nothing more of it 'until later that day when we had heard that Madeleine was taken it was only then piecing back. Who were these guys?'

I know that in 2012 Portuguese police started to investigate a former Ocean Club employee called Euclides Monteiro. They worked on a theory that he had been involved in a series of burglaries up the coast, which also involved the sexual assault of girls, although he was later cleared due to a lack of DNA evidence. I believe he may have been a friend of Brueckner's, as well as possibly convicted paedophile Raymond Hewlett, as said before.

Monteiro was an unusual man. The heroin addict had been working at the Ocean Club shortly before Maddie disappeared but was sacked for stealing from guests a year before the night in question. The 40 year old, who lived in nearby Lagos, aroused suspicions after phone records showed he returned to the resort a year after being fired. Detectives believed he may have wanted revenge against his former employers, and committed the kidnap as a form of retaliation. They also theorised that he may have been committing a burglary when he stumbled across Maddie sleeping and abducted her after being disturbed.

Could he have been visiting pals who still worked at the club's tapas restaurant when he spotted the note in the reservations book saying the McCanns and their friends would be dining there each night while their children slept in their apartment? Did he then tip off Brueckner?

Frustratingly, police were unable to interview him before he died in a tractor accident in 2009. And they cannot be entirely to blame, for it emerged that his name was inexplicably missing from a list of former Ocean Club employees given to police during the first investigation. Could this have been a deliberate omission from someone senior at the Ocean Club? Or could one of the detectives have removed his name?

It is certainly suspicious given Monteiro's criminal past. The drug addict, from the Cape Verde islands, was convicted of theft in 1996, but somehow escaped deportation. Given his connection to drugs and theft – not to mention his home in Lagos – it is very likely he would have known Brueckner. Did they hang around together? Even work together?

I have not found any evidence to support it, but there were certainly many local small-time crooks and ne'er-do-wells that he did socialise and work with. They include Helge Busching, Manfred Seyferth and Michael Tatschl. And then there was Nicole Fehlinger, who to my knowledge has never been convicted of anything.

I decided I could not conclude my investigation without a trip to Germany. I knew I had to put some questions to Brueckner's ex-girlfriend, who had managed to sail under the radar on the Algarve and continued to elude journalists in her home country. There was also her former charge Lina Valz, who had lived with her for three years, by my estimation.

I figured a week in Germany would also give me a chance to visit Brueckner's last official address in Braunschweig, as well as the famous box factory where he hid much of his child pornography and other stolen goods. And then there was the chance to grill the chief prosecutor Hans Christian Wolters about the state of play, as we reached the one year anniversary of the public appeal for information after announcing Brueckner was the prime suspect. I thought I might even get a chat with Brueckner's mother.

While the Covid situation was anything but under control, in June 2021 I booked a flight to Frankfurt, the nearest airport to Fehlinger and her family – in particular her father Dieter – who all live in Schweinfurt. It needed to be a carefully planned week. Firstly because it cost a small fortune, and secondly because I had to be back for my son Albert's birthday the following weekend.

I enlisted the services of a local English journalist Rob Hyde, who had worked with most of the British newspapers on the case in Germany. He was bilingual and knew the terrain well, plus had the addresses of most of the key characters in the case. However, having agreed to meet him in Schweinfurt on the Monday afternoon – and having compiled a list of 21 questions for Nicole – he suddenly said he was unable to join me.

There was the question of time and distance from his home in Bremen … but more importantly, there were the concerns he had about Nicole. It turned out he and a number of British journalists who had visited her home had faced a rather unpleasant welcome from her and her neighbours, and the police had been involved. He apologised and explained that due to German press laws he could be prosecuted and even extradited back to the UK if he was caught outside her house again.

He told me Nicole had 'screamed like a banshee' when he had knocked on her door asking for an interview, and had summoned a 'big, bouncer-looking guy' to send him packing. 'He was loud and aggressive and he told us he worked for the "Secret Services" and not only does Nicole seem to have him on tap, [they have] the local cops in train,' explained Rob.

He said the situation had got so bad that when he had visited a second time with Patrick Hill from *the Mirror*, the neighbours had literally ganged up on them and called the police, who were on the scene in minutes. 'One older neighbour screamed that the police should arrest us, although for what I don't quite know,' he recalled. 'The whole thing was very unpleasant.'

So it was with some trepidation that I arrived at the solid grey stone house divided into six flats, where Nicole now lives with at least one daughter. It was not long after 6pm in the neighbourhood of mostly terraced houses, which sits close to a number of parks in the industrial town of 54,000 people, and which is known for its ball-bearing factories.

I pressed the buzzer with the name 'Fehlinger' and stood there with my green notepad open at the page with the 21 questions. Within seconds I heard a woman say 'Hullo'. I explained I was a journalist writing a book on Madeleine McCann and had come over from Spain and could I just have a few minutes?

'No, go away or I will call the police,' she said in English before the intercom closed and that was it. I knew it would be pointless to ring again.

Just then an elderly couple (perhaps the ones Rob had met) came onto a balcony above the front door. 'What do you want?' the man enquired. I told him I was hoping to interview Nicole, and he stopped me dead. 'Get lost. Get off our property,' he barked. 'This is private property. You have no right to be here.'

'And if you don't we will call the police,' added his wife helpfully.

I figured it was time to go and I slinked back to my hotel, a new B&B franchise out of France that sat next to a motorway junction.

Plan B involved a chat with Nicole's father Dieter, who lived in a different part of town, and thankfully I had an address, care of Rob.

I had heard from Abul Taher at *the Mail on Sunday* that he was far more approachable than his daughter, although there was the suggestion that he would want paying for an interview, money I did not have.

The other issue was his lack of English and without a translator like Rob I knew I would struggle. Enter Sarah, the student daughter of the Polish owner of my hotel. Just 20, she was smart and personable, studying business studies at Frankfurt University and keen to practise her English. I asked her if she would be able to help translate for me the next morning, preferring not to mention I had neither an appointment, nor any idea how I would be received. She said we could go after her classes that were thankfully online and finished at noon.

It proved to be a masterstroke, as Dieter didn't speak a word of English, and he and his wife were utterly charmed by this sweet, switched-on young woman, who quickly explained that I had come 'all the way from Malaga to talk to them' and she was really enjoying helping me out. After two minutes on the doorstep, I asked if we could come in and Dieter's wife, who clearly understood a bit of English, beamed and ushered us into the kitchen and offered us coffee.

It was obvious that all was not well in the Fehlinger family. Blinking back tears, Dieter, 66, explained that Nicole had not spoken to him since he had done the handful of interviews for the British and German press the previous summer.

Worse, his other daughter Desiree and granddaughter Jessica (Nicole's daughter), who all now lived in Schweinfurt, had also closed ranks and stopped communicating with him.

'Nicole does not want to know anything about the case or speak to me,' he said. 'She has even turned my granddaughter against me. It is so upsetting and all because I simply wanted to help in a murder inquiry.'

I offered my condolences and said I was not expecting him to criticise his daughter, but merely 'clarify' a few of my concerns about Nicole and the time she spent in Portugal. He agreed to try and answer the questions I had planned to put to Nicole, before offering his theories on the case, over which he confirmed he had been interviewed by BKA detectives.

He started by telling us that Nicole had definitely not had a 'straightforward' life and had certainly chosen 'plenty of the wrong men'. 'Christian Brueckner is just one of many,' he said with a wry smile. He confirmed that she had indeed been born into the same hospital in Wurzburg as Brueckner just one week apart in 1976, but as far as he could work out, their paths had never crossed. 'But I really can't be certain and am beginning to wonder if maybe they did really know each other having met in Wurzburg in their teens,' he said. It was a tantalising thought.

Like Christian, Nicole had grown up in a small Bavarian village, surrounded by rolling green fields and the very picture of pastoral heaven. And Marktheidenfeld (population 11,000) is just 40km from leafy Bergtheim, where Christian was brought up.

And the parallels don't end there as, like Christian, family life was anything but settled with her mother Sonja and father Dieter splitting up when she was young. The divorce led to instability and she had left home at a young age, just 18, to settle down with a teenage sweetheart in Wurzburg. The son of a local baker, she began a two-year apprenticeship at his bakery, but by 20 they had broken up, and she started dating Andreas, another man with a tricky upbringing.

The couple had a daughter, Jessica, in 1998, but things didn't go well and Andreas, who was 'troubled' (that was all I could get from Dieter), tragically killed himself not long after her birth. Pretty soon she had met her next partner, Mathias Hamel, and they decided to move with 2-year-old Jessica to Portugal in 2000, as his sister, Barbara had a villa hidden in the folds of the inland Algarve hills in Goldra, near Loule, which had plenty of spare rooms.

But Barbara, whom I managed to speak to in June 2021, told me she kicked Nicole out 'and was glad to see her go'. Speaking on the phone from Germany where she had returned to look after her elderly mother during Covid, she said, 'Mathias really hates her too ... and even more so now after all this Maddie stuff.'

She confirmed how it was at her home where Nicole had undertaken a basic training course, which would allow her to look after troubled kids and led to her first association with the IAPRS, based in Messines.

She ended up looking after a number of teenagers, via IAPRS, with one of them, Thomas, eventually moving in with her and Mathias into the spacious Villa Bianca, in Foral, in 2004. It was seemingly a charming rural existence, recalled Dieter, who explained how he had

regularly visited his daughter there, sometimes with his second wife and occasionally on his own.

'She had the classic rural existence, with lots of dogs, most of them strays she wanted to save, plus a horse and a donkey.' The big house was big enough for Thomas to have a separate apartment. 'That was why Foral worked so well for them,' said Dieter.

He believes Nicole ended up taking in 'at least three children' during the time she lived there. 'They were difficult children, all youths, about 15 or 16 in age, from tricky homes back in Germany,' he said.

While he declined to comment on his daughter's relationship with Mathias, Barbara confirmed it was anything but perfect and had come to a sudden end when her brother, who had been working in Germany for much of the year, came back to discover a 'strange atmosphere' in the Foral villa, with his girlfriend inexplicably flush with money.

'That house was already an odd place and always attracted weird people,' said Barbara in her only interview with the media. 'Mathias came back from Germany and found the place in a really strange way. There was a lot of new furniture and she had a lot of new clothes. He was not happy with it all and took off very quickly after that.'

What we now know was that while Mathias had been away working Nicole had met Brueckner in December 2006 at a small party thrown by Bernhard Piro's wife Elke who had also worked at the IAPRS for a while. Nicole and Brueckner immediately hit it off and, according to Dieter, struck up a 'close bond'.

Dieter first met Brueckner at Villa Bianca in spring 2007. He had been picked up by Nicole at Faro Airport and driven back to the villa, where Brueckner was in the front garden, as we know, playing with his grand-daughter Jessica. 'They were playing right in front of the van, near the gate when Nicole introduced us, describing him as "a friend",' he recalled.

'I really don't know how long they were together or even if they were a proper couple. I really can't say. It was clear he definitely had eyes for her. I even asked her about it, but she brushed it off.'

Either way, Brueckner had certainly made himself at home.

Dieter told me he had two vehicles at the house – his trademark black Jaguar, as well as his huge Tiffin Allegro Bay RV, which was parked right in front of the house, parallel to the front door (Dieter drew a map showing me exactly where it was parked). His distinctive VW campervan was parked nearby.

'He was definitely a good driver and it must have been quite a mission to have got that huge winnebago bus parked in there,' said Dieter, adding to the testimony he had given to both the police and the press the previous year. He confirmed that he had looked inside this 'amazing' house on wheels, and that 'it definitely had an odd smell.' He also confirmed that Brueckner had indeed told him he could use it to smuggle 'at least 50 kilos of grass' and 'small children'.

'I was a bit shocked really, given he was so close to my daughter and granddaughter,' said Dieter. 'I played along though and pretended to be a bit naive. After asking him where he planned to hide the drugs, he made the shocking comment about smuggling children. 'In fact his exact words were "a small child",' added Dieter gravely.

'It was weird that he was so open and honest. We had met for just ten minutes. He also told me he had good connections all around Europe, and particularly with Eastern Europe, where he would sell this weed. He said he liked Romania and had good contacts there.

'Maybe he was trying to make a good impression on me. But it was the exact opposite. I wish I had asked where he hid things and taken a look. Nicole later told me he had reconstructed the van to create that hidden place. It really troubles me to this day. Could Madeleine have been taken in that space?'

He didn't get a chance to talk to Brueckner again. While they all had supper together in the garden that evening, he had left by the next morning, presumably on a 'journey north' towards Germany.

The date? He really can't remember if it was in April or May 2007. I think most likely late May. 'I've really tried to remember. Wracked my brains to try and get the dates and checked back on my phone diary. I know the timing could be critical as Madeleine vanished around then. But I just don't know.'

He said he didn't meet Brueckner again, but later that year – or early in 2008 – Nicole started dating her new boyfriend Romano.

'It was Romano who kicked Christian out. He didn't want him to stay there any more,' said Dieter. 'I don't know why. I wish I knew. But he said Romano himself was up to all sorts of things and he 'certainly wouldn't trust him'.

'He definitely lived off Nicole's money and didn't do any proper work. She was always hard working. You can never accuse her of not working hard to make money. How she made it, that's the question.'

He confirmed that his daughter had ended up having a baby girl with Romano, called Luana, and even that they opened a restaurant together somewhere on the coast, possibly around Lagos. He also confirmed that Romano began to treat Nicole badly.

Both Dieter and his wife believed Romano used to beat her and said she had 'grown increasingly frightened' of him. He said he could not imagine how it must have felt being one of the troubled German teenagers – such as Lina or Thomas – who had moved in to escape trauma back home.

It was so bad that by 2010 the Fehlinger family came together to plan a careful operation to get her out of Foral and back to Germany with her two daughters. 'When she was having problems with Romano and had to flee the home, I booked a flight to come down to sort him out with two friends, but we missed the flight,' explained Dieter. 'Luckily she was able to get away with the help of her sister and some other friends and came back to Germany.'

He is still unclear about what exactly happened while Nicole lived down in Portugal. It was obviously a murky time and it frustrates him that he was kept in the dark. 'I wish she had told me more about her life … and her boyfriends and lovers. But I guess fathers are often the last to know,' he said. 'If she had a problem, why didn't she come to me? I would have dealt with it fast.'

Speaking of the unpublished interview with Abul Taher of *the Mail on*

Sunday, he said: 'I helped set up an interview … for her to come clean and tell the truth. The paper gave her a fair offer and she even signed a contract. She was actually photographed and gave the interview, although she was very careful what she said, insisting she was not Christian's girlfriend and hardly knew him. I knew it was untrue.

'But then she suddenly changed her mind and backtracked. It was very odd and I don't understand why. It would have helped to clear her name. She claimed the interview would put her daughters at risk and endanger her life. I don't know exactly what she meant by that, but it makes me wonder.'

Dieter is still trying to piece together exactly what happened with Brueckner. He wants to ask Romano, but cannot located him, and even managed to track down Mathias. 'But he has blocked me now as well,' he told me. 'I wanted to know why they split, why he left Nicole. What happened in that house. What was she doing with Christian. But when I got hold of him all he would say was "You need to ask Nicole."'

He is particularly concerned about the reports from Portugal linking Nicole to robberies on the Algarve, potentially alongside Brueckner. 'The one at the villa where they allegedly stole 100,000 euros from those women [Isabel and Julia]. Money that was due to go to the bank and then someone robbed it the next day. And only Nicole knew about it. The police thought there was a connection but they couldn't find proof. Or didn't bother.

'There is definitely some truth to the story... and I just don't know if she told Christian by accident or deliberately that there was money in the house.

'Worse than that, it is not only this robbery there are supposedly more houses burgled. While I find it hard to believe it's apparently the case, so what can I say?'

He continued: 'Either way, the trust is now gone between Nicole and me. Our relationship will never be the same again. I have so many questions for her, but she is refusing to talk. She wouldn't tell me anything about what she talked about with the BKA police so many times. I don't even know what they asked her. She wouldn't tell me. It is so strange.'

He also knows that Nicole's connections with Brueckner did not end when she left Portugal in 2010. Dieter confirmed that Brueckner had turned up outside her house in Schweinfurt that Christmas. 'She told me he had turned up with an old bus and wanted to stay with her for the festive period. I think they kept in touch somehow through the years, probably through phone numbers,' he added.

'Why I don't know, but I am sure Nicole is definitely trying to hide something. In fact, I think she is the key to everything, maybe this whole case. My wife and I know something must have happened because of the way she is behaving. We have so many questions for her and I am sure she knows something important that can help clear up this mystery over Maddie.'

He is certainly not the only one, but how exactly could I find out?

I decided to have one last try at speaking to Nicole the following morning, before starting my travels around Germany. But it didn't go well.

It was shortly after 11am and I figured her youngest daughter would be at school. Despite reports suggesting she worked as a receptionist at a local hotel, I could find no evidence of that and she was certainly still at home, as I could see movement in her apartment.

I rang the bell and once again explained who I was when the intercom was answered. 'No, go away' was all I got from her, before two young women, who had been sitting smoking, and drinking what looked like beers at a table outside, stood up and asked me what I was doing.

I told them I had hoped to interview Nicole and one of them pointed at the road. 'Get out,' she said, while the other picked up her phone and started dialling. I remonstrated that I was only researching a book and asked what their problem was and they both stood up with one beginning to film me on her mobile.

It was time to leave and I walked back to my car, before driving around the block to see if they had gone. Incredibly, the two women, in their early twenties were both standing by the side of the road, talking on their mobiles, looking angry. As soon as they spotted me, one of them began filming again, while the other gesticulated at someone around the corner. When a big man emerged looking angry, I didn't hang around.

The incident had certainly not been unexpected after the warning from Rob. But it just didn't seem right to be so antagonistic of journalists simply doing their jobs in pursuit of the truth. As Rob later told me: 'In my books she is quite a nasty piece of work. All those reports of how she treated those kids in Portugal and the way she screamed at us. Combining all this with what Portuguese TV reported on her tipping off Brueckner to do that crime, I wouldn't be surprised if she was involved in something dark.'

•••

My hunch about Nicole just wouldn't go away and at the end of June 2021, on my return from Germany, I made a whistlestop trip to Portugal to meet Elke Piro, Bernhard's wife, who had held the Christmas party in 2006 that brought Nicole and Brueckner together, allegedly for the first time.

'I can imagine Christian now, suddenly appearing from around the corner, walking in with a big smile, saying "hullo"', said the softly-spoken woman sitting around her garden table on a bench where Brueckner had 'often' once sat. Like others I've spoken to, Elke described Brueckner as 'gentle, charming and lovely' until he got drunk.

'Then he would get really aggressive and … became the devil,' she said. 'Basically he had a split personality and I am now sure he was a classic sociopath or psychopath and can't bear to think about the things he might have done when he drove off from here at nights, heading towards the beach.'

Elke confirmed that she introduced Brueckner to Nicole (or Nikki as she calls her) as she knew her via her son Pablo (she and Bernhard also have a second son Flavio), who went to school with her daughter Jessica. They also had connections through the IAPRS institute, where Elke worked in administration for a while.

'I never really liked Nicole. She was very superficial, lacking depth and was all about money, money, money,' she said, as she busied herself knitting a colourful woollen doll for a friend. She recalled holding the small party in which they were introduced just after Brueckner got out of prison. She said there was 'an immediate attraction' and he became 'a king to her queen' and moved into her house in Foral soon afterwards.

She remembered how Nicole had gone shopping with her the previous autumn when the Piros had bought a warm jacket for Brueckner in prison as he was 'feeling cold'. When she finally met Brueckner, Nicole commented that she was 'at last meeting the man who had been given the jacket in prison.'

Elke reckoned the felon kept coming back as her family were the only people who gave him any real stability in Portugal. While he was incarcerated, they took in his beloved dog Charlie, looked after his vehicles, including his VW Westfalia, which Flavio used to drive, and little Pablo even received letters off Brueckner from prison. 'Bernhard took a few things to him in prison and even bought him some frozen pizzas from Aldi for a celebratory leaving party the day before he was released,' she said.

Chillingly, she said Christian Post (who seemed 'like a nice, normal, polite person') was also an occasional visitor and while Brueckner was in prison, Post brought some of Brueckner's belonging for them to store. 'We never thought to look at them and I have no idea what they were,' said Elke. 'I hope it wasn't awful child porn. I can't imagine if my boys would have seen it.'

When Brueckner was discharged, Elke says Nicole 'simply needed someone' and 'Christian fitted the bill, at least for a while.' Mathias had been away for most of the year, after all.

She doesn't know exactly how involved she got in his criminality, but she knows 'for certain' that she was involved in the burglary in Praia da Gale. 'I knew straight after it happened that they were both involved and Christian confirmed it to me later,' she said. 'I know it 100%, as he told me they had split the money half/half. Nikki told him everything and how easy it was to get the money. He told me that Nikki had given him the tip off and the villa was in Gale. She told him where the money was and how to get in. It was a lot of money and I can't remember if it was 70,000 or 100,000 euros, maybe Christian got 70,000 or he gave that much to Nicole.'

Elke said Nicole spent the money immediately. 'I remember going round to her house in Foral for a birthday party a few weeks after the robbery, and suddenly all the furniture was new, new, new. Everything, the TV, the stereo, all new. She also had all these new clothes … and this lovely new pedigree dog, which cost 800 euros.'

She continued 'I knew then straight away that something had happened, but when Christian admitted he had been involved I should have gone to the police straight away. Had him stopped again,' she said. 'Nicole should have been caught too. It's almost as bad tipping him off and she should answer for it. I wonder too if she tipped him off about other places to rob.

'To think Nicole was allowed to foster children. A simple woman like that with just a basic course. Being allowed to care for difficult children, a responsible, important job like that… . It was only about the money for her. If you knew Nicole you would not give her children.'

Of Brueckner, whom Elke now knows is a convicted paedophile, she feels utterly betrayed. She said he last stayed with the Piros for a month in 2016 when on the run from Germany, but was 'rude', 'drunk by midday' and talked 'nonsense about sex and women.'

He phoned again in 2018 to ask if he could stay once more. 'I told him not even to think about it,' said Elke. 'He thinks Bernhard and I will always be there to help him, but I told him not to ring again, or visit.

'When the BKA came and told me about the connections to crimes against children and women, I could not believe it. I actually sat down on my terrace and burst out crying.'

Chapter 41

Dig, Dig, Dig

I realised I would have to widen the search. I needed to find Germans who were close to Nicole or Brueckner back in the early 2000s. One person definitely worth a try while I was in Germany would be Lina Valz, now 29, and living with four children in a town close to the Luxembourg border, I discovered. I understood from Abul that she might still be in touch with Nicole, which might make it unlikely she would talk, but I thought it was worth a shot. After all, she had lived with Nicole in Foral from March 2007, right until her eighteenth birthday in 2010.

Apart from spending a lot of time with her, she would have regularly met Christian Brueckner, as well as Romano, whom I discovered was from Trier, close to where Lina now lived. Could they also be in touch? I figured if anyone had an idea what went on in Nicole's world, and the bizarre set up of the foreign foster home programme at the IAPRS it would be her.

I had already done a fair bit of digging into the organisation that sent children out to live with Nicole in Portugal. There was something not right about the way it randomly sent already troubled teens, many of them sexually abused, to live in often inappropriate situations that would surely only make their problems worse.

It turned out my hunch was right. Not only had the IAPRS become involved in a major investigation the year before Nicole left Portugal, but it closed down in 2014 amid claims of mismanagement and tax evasion.

I had managed to track down the former headquarters of this shady organisation in August 2020, to discover a modern, ugly building in the hamlet of Cumeado, on the outskirts of Sao Bartolomeu de Messines, beside the busy N124 main road to Silves. Now empty, it stood forlorn and dejected and the only proof of its existence was the doorbell, which had the letters 'IAPRS' etched over another name that had been Tippexed out. Very professional.

There were a few yellow plastic chairs out the back, an ashtray and a long string of wires along the ground. I could just make out a wallplanner at the back of an upstairs office that looked crammed with names. It reminded me of the boiler room operations that are so typical of the Spanish costas.

The only lead was the letterbox that had a photo of a lighthouse and the name: 'TULETORN LDA. & Peer H. Salstroem-Leyh' on it. I'll come back to that.

Locals who lived nearby described the place as 'a racket' that was merely set up to make money for the organisers, the authorities and the so-called 'carers'. I spoke to two neighbours, both of whom asked not to be named. One, a local artist, confirmed that police had twice visited the building, which had not been used for around five or six years. 'It was simply a licence to print money,' he spat. 'A total means to an end – flying in all these unfortunate kids from around Germany and sending them off to random local families, mostly German, who got paid thousands to look after them.

'The facts were they were hardly looked after, often left to their own devices. These carers hardly had any credentials and mostly just did it for the cash.

'I'm sure plenty got abused and a few actually died,' he added ominously. He didn't want to elaborate on that.

'The organisation itself got most of the money and those that run it must have got rich,' he continued. 'They sprinkled it around the local authorities to ensure that nobody asked questions and it carried on like that for decades.' These were damning words.

Officially inaugurated in Silves in November 2003, an old website for the IAPRS confirmed that it 'worked with' children and young people at risk, who due to their history 'are potentially delinquent'. It went on: 'These are young people whose families suffer from socio-economic problems, as well as emotional instabilities, which may expose their children to maltreatment, neglect or sexual abuse. They may also come from dysfunctional families with atypical social behavior, and whose way of life and experiences make group integration impractical.'

Its pledge was simple: 'Our work focuses on the uniqueness of each person, seeking to understand their reality, their problems and difficulties. We have "Respect as a Method".'

Yet following a series of alarming police reports involving the organisation's charges – one of those being Lina Valz – an investigation was launched by the Tribunal de Familia e Menores de Faro (Family Court of Faro) in 2009. It began after police came across a pair of German girls, named as 'Cindy and Jezeline', hanging about on a motorway lay-by on the A22 in Areeiro, near Loule, on June 8, that year. The pair were 'under the influence of alcohol and drugs' and 'displayed evidence of self-mutilation'.

It emerged that they had arrived in Portugal via the IAPRS and had been living with a German family, near Tavira, in a filthy and untidy outer annexe. Both had suffered 'serious emotional issues' back home in Germany and clearly needed intensive therapy to get over their problems. It didn't appear they were getting anything of the sort from their carer family, a German gardener and his wife, a nursery school teacher, who had only been living in Portugal for two years and may not have even spoken Portuguese.

The story was quickly brushed under the carpet before the media could turn it into a scandal. In the case of Lina, the report noted she had arrived in Portugal via the IAPRS on March 23, 2007, before having 'an unplanned and unexpected pregnancy' and finally moving out to live with 'a 22-year-old

Romanian builder boyfriend on her 18th birthday' in January 2010. Hardly a glowing reference for her foster mother Nicole Fehlinger, who was also named in the report, which I have seen and which was also reported on Portugal's RTP TV.

The court investigation discovered that in 2010 there had been around 500 children living in Portugal who had been sent from Germany. I estimate that around a third of them were administered through the base in Messines. It added that 'a total of 230 German families' were looking after these children, without any official authorisation from the Portuguese authorities.

It was unclear how the carers were selected, although Barbara Hamel told me Nicole 'simply did this course on the internet and suddenly she was able to have these kids.' She added: 'Everyone did it, all the Germans did it. It is a joke as the kids get left often in horrible circumstances and were not really looked after at all.'

Each carer would receive around 1,500 euros a month per child – an enormous amount of money for anyone based in southern Europe – while the organisation itself was sent around 3,800 to 4,500 euros per child, per month.

These were staggering sums to take in, and netted at least 2,500 euros per child per month for the organisation, or at least 30,000 euros a year per child, totalling, by my calculations, an incredible 15 million euros for the IAPRS a year (based on 500 children). Big bucks.

It is unknown how much tax was paid. And if so, where to, given that the families were 'evasive' and reticent to talk to the authorities when approached. The prosecutor at the Family Court in Faro was clearly shocked by the situation, describing it as a 'phenomenon' that the authorities had – apparently – never come across before; German kids living with German families in Portugal and all sanctioned by the German state.

And he added that from the very start of his investigation every professional body he spoke to, be it the police, the courts, or social workers, described it as 'deeply worrying'.

Officers at the GNR police station in Olhao, who dealt with Cindy and Jezeline, were extremely damning in particular of the IAPRS. They described the girls' predicament as 'awful' and reported that they had handled FIVE other similar cases linked to German children brought in by the IAPRS. One, involving a minor who was so unsettled at his new foster home, that he had threatened a member of the family with a knife.

'All these cases involved children in danger or at risk and I was told that on the eastern Algarve alone there could be around 100 youngsters like this,' the prosecutor ruled. 'In addition there are many more in other regions, including the Baixo Alentejo, the central and western Algarve.'

The court was able to trace these placements back to the 1980s when Portugal was considered to be the ideal location for the schemes, which grew and intensified in the 1990s with projects such as O Farol and Kaspar X among others.

Disgracefully, the probe ruled, none of these entities were 'licenced to undertake such work with children', nor were the carers 'officially classified as foster families'. In summary, he said the phenomenon involved:

- *Mostly Germans without professional occupations*
- *Who lived in isolated areas*
- *Who received minors often from more than one association*
- *Who were paid for by the German state*
- *Who showed great reluctance and adopted evasive tactics when approached by the Portuguese authorities*
- *Who were unable to provide documentation showing the placement was legal*
- *While the children were all between 14 and 18 years old and came from complex backgrounds, usually linked to alcoholism, abandonment and child sexual abuse*

But somehow, his investigation didn't find any specific crime that he felt had been committed (or at least one he felt could be prosecuted) and he archived the case.

He had not linked the pregnancy of Lina, then a minor at 16, to any criminal charges. How could he not draw that conclusion given she had vanished for 11 days to live with 'two Ukrainian men'? And then came back pregnant? Was this due to pressure from upstairs, from the local police or perhaps from someone in Germany? Someone with a deep fund of cash.

It led Sandra Felgueiras to angrily conclude that there appears to have been – yet again – some sort of cover up. She believes that not only was Lina prevented from speaking directly to the GNR on her return after 11 days missing (indeed, as I have noted because Nicole translated her statement, which took less than one hour), but that any mention of her pregnancy – or the fact that a convicted paedophile Christian Brueckner was at the house – were missing.

'What also stands out is that all the information that led to the shelving of this case is not included in the records of the Juvenile Court today,' claimed Felgueiras. She certainly has a point.

Unsurprisingly, the days were numbered for the IAPRS, which came under media scrutiny the following year (2011) in an indepth investigation by the newspaper *Publico* and German TV network ZDF.

A German woman, who had worked for the association, accused it of being a 'social mafia', only interested in keeping young people in Portugal for as long as possible to receive more money from Germany – the average length of stay being two to three years.

It led to Portugal's Social Security Institute ruling that the organisation was set up illegally and that 'most of the children were not receiving proper care.' Alarmingly, the institute revealed that two German children had indeed taken their own lives, while a number had committed 'minor local crimes'.

Its president, Edmundo Martinho, told *Publico* the authorities had only learned of the presence of these young people by chance due to the arrest of the two young girls on the A22 in 2009. 'We started to investigate and came across many more cases and they all followed the same pattern: Germany sends these young people to Portugal and other countries and gives them to German families, without ever establishing contact with the local authorities,' he explained.

When tracked down, the director of the IAPRS, German Ralph Dohlen – who lives in Cologne, but is a classic van lifer who, according to his Instagram feed, has a charmed life, regularly travelling around Europe in his converted VW van – played down the scandal, insisting there were only 50 to 60 children, and that the authorities in Portugal simply didn't understand the work they were doing. 'They actually do not want to know,' he added, patronisingly.

The same year, a lawyer based in Faro, Miguel Morgado Henriques, began preparing a case against the Portuguese Government to be presented in the European Court on behalf of the IAPRS. He said the reports of children being treated badly did not apply to the associations that he was representing. 'Claims that children have been treated badly are totally false,' Henriques told *the Portugal Resident* newspaper. 'All the children had good living conditions while housed through the associations and were all treated with respect.'

He added that 'thousands' of children had come to the Algarve through the associations and that there is documented evidence that they were not treated badly. His comments fly in the face of what happened to Lina in Foral, the two girls in Tavira, and, as I will explain, of Thomas, who was also living with Nicole.

The case obviously didn't go well as the IAPRS vacated the building in 2014, when the association's insolvency was officially declared.

Coincidentally, the mysterious name on the letterbox outside the empty headquarters today – TULETORN LDA. & Peer H. Salstroem-Leyh – has an interesting story of its own. It turns out that tuletorn means lighthouse in Estonian and Peer Salstroem-Leyh is a sixty-something businessman, based in Tallinn, Estonia, who has built up a foster home empire in seven European countries.

Half German, half Norwegian, the father of four insists his organisations are not for profit, yet his foundations (Leuchtfeuer in Germany is the biggest) appear to make huge profits each year, it has been claimed. According to one investigation by Norwegian newspaper *Verdens Gang* (or VG), his Norwegian foundation alone receives nearly half a billion kroner – approximately 49 million euros – a year and its managers get 'million-dollar wages'.

These dazzling sums led to an investigation by the Norwegian authorities, who have paid millions in public money to his foster home network. It is a lucrative business and it has been estimated that the foster care sector is growing rapidly in Germany where it is worth several billion euros a year and costs local authorities around 50,000 euros a year per child (hence perhaps why it is cheaper to farm them out to families in Portugal, or Estonia, say).

But whether this money is really used for the benefit of the children is hardly ever checked, as the youth welfare officers lack the time while their biological parents are usually unable to do so. In the case in Portugal there were no welfare officers, full stop. The entire operation was sailing under the radar.

Intriguingly, Tuletorn boss Salstroem-Leyh's story in the foster home business began in Portugal in the early 1990s, suggesting that he could even be the owner of the former IAPRS property in Messines. A former sailor, with a background teaching children to sail on holiday camps, it was in 1993 when he founded the Institut Algarve Projekt, based in Messines, no less. Described as 'individual educational projects at home and abroad', the institute appears to have morphed into the larger IAPRS institute around 2003/4.

There is remarkably little written about the institute online, nothing in Portuguese, and no press reports; all I could find were glowing annual reports. It was definitely time to visit Lina at her home near Luxembourg to see what she might have to say.

Her Facebook account showed an apparently happy woman with a brood of four seemingly content children. The oldest must have been the one born when she lived on the Algarve.

It was a good three hour drive south of Schweinfurt and I arrived, typically, to find her 'out shopping'. Having waited a couple of hours outside her flat in a small block on a busy road in the town, I realised she could be out all day. Even longer. So I wrote a nice letter and gave it to a neighbour who promised to give it to her when she returned. I also sent her a message on Facebook, which she replied to the following day telling me not to ever bother her again and that if I turned up again outside her house she would call the police. While disappointing, it was not unexpected due to her apparent continuing connections with Nicole Fehlinger.

Fortunately, one of the other teenagers who lived with Nicole in Portugal did want to talk and he gave neither her nor the IAPRS a glowing reference. His name is Thomas Milde and he had agreed to be interviewed by RTP in late 2020, from his current home in Cologne.

Talking to Sandra Felgueiras, while walking alongside the famous River Rhine that runs through the city, the 34 year old painted a decidedly grim picture of his two years housed on the Algarve with Nicole between 2003 and 2005, when he arrived at the age of 16.

In a damning indictment of his foster home environment, he insisted Nicole neither took care of him, nor gave him any mentoring. In fact, she used to leave him alone when she went out regularly 'to discos and nightclubs', and once 'abandoned' him on a beach more than 20km from home wearing only his swimming trunks.

'At first I thought it was a dream but something started to go wrong in paradise,' he said. 'Nicole, my foster mother, wasn't welcoming. She was the same as my own mother. She said, "I'm not interested in you."' He added that she only took him in due to the money she was getting from the German state: 'It was the reason she took care of me.'

Thomas confirmed that apart from earning 1,500 euros a month for looking after him, she had 'various other jobs' that brought in a lot more money. 'She was always buying new things,' he said. 'She lived like a rich woman and I estimate she spent 5,000 to 6,000 euros a month.' Where was all this money coming from?

Her focus certainly wasn't on his care. He recalled a trip they made to San Rafael Beach when they agreed to leave an hour later. 'I was maybe five or ten minutes late and when I got there she was waiting angrily in the car and said, "You're late! Goodbye" and left me there. I thought she was going to come back but she didn't. I was only 16 and felt really lost in a foreign country, where they speak another language, just in my swimming trunks and with nothing else.'

Thomas walked along the motorway for five hours until the police picked him up 'because you can't walk on the highway... but it was literally the only way I knew how to get back home.'

The police then fined him 30 euros for 'jaywalking', which Nicole made him pay. 'She was the one who left me on the beach, yet I had to pay the fine,' he said.

When he tried to complain to the IAPRS, they laughed it off. 'I tried to speak to the supervisor several times,' he said. 'But the only reaction I got was that I was a criminal – and a child – and so I had better just shut up.' He added: 'The only alternative solution they gave me to get out of there was to go to prison. So I simply had to comply.'

It was little surprise that on the day he turned 18, he got the hell out of Portugal, went back to Germany and never spoke to Nicole again.

Chapter 42

The Circle of Life

It was already clear Christian Brueckner had had a tough upbringing, so while I was in Germany, I decided to try and understand quite how bad it was. Conveniently, the village where he grew up was just a short drive from where Nicole Fehlinger lives today in Schweinfurt.

Almost exactly halfway between Schweinfurt and their hometown of Wurzburg, Bergtheim proved to be a surprisingly attractive place. Surrounded by rolling fields of mostly wheat and long lines of apple orchards, the village also boasts a series of vineyards, including the popular Weingut Schmitt, which produces some excellent whites and a red. 'It's a lovely place to live and a good place to bring up children,' teacher and mother-of-two Saskia told me over her picket fence, while her 3-year-old daughter, something of a spit of young Maddie, played in a sandpit in the front garden.

While not from the village, the 43 year old told me her husband grew up there; just two years younger than Brueckner, they went to the same school and he remembers him well. 'Everyone remembers the family,' added Saskia, who asked not to give her surname. 'There is always one bad family in every town and village and he and his brothers were a bad bunch and his mother, in particular.

'The thing is nobody will want to talk to you. We have all tried to forget about them and, quite honestly, nobody really mixed with them. The oddest thing is the two brothers, who have literally disappeared off the planet. Nobody has a clue what happened to them.'

Just then, a bird swooped over and a big wet poo dropped on my arm. 'It's good luck,' I told her, as she handed me a tissue. 'Maybe Brueckner's mum will invite me in for tea. We both laughed. 'I very much doubt it,' she said.

I took a wander around the village looking for his childhood home, where he was adopted by Brigitte and Fritz Brueckner in the late 1970s, through the German Protestant church's charity Diakonie. (Ironically, and, as I have noted, possibly coincidentally, little Inga Gehricke went missing from woodland close to a Diakonie-run institution.) Saskia was right; nobody wanted to talk about Christian Brueckner. Birdshit or not. A few people shrugged their shoulders and pointed me in the direction of where he lived, but most smiled and walked away. There had clearly been a fair few journalists in Bergtheim and you could sense the hostility in the air. Understandably, they didn't want their village to be just known for 'that monster'.

I eventually came across his former home, a big austere place, now divided into three flats in the heart of the village. What particularly interested me was the cellar, knowing Brueckner's apparent fixation with them. By chance, a downstairs door was open leading to the basement and, with nobody about, I took the opportunity to stroll down to look. It was clearly being used as storage space for the three flats, with all sorts of items scattered about. But there was something about the dankness and vaulted ceilings that gave me the creeps and I decided not to stick around.

Instead I rang the trio of doorbells until one fellow on the top floor, a friendly chap, came out to say hello, although sadly he spoke no English, and I could tell he really didn't want to talk about the former resident. Hardly surprising, given that the very week of my visit a story had been published in German newspaper *Bild*, that painted anything but a rosy picture of Brueckner's life in the village and of his parents, in particular.

While previously the media had given Brigitte the benefit of the doubt, invoking some sympathy for her as they pictured her looking sad shuffling around the village, now it looked like the gloves were off.

According to the report he had been treated like something of an animal by his adoptive parents. The paper wrote that he had suffered 'horrific abuse' that probably involved him being locked in rooms (probably the cellar, I figured) for hours on end and 'not even allowed a glass of water'. It added that he and his two brothers were yelled at and badly beaten with a belt, while his mother was 'brutally domineering', insisting that adopted children like them 'had to be strictly disciplined'.

Their father Fritz also used to 'whip them properly on the bare bottom' yelling, 'If you cry, they'll be more.' And when a teacher noticed the bruises, she was told that Christian 'had fallen down the stairs.'

It was starting to make sense … and more so with locals telling *Bild* that the couple had only taken in the three boys due to the benefit money they received from the German state. 'It was just business to them,' said a former friend. I'd seen all this before in Portugal, of course. And it didn't half make me sad. And angry.

What was also particularly interesting was the insinuation by the newspaper that Brueckner's birth mother had been a prostitute, who was unable to look after her child, which led to him becoming a ward of court and being put up for adoption. It said that his biological mother, Frau Fisher, 'lived above an inn and socialised with local criminals' and his adoptive parents frequently reminded him that he was 'the son of a crook and a whore' when they beat him.

Other locals recalled how the brothers had really started to run wild when Fritz had a bad traffic accident in the early 1990s and was left in a wheelchair with brain damage (he would die in 2004). They had formed a local gang that terrorised the village, shoplifting, pickpocketing and vandalising local buildings. They broke into sports halls, stole bicycles and smashed up street vending machines. 'If something happened in the village, it was the boys,' said a former neighbour.

It was all getting too much for Frau Brueckner. With her husband now in a wheelchair, she was unable to discipline the boys. She was most likely now getting benefits for him and probably didn't need the money for the children. And so in 1990 or 1991, Christian, then 13 or 14, was sent back to the Diakonie charity in Wurzburg, and put in an orphanage with other boys, where he would live until 1993, when he was sentenced to two years in a juvenile facility.

It was time to ask the beleaguered Frau Brueckner first hand what had really happened when Christian was a child. I discovered that she still lived in the village, having moved to a small bungalow in a quiet cul-de-sac, next to open fields and a footpath north. It was a carefully tended home with a row of multi-coloured flower pots outside, full of geraniums, and net curtains in the windows.

I walked up with the silence punctuated with the giggling of children in a nearby back garden. At first there was no reply to my knock, so I tried again and finally the door swung open. A small curly haired lady looked me in the eye and grimaced. I hardly had time to introduce myself when she barked loudly 'No!' and slammed the door. I knew there would be no point in trying again.

It was the end of the line in Bergtheim and time to move on, but just as I was about to return to my car, a little man a few doors up came out of his front door, and presumably having spotted me walking past with my notepad asked me if I was there 'on the Brueckner story'.

I told him 'yes' and he came over to talk. The problem was he hardly spoke any English, so after talking rapidly in German for a few seconds, he pointed to Frau Brueckner's house and held his hand to his heart. He then did the universal symbol for tears. I'm still not sure exactly what he had wanted to tell me, but it seemed poignant.

It was just 20 minutes up the road to Wurzburg, where Brueckner had been shipped off as a young teenager after his adoptive parents, Brigitte and Fritz could no longer cope. Interdeep Bains at *the Daily Mail* had given me an address for the orphanage so I decided to take a look.

The home was nothing more than a terraced property on a leafy residential street at one edge of town. I knocked on the door and discovered it was no longer an orphanage, as the charity stopped renting it a few years ago. It was now back in the hands of the owner, who was living there and who gave his name as Roland Straub.

He confirmed Brueckner had been there for around two or three years but added there was little to say as he really had no involvement in the work of Diakonie, who had just rented the four-bedroom home from 1985. He explained that they paid a good rent and took over the entire running of the property, including all bills. He added that the charity had also taken over the property next door, which had three bedrooms.

As noted earlier, a former orphan who lived there at the same time, described the conditions as 'violent', with Brueckner regarded as 'one of the most aggressive' children evidenced when he once threw a glass bottle at a carer. With food in short supply and the home 'full of cockroaches and moths', it wasn't homely. The unnamed flatmate said Brueckner was 'always getting into trouble' with drugs and burglaries 'and once stole the minibus'.

According to the recent *Bild* report, it was here that Brueckner started to develop his sexual attraction to children, with a former neighbour, a postman, telling the reporter that he was so concerned for the welfare of his 8 year old daughter that he moved to a different part of town. He said Brueckner had become fixated on the little girl and always 'talked stupidly' to her and he feared he was set to abuse her.

It was an astute move because in 1993 he grabbed and sexually assaulted another young girl in a playground, near the home. It was to be the start of many such crimes, most of which I'm sure he got away with.

By something of a coincidence, the next door neighbour to his former home in Wurzburg was a child psychologist, who was more than happy to talk to me. Giving her name as Christine, she not only knew the boss of the local Diakonie charity but she vaguely remembered Brueckner, having bought her neat red property in 1993.

Working with some of the most troubled children in the area, she understands their needs, in particular boys who have been sexually abused, as she believes Christian probably was. 'We often work with teenage boys who suffered sexual abuse in their childhood. What they need is very intensive therapy and you have to spend a lot of money on it, unlike for girls, who have a different way of dealing with it.

'For boys there is the shame of being abused by men - which is normally the case - and they blame themselves and think they must be gay which is why it happened to them,' explained Christine. 'It often leads to a lot of anger and them needing to have control over something and the feeling of having the power to break someone. And we know if they do it once, they are likely to do it again and again. They get addicted.'

She added 'I think the boys who lived here didn't have enough intensive care,' she said. 'There were not enough educators or carers here and the ones who came were not experienced enough – sometimes straight out of university and some of them young women. They also used to change them too often so there was no continuity. It's not surprising that kids like Christian went off the rails.

'I've even taken it up with the boss of the Diakonie charity, but I have no idea if he listened,' she said. One would like to think they have learnt a little from their mistakes.

Chapter 43

A Shallow Grave

Scattered over a couple of hectares of despoiled scrubland in a backwater of the former communist German Democratic Republic sits a collection of derelict buildings, strangled with the detritus of a half century of neglect. Weighed down by history and choked with weeds, the former box factory in Neuwegersleben was for my journey into the very heart of darkness.

I was heading north through Germany to meet the chief prosecutor in the case against Brueckner, and this was one place I could not fail to visit. The former plant, which once made egg boxes and crates for fruit, lies isolated, half a kilometre outside the tiny Saxony village, in the province of Sachsen-Anhalt. At the end of a dark, narrow cobbled track, it sits on its own, apart from one house, lived in by a giant of a man, who understandably has two huge Rottweilers and is covered from head to toe in tattoos.

It was here that Brueckner invested 36,000 euros of his own money through an auction in Leipzig in either 2008 or 2009 … and here that police found more than 8,000 sickening photos and videos he had hidden in a Lidl bag under the body of his buried dead dog Charlie.

I arrived on a sunny afternoon to find nobody else about, although I recognised it from numerous press reports. It had taken some time to find, given that nobody in the village spoke enough English for me to explain what I was looking for. In the end I had to show photos of Brueckner and his factory, until someone finally clicked.

The rusty old gate was chained shut and had a 'Stop' sign alongside it. The gatehouse next to it had almost no roof to speak of and little of interest once inside.

It was walking into the wide open expanse that you began to realise what an incredible opportunity this could have been for a pervert like Brueckner, who officially told friends that he wanted it to be a car repair garage or some sort of sculpture garden.

If you looked down on it by air, you could see it had once been divided into a grid of concrete squares and comprised of around half a dozen big buildings. The first thing I noted was the amount of underground areas it had, suggesting that it was once used for something rather more sinister than making boxes. Perhaps armaments. There were dozens of openings that led down to dark spaces, some interlinked and others full of rubbish.

I clambered into the first building, which had a collapsed roof and rubble piled up at least a metre high. On one wall the word Arbeit (job/work) and two shorter words could just about be made out, not dissimilar to the words on the entrance gate at Auschwitz concentration camp: Arbeit macht frei (work sets you free).

In the next building, there was a huge collection of junk scattered around, including a crate full of empty Jagermeister miniatures, almost certainly stolen, while, in red, scrawled on a wall were the prophetic words: '*Mein freundin hat mich beloneen betrogen zum hass erzogen*' meaning: 'My girlfriend lied to me, cheated on me and raised me to hate.'

Alongside was a weird hippy-style drawing and something about 'peace'. I checked the handwriting on a letter Brueckner had written to a landlord and while very similar it was not conclusive. Which girlfriend could he have been referring to?

I clambered about looking for anything of relevance until I stumbled across a side annexe with four huge plastic vats, presumably used to store the diesel that Brueckner stole on many occasions. Just outside, in a neat line, were four more portable plastic petrol canisters, beside a pair of colourful juggling clubs, which I can imagine Brueckner using at festivals.

Next to this was another small annexe with one big, heavy garage door slightly ajar. I pushed it open and wandered in to find a pair of dirty mattresses propped up against the wall, a tub full of empty alcohol bottles and a pair of broken women's sunglasses.

Could this be where Brueckner made some of his videos? Did he keep women, even children, chained up here?

There was only one small window with reinforced glass, so this would be the place for it, and given his 2013 Skype chat about 'capturing something small', it would fit the bill. 'Particularly if evidence is destroyed afterwards,' he had replied to his online friend.

I had those words etched in my brain so when I wandered to the back of the small annexe I did a double take. Looking recently dug up, and certainly not appearing in a single photo or video I had seen of the box factory, was what looked like a shallow grave, about 5ft in length and a foot and a half in in depth. A pile of rubble, with chunks of concrete at the bottom, was next to it, while an empty bottle had been thrown in, almost for decoration. It was extremely sinister.

I was just coming out of the building, having taken some photos, when I heard a bang and a rush as a deer bolted right by me. I jumped. I was all set to run for it myself.

I calmed down and continued the search, next coming across the biggest building, around 80m in length and 20m wide that had, according to locals, once housed around half a dozen of Brueckner's vehicles. This included his Tiffin Allegro, Halle police later confirmed to me. Today there was only one, a small light blue Renault Twingo, which I later established he had driven over, laden to the gills, from his allotment home in Braunschweig on April 2, 2016, just before he fled again to Portugal. He would have driven it in furtively knowing the BKA in Halle were already investigating the property.

243

It was in a woeful state with all its windows smashed, number plates missing and, curiously, it was riddled with bullet marks. Lots of them. It was first registered to the garage, Autohaus Hartel in Osnabruck, and, at first, there appeared to be nothing else of note.

However, when I opened the boot I noted that the spare tyre was still in place and out of curiosity I lifted it out of position to see if anything was underneath … and there standing out like a sore thumb was a pair of surgical scissors, that I later brought up with the prosecutor Hans Christian Wolters, with him scoffing 'what would I be expecting to find on it?'

I might as well have replied, 'DNA of Maddie's', and had there been gaffer tape and a mask, we could have been in the realms of a Sopranos episode.

This factory would have been one hell of a job for the police to examine and, it was reported that 100 of them had been in situ for the first few days of the search which began on January 14, 2016. All around the site I found holes in the ground, openings leading to cellars and tunnels. Some areas had obviously been excavated by police, while many others appeared to have been ignored. But that is only guesswork.

The downright spookiest building was the one I'd seen photographs of Brueckner posing in, which had been published in the media. A large place, it was almost certainly once the factory office and it was the most intact, and the closest to the heavily tattooed neighbour. I had somehow missed it during my first tour round the site and by the time I reached it, my mobile battery had, typically, run out.

Frustrated as hell I retraced my steps, jumped in the car and drove into the village to find not one single place open (it was by now after 6pm), so I carried on until the next village, where by good fortune there was a hairdressers still open, who agreed to let me plug my phone in to charge.

Half an hour later I was back at the building, with the loud barking of the neighbouring Rottweilers – who had clearly heard me return – in the background. I pushed open the door to go in and found a trapped bird flying around and tried to let it out, unsuccessfully.

This had obviously been the hub of activity and according to one of Brueckner's friends whom I talked to later, this was where he stored most of his stolen goods, including dozens of computers, solar panels and many other items. There were pots of paint, cutlery, countless chairs and tables, over a dozen computer monitors. A nasty looking circular saw cut into a workbench.

There was a kitchen, two bathrooms and a big room with dozens of shelves, which had up to 1,000 books on them (many more were strewn on the floor), as well as hundreds of old records, presumably all once stolen by Brueckner, including one by Barry Manilow, which I imagine wasn't his taste.

The weirdest thing I found as I sifted through the cornucopia of neglect was a large series of circular symbols sprayed on the floor at the threshold of each room, a neo-Nazi-type Celtic cross in an electric orange colour.

Journalist Rob Hyde later said he thought it was probably sprayed by police as they finished inspecting a room. They did appear to have been added recently, suggesting the police may well have been back over the last year – a fact Wolters would confirm to me the following day.

With dusk falling I took my leave, not wanting to be stuck here at night and with an appointment already made with Rob in Braunschweig, an hour's drive away. I picked up an atlas of Germany, from 2002, with hundreds of detailed colourful maps of all the country's regions. I figured if my phone ran out of battery again (it did) I could use it to steer me towards my hotel.

I met Rob in Braunschweig shortly after 9pm and was surprised to see him in a smart suit and with a briefcase. A convivial chap with a bushy Bavarian moustache, he impressed me with his knowledge of Brueckner and the town, where he had spent many weeks helping the British press investigate the McCann case the previous year, and where the prosecution had been launched.

Braunschweig, I learned, was where Adolf Hitler had been given citizenship in 1932 to allow him to run in that year's German presidential election, and he was rewarded with a series of ministries once the Nazis took power the following year. They included the administrative centre of the Hitler Youth and even the SS training schools base, while a number of key armament factories were set up here.

Despite being heavily bombed during the Second World War, it still has a number of charming buildings dating back to the Middle Ages, including the Hotel Ritter St. Georg where we were staying for the night. It was conveniently near to a rooftop bar that served a wonderful pint of Duckstein, a specialist beer which has been brewed in Beechwood since the fifteenth century.

We swapped notes until the early hours and, in the true pursuit of seasoned journalism, were the last to leave well after midnight.

Chapter 44

Life Falls Apart

It was here in Braunschweig that the endgame for Christian Brueckner started to come into play when police sent him a summons over Maddie at his rented kiosk in 2013. A simple place in a scruffy part of town, it was shuttered up and looked like it hadn't been open for some time when I visited with Rob Hyde in June 2021. I wasn't surprised to find it had a big cellar, where Brueckner 'kept a lot of things, a lot of them stolen,' Rob explained.

Brueckner had taken on a lease at the kiosk on December 7, 2012 and threw a launch party for the locals and a couple of friends later that month. 'There was champagne and Christian showed off his new girlfriend Nakscije in her bright red dress,' said Rob. 'Wouldn't that make her 15?' I enquired, going on my calculations. He wasn't sure, but we agreed she would certainly have been a young teenager and far too young for Brueckner, who had turned 36 that month.

We banged on the door hoping to speak to the current manager Norbert, who had taken it over from Brueckner in 2015. His family actually owned it, but he wasn't inside and none of the neighbours upstairs in the four-storey block of flats had seen him for a while. Having taken a couple of pictures, including the obligatory one of me outside, we were set to move on when a pair of young women arrived. They introduced themselves as Inga, 19, and 21-year-old Melina and claimed that Norbert was their uncle and he was away for 'a month or so, maybe longer'. It sounded suitably ominous for a man that Rob had described as 'pretty dodgy' and 'only talked to the media for money.'

But his nieces seemed sweet enough and were curious about what we were up to outside their uncle's kiosk. Melina, in particular, seemed switched on. German-born but of Serbian descent, she spoke four languages, including Russian, Polish and fortunately English, which had improved massively since she started watching the crime shows Killing Eve and Line of Duty over the previous year. She explained that her father was the actual owner of the kiosk and that he lived nearby. Across the road, in fact.

I asked if she remembered Brueckner and she pulled a face of disgust. 'He was a really strange guy. Not a nice man at all,' she told me. 'He was always drinking and looked like he was on drugs. He constantly appeared busy, but didn't seem to know what to do with himself, which way to turn, left or right. He was always starting something and not finishing. Basically he was a mess.'

It seemed like an apt way to describe him, although as I pointed out to her, surely there was a method behind his apparent madness. 'Well he definitely wasn't kind and he didn't show any empathy,' she said. Her eloquence is worthy of note.

I wandered across the road to talk to her father, who was lying on a sunbed in a small back garden, with a towel over his face, apparently taking an early siesta. His wife was sitting reading a book at a garden table. Initially he said he didn't want to talk to the press. He then told his daughter to explain to us in English that it was 'a bad time' and they wanted to 'forget all about Brueckner'. After all, his brother Norbert had been threatened by Brueckner at knifepoint when he stole various items from the kiosk and there had been a trail of police and trouble ever since, it appeared.

I apologised and said 'no worries', before complimenting him on his charming, clever daughter and all her languages. It struck a chord and he smiled. 'Listen, I'll tell you one thing,' he said. 'He was a really bad man. You could see that from his eyes. Those eyes said it all. He was crazy and definitely a serious criminal. It was good to get him out and I hope we never see him again.'

We crossed the road again and took a stroll around the corner to another sizeable beige property, split into flats, on Hohestieg Street, where Brueckner's friend Bjorn had lived – and Brueckner himself had been registered officially for some time. Why he hadn't used the kiosk address was not clear. He did plenty of other times.

That evening Bjorn told me that he had 'only used the internet there' and one trusting neighbour called Momo had allowed him to use his wifi log-in and even lent him his purple Volvo a few times for business. It turned out to be a disaster for Momo as it was from that flat in Hohestieg Street that Brueckner had allegedly undertaken his infamous Skype chat about 'trapping something small' and, probably, many other dodgy conversations and deals. Crafty and cunning are the words that come to mind.

'The police smashed down Momo's front door and completely scoured the place, taking quite a few items,' Bjorn revealed. 'We thought they were after Momo and he had been involved in something serious and after all that, it turned out to be Christian they were after.'

Bjorn was a classic happy-go-lucky German who had worked for Brueckner in his kiosk for nearly two years. They became good friends and spent a lot of time together, both in Braunschweig and out in the countryside near the city, particularly at his box factory an hour's drive to the south.

He describes it as 'a total betrayal' discovering what he was up to in private, and told me he felt 'totally bereft' on discovering that his former pal was not only a dangerous paedophile and rapist, but was also now being probed in a murder case. 'I'll be honest, I still find it difficult sleeping and feel very betrayed,' he said. 'More than anything I'm angry with the police for not tackling a sicko like him earlier … not to mention the appalling mistake they made with the summons in 2013.'

He revealed that he had actually been in the kiosk with Brueckner the day the police summons about Maddie was delivered to him, and he had since been brought in for questioning over his former friend.

Rob and I were sharing a couple of beers with Bjorn while sitting by a lake in a different part of the city, where he now lives. He told us he had first met Brueckner when he had visited a friend who lived beside the kiosk who had just lost his dad. 'I was consoling him when Christian came back from the supermarket having bought beer. We got chatting and a little while later Christian, who had only been running it for a couple of months, asked me if I would mind keeping an eye on the kiosk while he went off for an hour to get supplies.

'I said I didn't mind as I knew the place well as there was a small bar inside called the Flüsterkneipe, a sort of speakeasy, and I used to drink there now and again. And that was the start of it as within a few days he had me working there for five or six hours at a time. Basically for no money, but with plenty of free beer, so I thought fine, why not. Now of course I can see that I was being used by him.'

Nevertheless, the personable German had become friends with Brueckner and would regularly end up drinking with him at the weekends at his allotment and even at his box factory in Neuwegersleben, where he used to hold barbeques. 'He kept all his stolen things there,' said Bjorn. 'The computers, solar panels, furniture and fuel. I also remember his huge bus that he had there.'

Bjorn met several of his girlfriends, including Anja P, another Turkish woman and the Kosovan teenager Nakscije Miftari [whom he called Nadja] who Brueckner met in late 2012. 'Nadja was pretty stupid and could be really annoying, no surprise considering her age,' he recalled. 'Christian ended up teaching her how to read and write, which I thought was really nice of him, and she really loved him and would cuddle up to me and tell me when Christian was not there how much she wanted kids with him.'

He reiterated that they frequently joked with Brueckner about his alleged links to Maddie, particularly after he received the summons in 2013 at the kiosk. 'We teased him ever since he went to make the statement at the police station,' recalled Bjorn. 'So, every time he went down to the cellar to get supplies we would joke, saying things like, "Oh, bring back Maddie with you while you are down there." It was a bit out of order as we could see he was losing his rag about it all. But it was fun to tease him anyway.'

He also confirmed what kiosk worker Lenta Johlitz had told *Bild*, that Brueckner had barked about pigs being able to eat bodies. 'I don't remember exactly what he said as I was really drunk,' said Bjorn. 'But I do remember having a go at him saying, "How can you say things like that?" Apparently I went on about it and he got really aggressive and we nearly had a fight. But I only know this because the next day he came and apologised to me for having been 'so aggressive.'

He continued that Brueckner had been away in Portugal for much of

2014, but that through 2015 and into 2016 the police started to probe him with more intensity, and he became increasingly stressed. Bjorn said it was obvious they had some 'pretty serious stuff on him'.

Indeed, they did, for they later launched a prosecution over his links to child pornography and that led to missing Inga, the raid on Momo's house, and also the long searches of his box factory in early 2016.

'Christian told me that the first time they raided Neuwegersleben, he had actually been there, hiding,' revealed Bjorn. 'He told me he watched this 7-ton police truck back up to the main building where he stored his things. He said they had completely loaded it up and took "everything", apart from the solar panels and his fuel. He was really pissed off, but pleased they hadn't arrested him.

'He said he had hidden in this annexe at the back, from where he could peek through a hole where a brick was missing and see what they were doing. When they came over that way he could vanish into the undergrowth. He basically watched it the whole day.'

Had Brueckner also watched police find and dig up the body of his dog Charlie during the January raid, when they found the stash of photos and videos at the box factory? He might have also been tipped off. Both seem possible.

'He knew the walls were crumbling in and he told me they were going to arrest him at any minute and he needed to go,' said Bjorn. 'We had a few drinks for my birthday in early April 2016 and two days later he was gone, away back to Portugal.'

The next time Bjorn saw him was in 2017, briefly, after he had been extradited back to Germany from Portugal and served his sentence for abusing Anja P's 5-year-old daughter. He should, of course, have been kept inside to serve other sentences, including the drug dealing offence in Niebull, not to mention the rape of Diana Menkes. 'The cops had been forced to release him because they hadn't managed to get the paperwork sorted with the Portuguese authorities. They didn't have this amendment to the arrest warrant, so they couldn't hold him,' Bjorn confirmed. 'As a result the SEK, the German secret services commando unit, was tasked with supervising him. Basically following him.'

But Brueckner was always one step ahead. 'Christian knew exactly what they were doing,' said Bjorn. 'He thought it was funny. He even stepped onto a tram and they all got on, and at the very last second he jumped out and they were left in the tram. They didn't like that.

'He knew how to play games with them. It was all about power. They would go up to him and tell him they had their eye on him but they still messed it up again. He managed to get on a bus to Holland with them following in the car. Yet when the bus arrived in Amsterdam, Christian had somehow avoided them, so he couldn't be arrested. I just can't see how they managed to let him slip away yet again. How hard could it be?'

He hardly had a good word to say about the German police, particularly the 'bungling' BKA. 'They are absolute idiots,' scoffed Bjorn. 'I mean how can you go and search the box factory and not find Christian hiding there? And earlier send him an invite for a summons and let him know you are looking into him in connection with Maddie, and let him reply "I have nothing to do with it" and just let him go. They should have done more but they just let him go off and do more things. And I bet he has done many things which we don't even know about. There has been this constant pattern of crime and of child abuse running through his life. But in the case of Maddie, I'm sure he did it and I really want him to hang for this, so this is why I want to help in every way I can.

'Sometimes I really fear that the truth will never come out, particularly if the police continue to bugger things up as they have done so far. I just fear sometimes that the poor parents will never know what happened to their little girl.'

He admitted that, having been duped by Brueckner, he was now wary of befriending people. 'I just can't get past the fact that a person who used to stand in front of me every day; a person who was my friend – a great friend – was not the person I thought he was. But much worse than that, he was an abuser of children. And who knows, maybe a child murderer too.

'It brings me to tears when I think of the young children I am very close to and who I help look after,' he said. 'If anyone did anything to them, I would kill them. In my view there are only two types of people. Whether you are rich or poor, left wing or right wing, at the end of the day you are either someone who abuses children or someone who beats up child abusers.'

• • •

There was one final visit in Braunschweig before our interview with prosecutor Hans Christian Wolters, and that was to see Brueckner's second allotment on the outskirts of the city. A ten-minute drive from the centre, or just over 3km by bike or shanks pony, Brueckner had taken on a lease at Am Fullerkamp 97, with a small home on it, on October 1, 2013.

Signing the lease two weeks earlier on September 15, he had paid 1,000 euros, plus 86 euros a year in rent, and given his date of birth, his kiosk's address at Altstadtring, 33, and his phone number as 0152 27145924.

Plot number 44 was 510 metres square and sat in the far corner of the Vereinsheim Kennelblick community gardens, which comprises 77 units and its own small bar/restaurant. Rob and I took a walk down to have a look at the plot with its quaint-looking gingerbread house that I had seen in various photos and on TV. Its garden was beautifully tended by its new owner Sabine Sellig, who was not around, and its blue-tiled roof stood out a mile away.

There were few people about, it being a weekday afternoon, but luckily the site manager Juergen Krumstroh was on hand to field some questions. It turned out to be fortuitous as not only had he kept a copy of the contract, he also had the original termination note that Brueckner had signed on his departure on April 2, 2016.

Juergen explained that he had insisted Brueckner leave an official note, before vanishing for good. 'He was all set to leave when I stopped him,' he recalled. 'He had packed up the blue Twingo car, which was literally bursting to the seams, and just popped in to say goodbye.

'He was with this strange young girlfriend, a really young one, definitely less than 20 years old. He said, "I'm giving you the plot back" and I said, "No, you need to come to the office and give me an official letter of termination and pay the outstanding money you owe." He didn't argue and came over and gave me the 120 euros that he owed in cash. We never saw him again.'

Juergen, who takes care of the community and runs the bar, remembers well the 'strange' man who mostly 'kept himself to himself'.

'He was always friendly when he visited, which was mostly on Sundays. He would come in for a beer and would chat about this or that. He sometimes came with girlfriends and there were a couple of them. We had a few problems with his garden as he didn't do much and left it in a state of disarray. But other than that he wasn't a terrible tenant.' He said he sometimes arrived in a Mercedes Sprinter van or in his Twingo.

He was unsure if Brueckner had tried to dig a cellar at the property, but thought he would hear from the authorities soon. 'I expect the police will come and dig the place up at some stage,' he added. They still hadn't as the book went to press.

Chapter 45

The Prosecutor's Verdict

'It is still a murder inquiry and we still only have Christian B as a suspect,' Hans Christian Wolters told me definitively as we launched into a nearly three hour face-to-face interview at his office in Braunschweig in June, 2021. 'But yes, we are missing some key information and I can't say if I am confident of solving the case or not.

'All I can say is Christian B is our only suspect in the Madeleine McCann investigation. However as you can see from the fact we have not pressed charges yet, the evidence could definitely be better. Equally though, it hasn't worsened since last year and if we had been given an alibi that Christian couldn't be the perpetrator, then we would obviously cease investigating. Just because we don't announce anything new doesn't mean we have not found anything new. I heard Christian's lawyer insist he has nothing to do with it; saying he had found all these interesting things on a research trip to Portugal. But in the same way we have not shared our results, he has not shared his.

'Rest assured though, while German tourists may not have a great reputation our judicial system does and Germans are known for hard work. We take our jobs seriously, so you can be certain when we do release more information it will be reliable. The time has simply not yet come for us to put all the evidence together and work out whether or not it is enough to press charges. We will only do it when we reach the end of the investigation, when we are of the opinion we have investigated as much as we possibly can. We are not there yet.'

It was a brutally honest summing up of the progress his department had made since its public appeal, in June 2020, over a German they believed was involved in the abduction and murder of missing toddler Madeleine McCann.

We were sitting on the second floor of the rather nondescript Braunschweig prosecutor's office, based in the heart of the city centre. We had arrived a little before 3pm, with no idea how long we would get with the busy chief prosecutor in the Maddie investigation. 'He normally gives the best part of an hour,' Rob volunteered, as I sat nervously with a list of 27 questions I had put together on the flight over from Malaga. It was Rob's third visit to the conference room that doubled up as a sort of library, with rows of legal tomes.

Herr Wolters breezed in uncharacteristically late for a German — albeit just ten minutes – apologetic and clearly in a good mood. Rob had told me I would like him, and he was an open, personable chap with a no-nonsense approach.

We immediately got onto the subject of summer holidays, with Wolters revealing that he would stay in Germany and would probably head to the Baltic, or 'Eastern sea' as he called it, with his two boys, one who loved basketball. He said it had been an 'incredibly busy year' and he was working flat out, 'over ten hours a day', much of it on the Maddie case, while also having to keep an eye on many other local crimes. He said he mostly worked on murders and manslaughters, but there were around 40 to 50 cases a month coming into his team. 'Some are complete nonsense that we stop investigating quickly, while others, like theft, I can write up the charges in 20 minutes or so,' he said. 'Luckily, of the complicated murder cases, I only get a few of these a year and I always have a few colleagues to help.'

But we were here to talk about Madeleine McCann and it was a total coincidence that we were sitting down exactly a year since his dramatic press conference in this very same building in which he launched a public inquiry into a German suspect police believed could be behind the disappearance and murder.

It quickly became apparent that I knew a lot more about the case than most journalists he had met. And, as Rob said later he was 'really taken aback' and 'defensive' on at least three occasions with my line of questioning. 'He was definitely covering things up a few times,' he insisted.

I was pleased to hear it, as ostensibly, he hadn't given me anything hugely groundbreaking. Colourful yes. Anecdotal, in part. But not groundbreaking. What he did do was help me understand exactly how seriously the Germans were taking the case, and precisely what he thought of the previous Portuguese investigation. It was also interesting - and refreshing - to hear him admit to various mistakes the Germans had made (something you never get in Spain or Portugal) and explain exactly why it had been so difficult to keep tabs on Brueckner over the years and catch him.

He confirmed that his department had been working on the case since the summer of 2018, but that German police had actually launched an investigation a year earlier in 2017, having received a second tip from a member of the public, following the ten-year anniversary TV appeal.

He also admitted that the first tip on Brueckner had come into the BKA police department in 2013 and, in retrospect, it could have been handled better.

'I only know it was a tip off from the UK without any details,' explained Wolters. 'There was no concrete reason or suspicion. No-one said how he might be involved. It was just; "take a look at Christian B." So, the British police didn't know anything. They just thought, "What is this? Who is this?" In Germany there was no investigation at the time into Christian B and because the BKA didn't know Christian B, they gave it to the Braunschweig Police department, and they then spoke with him as a witness and they only asked him a few questions. And basically he answered the questions and did not seem suspicious, so they sent the information to the BKA, and the BKA sent this to the British police. And then nothing happened.'

When pressed on why they hadn't done a bit of probing first, cross-checking with his previous record, other federal regions of Germany or other European countries, he skirted around it. 'Look, we had no concrete evidence, nothing to go on, so we had to approach him in a very open way and write to him to tell him what it was about,' he said. 'And he insisted he had nothing to do with the crime and so that was that, done and dusted. Because one couldn't hold anything against him. One could not confront him with any findings.

'Looking at it today, with hindsight yes it was unfortunate, but at the time we didn't have any knowledge.'

Fortunately things were a little different in 2017 when the second tip came in. By then he had recently been convicted for molesting the 5 year old, among others, had a drugs conviction in Niebull and the police should also have been aware of the findings in Neuwegersleben.

'An investigation was launched in 2017 and the BKA gathered all the information they could get and a year later presented it to the prosecutor's department here in Braunschweig and we then launched a formal investigation.

'At first I couldn't believe such a huge case would end up landing up in this small German town. I mean Maddie was British and went missing in Portugal. It seemed so far away and so we came to this case as a virgin comes to a child, as you say in Germany.

'But we started investigating in depth, reading into all the background and had been working in silence for two years before the appeal – and I can tell you we investigate much better when nobody knows what we are doing. From 2018 to 2020 nobody knew what we were investigating, even though there was a very large contingency of police and investigators involved.'

How many, he wouldn't say, but he insisted the group had only increased in size since 2017. 'I am only allowed to tell you that we have had between ten and 100 police officers working on the case since last year due to potential public complaints over numbers compared to other cases. But it is towards the upper figure and the number has not shrunk at any point. It has only got bigger and we still have plenty of work to do. Another thing, Germany does not have enough police officers, so if they weren't busy with leads they would simply be pulled off and put on other cases.'

He was adamant that the June 2020 appeal had not only been vital, it had also produced a lot of valuable information, in fact 'more than 1,000 tips' from the public. 'The majority are from Germany and the UK ... and we have been getting at least one tip a day, of varied quality,' he said. 'There are not only thousands from Germany, but also thousands from Great Britain and other countries.'

It was very encouraging. He also admitted they did still have other key information in the Maddie investigation - 'maybe video, maybe phone evidence' - that hadn't been released to the public, and it was not the time to confirm exactly what. 'There are quite a lot of things I am still unable to tell you,' he said.

He was, however, happy to explain the circumstances surrounding last year's appeal and clarify a bit more detail on the phone that Brueckner was thought to have used in Praia da Luz on the night of Maddie's disappearance. He said the discovery had come about 'due to good German policing' and because, by something of a miracle, the Portuguese authorities had managed to keep the data.

'Thank God, the Portuguese managed to secure the cell tower data back in 2007 so we could take a close look at it over a decade later. And we didn't find it because it was registered to Christian B, rather because we had other information that he had used this number. The British didn't have these clues and the Portuguese didn't have them either. It was us, the Germans, who were able to assign one of those thousands of numbers to Christian B.

'We know that he used this number. It was his own normal, personal number and we know that he was in contact with another Portuguese mobile number that night in Praia da Luz. But we still don't know who used this other number.'

He said they had got the name of the person the SIM card of the other number had been registered to – one Diogo Silva – as it was 'relatively easy to investigate this sort of information in Portugal. (He did however, confirm what I already knew: that it was not THE Diogo Silva who lived in Praia da Luz and ran a restaurant.)

What WAS intriguing though was his inability (or refusal) to confirm in which shop, or even area, the SIM card had been bought, as that could, of course, give me some invaluable clues as to who owned it. 'I can only say that we have not found out who used this number. In fact we have found out nothing about the user of this phone,' he said. Could I believe him?

He continued: 'We got a whole load of info about who this number was registered to (Diogo Silva), but it was unfortunately not the person he telephoned. In Germany you could also register a SIM card under a fake name. In fact until a few years ago it was possible to register it in the name "Mickey Mouse" without any problem. You even had people registering their SIM cards in the name of lawyers, as they had just found their addresses online. Now the process of authentication is a bit different and they do check if this person really exists. But there are still ways of being able to use fake names.'

In reference to the photos released of a pair of vehicles Brueckner was allegedly using in May 2007 (the VW van and the Jaguar) and two photos of a property he was allegedly living at, he expanded a little. He said his department was interested in all the vehicles he owned or had been driving, but in particular the ones he had around May 2007. They knew about various other vehicles, he said, and had some impounded, but they had only released photos of two of them because they were particularly memorable. In particular, the Jaguar as they knew 'not many Germans would have been driving a Jaguar around Praia da Luz.

'People would immediately remember him from it … and plenty of them did,' he explained.

The fact that this Jaguar was re-registered the day after Maddie went missing was, in his words, 'remarkable' and of particular note. I think he meant 'suspicious' but he didn't wish to speculate further, nor discuss why they hadn't released details of his huge Tiffin Allegro. 'We knew that he had this Winnebago [the Tiffin], but when he bought it, etc, I really can't say.' Nor would he confirm if police had interviewed its previous owner, Hubert, who he seemed surprised I knew about.

Concerning the internal house photos that had been released during the appeal, he was also a little vague. I couldn't understand if it was deliberate, or if he genuinely didn't know. 'I can't tell you exactly which house it was, I can only say that the photos we released are of a property which we believe Christian B was living in, at least for a short while, around the time of Maddie's disappearance.

'In particular this house had a big wooden beam. Where is it in Praia da Luz? I don't know exactly as I haven't been there.'

When I insisted the police must, at least, assume it was near Praia da Luz, he would only add, 'Near Praia da Luz? Yes, I can tell you that, but not exactly how near, nor when exactly he lived there, and he lived in quite a few houses at the time. We just know that he spent some time in this particular house. As to what it looks like from the outside, that is something I really can't answer.'

It made me wonder if he was deliberately putting the media off the scent. Perhaps this was not the infamous Yellow House that got cleared out by his friends while he was in prison. It was, after all, close to other neighbours, who would have certainly heard screams, or other noises, if he was making videos and torturing people there. And, I figured most criminals are careful not to shit on their own doorsteps. He appeared to have been very careful around that Yellow House; no doubt that was his sanctuary and safety net for not far off a decade.

Could those photos have been taken at the Old Schoolhouse in Bensafrim (which might explain why the highly sensitive British tenants wouldn't let anyone in), or possibly a different property altogether? One of his friend's homes? Even the house in Foral? No one had been inside there. I had tried on a few occasions, but Lia was insistent no-one could see it. Maybe it was Christian Post's home near Odiaxere?

On that Wolters most certainly would not be drawn. There were key questions on my list about Brueckner's old friend Christian Post, but when I asked Wolters how many times police had been to question Post in South East Asia and how many videos and other items he had taken out of Brueckner's house while he was in prison, he went quiet, uncharacteristically quiet. Then he answered: 'It's possible we've spoken to him, but I can't say anything about this.'

I pressed again, asking the same questions and more specifically if

Post had been out with Brueckner on the night Maddie went missing, or in 2017 when the abuse of the children in Messines took place, to which he snapped: 'I can't confirm with whom we have spoken, or not spoken. I can't confirm or deny it. I am only involved primarily in the press work, so I don't know everything in detail. I only know things in general terms. Because, thank God, my colleague who does all the investigation, she doesn't tell me everything, so, I don't run the risk of blabbing everything.'

And then he added: 'And if I knew, I would probably not tell you.'

'He was really spooked when you asked him about Post,' Rob said later. 'He was rattled.' It had certainly been an awkward part of the interview, and it didn't get any easier when I introduced a few more characters that I knew the German police had been keen to track down. In particular, the so-called 'Russian brothers' who lived in Spain.

The questions went down like a lead balloon. He obviously didn't want to talk about them, despite being quoted as saying he 'would like more information' on them during an interview with Sandra Felgueiras the previous autumn. 'It is true that during the course of the investigation we came across these Russian-speaking people, but we don't know if they are Russian,' he insisted, pouring as much cold water on it as he could.

'We mentioned them because they had contact with Christian B and we assume they can give us information about him. But this is not about direct contact with Maddie, rather it is about gathering fundamental information. I can't add anything more than what I said to Sandra.'

I asked about Nicole Fehlinger. How much had they looked into her? Once again, he was cautious, but his answers were telling. Initially, he said he couldn't say anything as it concerned 'details of the investigation', but he went on to confirm Nicole as 'a girlfriend' of Brueckner's (a term we double-checked with him twice) and said people like her told them an 'awful lot about Christian B.'

'But she is not a suspect, just a witness,' he insisted, rather too pointedly.

When I later returned to the subject of Nicole and asked him about the claims that she and Brueckner were involved in the robbery of the two Portuguese women of 100,000 euros, in Praia da Gale, he confirmed he knew about the case and added, 'Maybe that's where the money came from for the Winnebago.'

I didn't say that it was most likely bought around six months earlier, but maybe he was right. After all, he was the prosecutor working on the case for three years. Maybe Christian had bought the 'Winnebago', or Tiffin Allegro, a few months later.

Pushing him on the subject of the robbery, he said the German police 'certainly have their eyes on this theft of 100,000 euros.' Note, he said 'have' not 'had'.

'Because there is indeed a connection to Nicole F, and she was a girlfriend of Christian B,' he said adding that they 'knew' she had made 'a telephone call to someone in German on the day of the robbery'. She later told police it was Brueckner. Did they have her phone records? Or his?

'Obviously it was not enough to charge her or Christian B in Portugal. But more to this I really can't say as I don't know what the police asked her there exactly,' he said, adding cryptically, 'Sometimes you have the feeling that you know what happened, but you are not in the position of being able to prove it to charge someone.'

Wasn't this similar to the German foster children neglect investigation, launched out of Faro in 2009?, I asked. He really didn't want to be drawn on that, but said, 'If we were to get information that crimes had been committed then of course we would start appropriate investigations there. We are legally bound to do this. And because Nicole F is a German citizen, this would be a matter of German jurisdiction. Maybe not the jurisdiction of Braunschweig, but we would pass on our findings accordingly. So nothing would get lost.' It was comforting to know.

The conversation moved on to the cases that Brueckner was being investigated over. And it was interesting to discover how many other cases the German police were linking him to. Wolters could confirm at least five separate cases. These included the rape of Hazel Behan, the abuse of the children in Messines, the sexual assault of Joanna Eilts, missing Inga Gehricke and even Carola Titze, who was killed in 1996 in Belgium.

'A Belgian prosecutor had some concrete questions about Carola not long ago,' he confirmed. 'They needed some information about Christian B and we gave it to them. I have not yet heard what the result is, but there was definitely contact between us over the last year.'

Regarding Behan, things were progressing well but it would take 'a few more months' although 'probably not be as long' as the Maddie case. 'We only have Christian B as the suspect. However some information is missing, which we are in the process of pulling together. We are working with the Irish and Portuguese authorities and it takes a bit of time to get all the information we need. Once we have it all we will close the case. It will continue for a few more months, but not three months as it was recently reported.'

He continued: 'We cannot yet say with all certainty that he committed this rape. I can only say that the victim got in touch when she learned about our case with Madeleine, and also of the case of Diana Menkes. As to whether there are any parallels, I really can't say anything as the investigation is still running and I don't want to give out any details here.'

Concerning the two child abuse cases in Portugal, he said his department was continuing to investigate them, albeit slowly. Of the case in Messines, where Brueckner exposed himself to four or five children in a park during a town fiesta in 2017, he said, 'I think that case was a little bit forgotten because he was extradited back to Germany.' He confirmed he was now working closely with the Portuguese authorities over the case: 'We have now picked up the investigation and he is facing several years in prison. I cannot say exactly, but it will be two, four or six years. And it will be higher because it is not his first offence.'

He added: 'It is perhaps fair to say that the evidence is better than in other cases, but I don't want to commit myself to saying anything until we have made the decision to charge him.'

He was more tightlipped about the case against Joanna Eilts near Praia da Luz in April 2007. 'We are investigating Christian B's possible involvement in this and there is a good basis for our suspicion,' he said, before adding once again, 'I am not allowed to tell you anything at this stage.' It actually sounded encouraging.

He said there had been some involvement in the case of Inga, but the case was in the hands of the Stendal Police, who would make any decisions on whether to charge Brueckner or not. He didn't wish to comment on the case of Rene Hasse, Joana Cipriano in Portugal, or 13-year-old Tristan Brubach's murder in Frankfurt, in March 1998 (the prosecutor there had officially made Brueckner a possible suspect in 2020).

It was the subject of the Portuguese inquiry and policing in general that was most illuminating. While he was extremely careful about what he said and bit his tongue on a number of occasions, it was clear what he thought of the PJ's endeavours on the Maddie case back in 2007.

Of former inspector Goncalo Amaral he was the most damning. Describing him as 'a special personality', he insisted he had no intention of meeting him or reading his book: 'It is enough to see him now and again on various TV programmes. Thank God he is no longer a police officer. Please don't write that though.'

Regarding Amaral's deputy Paulo Pereira Cristovao, he said it was 'incredible' that he had gone on to run Portugal's missing children's bureau after being involved in the Joana investigation. 'All in all it is a very interesting police department that one. The opinion you form on them is probably very valid and they get criticised all the time. You practically read this every day and maybe you could write a whole book about them alone, but really I don't want to express anything here or judge them because their willingness to cooperate with us would diminish.'

I then went on to tackle the investigations at the Neuwegersleben box factory and what I had discovered on my recent trip there. I wanted to try and understand from Wolters what exactly they had found there and to what level they had really scoured the place. Initially he tried to palm me off by saying the factory was not under his jurisdiction and had nothing to do with the Maddie investigation. When I asked him about the 8,000 files buried there, he added 'there were actually many more', but refused to give me more details, insisting we would need to file our questions to the police in Halle, in the region of Sachsen Anhalt.

Incredibly, he added, 'I don't know about the photos or videos or even if he was in some of them, as it was not our investigation. In fact I don't know exactly what they found there.'

It was absolutely baffling as to why his department, which was investigating possibly the world's biggest criminal case, was insisting he did not know, nor could talk about the main suspect in connection to a horrifyingly large stash of child pornography – some that Brueckner was even starring in. It surely had a massive relevance to the case. He was surely bluffing.

I ploughed on insisting that I had been to the factory the day before and found some remarkable things, including the surgical scissors hidden under the spare tyre in the Twingo. I said it was clear they had not been found by the police and I was sure they had not been tested for DNA or potential evidence. I also told him that I had found what looked like a recently unearthed shallow grave, although I could not show him a photo as I was recording the interview and didn't want to interrupt it.

He looked taken aback. 'We can't expect a pair of scissors to help us much further,' he barked. 'That there are other things with his DNA on them – we already assume this. Finding his DNA won't help us further. And we don't expect to find any DNA of kids or anything.'

It seemed incredibly defeatist, and I said as such, at which point he opened up a little. 'OK, perhaps we were there again,' he said with a sudden grin on his face. 'It could be that we went back and had another look.'

'I knew it,' I told him. 'I had a distinct feeling something had been going on recently. I would suggest that you found something interesting?'

Once again he smiled, and this time he winked. 'We really didn't find anything there and, look, I am not allowed to talk about the details of our investigation, but yes, OK, we do have the factory in our sights and it could be that we went back and had a really big look around.'

I told him I was pleased and mentioned what a 'spooky, weird' place it was and said I had got the oddest sensation while going around it. 'And there are absolutely no neighbours,' he interjected. 'If you want to sexually abuse kids, that is the right place, as nobody would see or hear anything.'

I brought up the children's swimming costumes that police had found in one of Brueckner's vehicles. 'You can only speculate about what he did with them, although it is of course of note that an adult man has so many [children's] swimming costumes, but we don't know what they are supposed to be used for or how he used them,' he said. 'There is nothing to indicate that these swimming costumes were in any child porn photos or videos though.' And he added, 'I have never heard of any parents coming forward, but as I said this is not part of our investigation. This is something which the colleagues in Halle have to answer. But only my colleagues there know what they examined and when.'

It was starting to get a bit ridiculous and he admitted that the federal situation in Germany made it anything but easy to pursue and monitor dangerous criminals such as Brueckner.

'In Germany every public prosecutor is responsible in the district where the crime was committed,' he explained. 'So when you get a person who moves around a lot, you can very quickly lose track of what they are doing, lose perspective.

'Most criminals in Germany stay in their hometown or nearby, so usually we know our local suspects, and the police too, but when you have a person like Christian B, who is only in one place for a few years, it makes it hard for the police to keep an eye on them.

'Add into the mix someone who is moving abroad time and again, then it is even more difficult to keep track, because then no one even knows when you are abroad and when you come back to Germany.'

This has certainly been one of the failings of a bigger federal Europe and the Schengen agreement. I told him it had been a constant theme of my book.

But what excuses do the local federal regions have for not communicating within their own country? I had seen this between the National Police and Guardia Civil in Spain, when one tries to keep a case under its wings, not pass it on, and not communicate key information that would help another investigation. But in Germany, I thought they would be more organised.

This lack of communication between the different police departments and prosecutors' offices has led to criminals such as Brueckner getting away with serious crimes or, at the very least, getting off more lightly.

His 2016 prosecution in Braunschweig for child abuse and child pornography was a good case in point, I discovered from Wolters. I had previously not understood why he had got off so leniently: he was caught possessing 8,000-plus videos and photos of child abuse, plus prosecutors had pictures of him directly abusing the girl in Braunschweig. Surely he deserved a decent spell inside, much longer than 18 months, particularly after dozens of previous convictions, two for sex assaults on children?

Wolters confirmed that no less than three forces (Stendal, Halle and Braunschweig) were in contact about Brueckner over a series of similar crimes, from the possession of child pornography to child abuse, and as a potential suspect in the case of missing Inga. And he admitted communication could have been better and insinuated that there had been some errors, which handed Brueckner a far more lenient sentence.

The issue had arisen when police in Braunschweig had raided his flat in 2014 and found his Olympus camera and photos of him and his girlfriend Anja P's 5-year-old daughter. 'You could definitely see he had taken the pictures and in one you could even see his penis in the foreground with the young girl at the top of the slide,' explained Wolters, who confirmed they had found the park and had both the mother and daughter as witnesses.

But somehow it took a long time to gather all the information they needed and they didn't charge him until 2015, the year in which they had suggested Stendal Police take a look at him over the Inga case. Meanwhile, in the same year (possibly even earlier), a third force in Halle an der Saale started investigating him for possession of child pornography. What they had found, where they had found it and why they had started to look into Brueckner is still unclear.

'They obviously had various findings, but I don't know much more about the case,' he said. 'But they were the force that got the search warrant in Neuwegersleben, where they did indeed find child pornography.'

This was where the problems began, because among the 8,000-plus images and videos they found in early 2016 was the series of Anja P's daughter. 'They were the same files we used to prosecute him over and that is why he could not be sentenced again. In Germany, if you get charged for one thing, you can't be sentenced for the same thing.

'It was basically impossible for us to prove that when his flat was searched in Braunschweig he didn't already also have all those photos in Neuwegersleben. So we ended up only charging him for a small proportion of the material he already had.'

He admitted Brueckner had been 'incredibly lucky' as if he had not already been sentenced in Braunschweig on the far fewer files, 'we would have been able to sentence him for all these files in Neuwegersleben. He would have got a higher sentence.'

It made me wonder if that huge stash of appalling images and videos had been properly checked and cross-checked. Had any of the children in those photos been abducted? What about the 100-plus videos and pics that Brueckner is allegedly in? 'I really don't know, I am unable to say,' said Wolters. 'I don't know if they actually found any other evidence that he had abused other children. You would need to speak to the police in Halle.'

However, he said he 'very much doubted' they would help and he was unable to give us a good contact there. Just before this book went to print some of the questions I sent to Halle BKA and the prosecutor's office, via Rob Hyde, came back answered. Only some mind. A spokesman for Halle stated, no shit Sherlock, that 'only little information has reached the public from here so far', confirming that they had initially found 6 USB sticks and 2 SD cards full of pornographic material. He added that during subsequent searches, further data storage devices were found and swimwear in children's sizes… predominantly in a large garage and in the Allegro. 'As the seized data and objects are still the subject of investigations by another prosecutor no further information will be provided.' So they basically passed the buck back to Wolters.

My final questions for Wolters also mostly came back unanswered. They included the discovery of a SIM card of the British holidaymaker whose apartment had been burgled around the same time as Maddie went missing. I told him I had been told by a very reliable source that it had been found at the box factory and linked Brueckner directly to the Ocean Club. But he insisted he had 'never heard about it' adding that we would 'also have to talk to Halle about that'. For the record Halle's reply was 'no comment'.

It certainly seemed like a legal minefield working as a public prosecutor in Germany. There seemed no end of politics involved and banana skins waiting to be trod on.

The new German investigation into the murder of Madeleine McCann was taking a lot longer than everyone had originally hoped and it was perhaps not surprising, as we reached the year's anniversary of the public appeal, that a string of barbs had been launched at both the Braunschweig prosecutor's office and Wolters himself.

They came predictably from the Portuguese police and British media, but ironically the worst came from within Germany, from Brueckner and his lawyer. The first came from his brief, Friedrich Fulscher, when he criticised the prosecutor's office claiming they had not shown him a shred of evidence that his client was guilty, and adding that Germans were 'arrogant' in believing they were superior to all other police forces in Europe and could easily solve such a complicated crime.

The second more bizarre attack came via a letter sent to *Bild* on May 8, 2021, from Brueckner in prison. In neat, tidy handwriting (that would come back to haunt him after being analysed by handwriting specialists who said it showed he was 'secretive and deceptive'), he insisted police and the prosecutors should simply 'give up'. He later sent a cartoon, again mocking Wolters and his team.

In his first public comments on the case, the convicted paedophile branded the investigation against him 'scandalous' and said the prosecutors had 'brought shame to the legal system.'

He wrote: 'Charging an accused is one thing. Something completely different, namely an unbelievable scandal, is when a public prosecutor starts a public prejudgement campaign before the main proceedings are opened.

'I call on the Brunswick public prosecutors Wolters and [Ute] Lindemann to resign from their offices… . You both prove through scandalous prejudgement, that you are unsuitable for the office of an "advocate for the honest and trusting German people" and that you bring shame to the German legal system.'

When I put all this to Walters he laughed out loud and continued to say they had 'concrete evidence' that Brueckner was guilty and that it would 'just take more time to conclude the case.'

He also said some illuminating things about Fulscher, including how he was being paid and also about his personal life – but he insisted I did not publish them. I have agreed not to do that.

In summing up, he described the case as anything but an easy job and admitted the speed of the investigation was slow, in part due to Covid. He also once again appealed for British tourists who were in Portugal and Spain at the time Maddie went missing to scour holiday snaps or videos, to see if anything relevant can be gauged from them. 'Maybe something has been recorded which helps us further,' he said. 'I cannot tell you exactly what we are looking for, but of course the best thing would be a photo of Madeleine on it, then we would know who she was with.

'It has been difficult and given it is a year since our appeal, the chance of us getting anything that will really help us now is pretty low. But who knows, there might be someone out there who suddenly realises they can help. We remain focused on everything about Christian B, particularly involving his life in Portugal in May 2007.'

He admitted the problem of having to work with two other countries and two or three other local federal states 'made things more complicated'. But he insisted the three forces – in Portugal, Britain and Germany – were speaking regularly. 'I don't know if frustrating is the right word but it would be nicer if it went quicker. It would be a lot better if you could just pick up the phone and the police in Portugal could tell us if something was true or not. It is a typical problem when you have many countries involved.

'There is also the second level to it all, that's the police level – via Interpol. This is somewhat quicker, but information from the police on its own is not sufficient. If we get good information at a police level, then we still have to get this re-confirmed at a judicial level. Sometimes you are left wondering if it is actually worth all this (bureaucracy).'

I reassured him that it certainly was and that he and his team would become 'global heroes' if they could solve this case. I gave him my theories, in particular, that I felt there was a senior police or judicial cover up in Portugal, perhaps linked to people involved in the Joana Cipriano case, and that I felt there was a big paedophile network involved. His reply was revealing: 'Could be, could be. And one certainly starts to wonder about the people who are involved in these sorts of crimes – the crimes of child abuse and child pornography. So I would never exclude the possibility that certain (high level) people were involved in this.'

Chapter 46

Is Maddie Alive?

While the German prosecutors are convinced that Madeleine McCann is dead and the investigation is a murder inquiry, the British police continue to call it a missing persons inquiry. Some suggest this is out of respect for the family, but I think it is entirely justified until German police offer up the evidence that proves she is dead. And there is some possibility that Maddie may still be alive.

I have long been intrigued by the many claimed sightings of Maddie on the Spanish coastline in the years after she vanished. She was seen in up to a dozen places, as earlier mentioned, a number of which I personally investigated and two I believe could genuinely have been her.

I think it is highly likely that after Brueckner snatched Maddie he drove her inland to the village of Foral where she was kept for one or two weeks – perhaps abused by a group of paedophiles – before being driven across an inland unmanned border into Spain near Rosal de la Frontera in the Sierra Morena, of Huelva.

From there, he would have dropped down the empty N-433 through the Aracena Natural Park, past Sevilla, potentially towards Malaga before heading inland into the Alpujarras where his best friend Michael Tatschl had been living since March 2007, and an area he knew extremely well. He could equally have headed north up towards Badajoz and then taken the rarely travelled E-903 from Merida east towards Ciudad Real and Albacete, before taking the E-901 that skirts up to Valencia on his route north towards Germany.

What I think is highly credible is a sighting of him on May 28 at Tunnels restaurant in Alcossebre, a small little-visited seaside town in the Castellon province, north of Valencia. This is an uncommercialised part of the Spanish coastline, with few British tourists, which would have been important for Brueckner if he was travelling with Maddie, who was by then known to everyone in the UK. It is also popular with people living the camper-van lifestyle, such as Brueckner himself.

The restaurant sits in a wild, isolated place called Capicorb, and I have spoken to two witnesses who are certain they saw his yellow and white VW Westfalia van parked there. It was on German plates and one of them saw a girl 'identical to Maddie' walk out of the restaurant around 11am and get into it. They were so sure, they even made a note of the number plates.

Dutch expat, Jorge, who asked me not to reveal his surname and who has lived near the restaurant for years, remembers the day well. He told me it was 'the talk of the town' and his friend Juan, a handyman at the restaurant, 'still swears it was Maddie.'

'I remember seeing the Volkswagen from my balcony, but I don't remember seeing the girl,' Jorge told me. 'Juan though was convinced he saw her that day, and he asked the owner of the restaurant to phone the police. He has been saying it for 13 years that he saw Maddie that day, but nobody believed him because it's 1,000 kilometres from Portugal.'

Juan himself eventually turned up to talk. Now in his sixties, he does a lot of different jobs in the Capicorb area in the Alcala de Chivert municipality, and is by all accounts a reliable and solid chap. 'First of all, I remember the van, because it was very eye-catching,' he told me. 'I'm a car fanatic and we often get car shows down here. And so it caught my attention. It was one of those old Volkswagen Westfalias. It's exactly the same as the photos that came out, and the van I saw was in a bad state and had a yellow stripe running around it.

'In Spain, collectors usually have these vans with a historic number plate. So I remember seeing a foreign number plate on this one. Secondly, the girl's face was also strangely recognisable. I remember coming home and thinking, "Where have I seen her face?"

'And later I remembered I had seen her on the news: it was the English girl, Maddie, I had no doubt it was the girl I had seen. We get a lot of tourists down here with children and families and all sorts. So I remember thinking, "Why do I remember her face in particular?" I remember her face, the blue eyes and blonde hair down to her shoulders. It caught my attention because of course she doesn't look like any other Spanish girl and I remember her with the man and the van.'

He said that even after all these years, the image is clear in his mind. 'Then there's that man,' he added. 'The Christian guy. When I saw his photo in the press, I knew immediately it was him that day ... I'm sure he was driving that van and I've seen him around here a few times since.'

He insisted the owner of the restaurant, who is also called Christian, call the Guardia Civil, which he did the following day. His son Jan, the current owner, told me he remembers the Guardia Civil coming to ask for CCTV, but that the restaurant did not have cameras. Jorge and Juan had, however, noted down what they thought were the number plates, which were 'BMS 1049'.

Incredibly, I managed to find a link to the tip off in the detailed PJ files and discovered that it was in fact taken seriously. I discovered that a Leicestershire policeman DC John Hughes issued an international Interpol alert with a 'risk to life missing person' warning demanding that both Spanish and German police investigate the claims.

He urged Spanish police to check the location for CCTV and witnesses and asked for the German van's details. The police report, issued as part of

Operation Task, explained that the restaurant was in an area called 'Cap Y Corp' and that the witness had an 'unimpeded' view of the girl who walked straight past him.

This led to a request via SOCA (the Serious Organised Crime Association) to search for the German owner of the van. 'We request the Spanish police check the location for any CCTV or witnesses,' reported the PJ files. 'We request German vehicle details. Can the vehicle be circulated for stop and check to be carried out if seen?'

However, I've tried to look further into the request and don't believe police ever acted on it properly.

While I know Spanish police did turn up at the restaurant and German police were requested to track down the number plate BMS 1049, the only conclusion I could find was a handwritten note on top of the printed request from SOCA, in the PJ files, which said, 'Spanish police traced a German man who is not connected to the missing girl.' No names, nothing more.

Having worked here as a journalist for nearly 20 years, I know the Spanish police well. I also know that in any case involving a foreigner they can be laid back, at best, and I am simply not convinced they went out of their way to locate and eliminate this 'German man' from their enquiries. Maybe they actually did locate Brueckner and, as in 2013, he managed to easily brush it off and evade them.

This could well have been the best chance to have caught Maddie alive so far. We must never give up hope that she might still be alive. And the police finally charge Brueckner with her kidnapping. Only time will tell.

•••

As this book goes to print there are so many unanswered questions. Why hasn't more been done on the ground in Portugal, and Germany, digging up Brueckner's former properties and places of interest, looking for evidence? Surely if he buried 8,000-plus files at the box factory, he could have buried more elsewhere? Yet despite a couple of haphazard searches in wells by Portuguese police in late 2020 there has been remarkably little activity going on in the Algarve to solve the case.

Why haven't they excavated his infamous Yellow House in Praia da Luz? Why haven't police dug up Villa Bianca in Foral where he spent considerable time? The villa's owner Lia welcomes it but the police don't seem interested. Sabine Sellig has pleaded with police to dig up the grounds of the allotment home he lived in near Braunschweig, saying she worries she could be sleeping on 'top of the body of Madeleine McCann'. And nothing. It does make me wonder if someone, maybe someone in authority, is protecting him.

Appendix I

The Rise in Child Sex Abusers

Of the ten most wanted criminals sought by Operation Captura (the multi-agency operation to detain criminals wanted by the UK, who are hiding in Spain), three of them are child sex offenders. And paedophilia is a rising global problem.

It is a fact that 10% of adult men are involved in child pornography and one in 13 adults in the UK was sexually assaulted as a child. According to an official Office of National Statistics (ONS) report, in the year up to March 2019, 3.1 million adults aged 18 to 74 experienced sexual abuse before the age of 16. That's 7.5% of the population in that age group.

'The numbers are getting higher as more and more people are using the internet,' said Tom Powell, who works on the UK's Independent Inquiry into Child Sexual Abuse (IICSA). 'So much more could be done by social media companies to try and tackle the problem.

'In particular, the increased use of live-streaming services that can cost less than a euro, substantially adds to the problem.'

This certainly seems to be the case, with the British Government highlighting the 'ease at which indecent images of children can be accessed and shared online' in an ONS report in 2019. It added that offenders commonly had hundreds of thousands 'and sometimes millions' of indecent images on their devices.

And it's little wonder the IICSA ruled that it was 'unconvinced that internet companies fully understand the scale of the problem of live streaming on their platforms' while it appealed for them to hire considerably more monitors to watch their own networks for evidence of abuse.

The volume of offending is growing so fast that the British Government described it as 'a national security threat' in 2020. In one year alone (March 2018–2019), 552 victims were identified by the images seized by police in the UK, according to the National Crime Agency (NCA).

And in the same period, there was an alarming 11% rise in calls (9,232) about child sexual abuse to the National Society for the Prevention of Cruelty to Children (NSPCC) helpline.

Furthermore, between April and September 2018, police recorded more than ten grooming offences a day in the UK. These commonly take place on Facebook, Snapchat and Instagram. Even more shocking is that just a quarter of those abused told someone about the abuse and only one in seven (14%) told the police. Some 58% of those who did not tell anyone said it was due to 'embarrassment', while 22% thought nothing would be done about it.

Most alarming of all is the substantial rise in the levels of depravity, plus the lowering of the ages of children being abused, with 7,618 offences taking place against children aged between four and eight in 2019. An IICSA report from 2020 reported that police 'frequently encounter images of babies and toddlers being raped by adult males as well as children being sexually tortured.'

Yes, that is the society we live in … and it is a highly profitable industry that makes more money each year. It is no wonder that gangs are increasingly muscling in on the child abuse industry that has been estimated to make $36.6 billion a year.

'The scale of the problem is vast and our remit is looking into institutions that have any connection to children,' continued Powell, a former journalist. 'That includes councils, schools and churches in particular, with the idea to gauge how widespread it is and how we might tackle it.

'Perhaps we should also be looking at the police force too and definitely more at British sex offenders abroad.'

According to statistics sent by Powell, 80,000 British abusers are a threat to children at home and abroad. 'Abusers are highly likely to operate in a wider range of countries than official data indicates,' he explained.

While he didn't want to get drawn into estimations, he felt it was highly likely there was a higher proportion of paedophiles living amid the vast expat populations of southern Spain and Portugal. It is guesswork, but I would extrapolate that the 'normal' 10% of adults believed to have an interest in child porn in the UK, is most likely to be at least 15% among expats in southern Europe. I would also argue that a larger percentage of the more aggressive, hardcore offenders are based in Spain and Portugal. One Scotland Yard detective from SOCA told me privately that he had a list of 'at least 230 [British] criminals' who were sheltering in Spain. The Spanish police don't have the resources – or the desire – to flush out these lawbreakers. It's that famous blind eye again.

The IICSA is equivocal that poverty and corruption leaves children vulnerable, and Spain and Portugal certainly suffer from these afflictions. 'Abusers often target poor children who may already be sexually exploited,' stated the inquiry's annual report in 2020. 'They also target poor families where family members or other third parties are willing to act as facilitators.

'In those cases the disparity between the financial position of the abuser and the victim and their family is a key factor. Abusers establish trust with vulnerable children and families by masquerading as philanthropists by providing money and subsistence, before sexually abusing the children.'

It added that when abusers put down roots in a foreign country, 'they are better able to exploit victims in institutional care, educational establishments, charities or religious groups.'

It highlighted one popular 'offending pattern' where individuals set up a shelter, orphanage or school, perhaps with other volunteers, specifically to create an opportunity for the sexual abuse of children. Abusers then share strategies to avoid detection, in particular regarding law enforcement and local legal frameworks … and 'share information about what to do if caught, including the amount of money they can expect to pay to bribe their way out of it.'

While this is obviously highly relevant to poor south-east Asian countries, the poverty and low wages in most of southern Spain and Portugal (including police on ridiculously low salaries: I was amazed to discover a Spanish friend I played tennis with, who was in the Guardia Civil, earned just 14,000 euros a year, albeit over a decade ago) has led to high levels of bribery and corruption.

I have long suspected that a number of expat paedophile rings exist on the costas and I have heard plenty of claims from readers of my newspaper and contacts confirming this. It is a fact that there are many odd, eccentric men of a certain look and age who drift in and out the myriad charity events in the region, often larger than life and giving generously.

I can think of a number who we at *The Olive Press* have tackled, such as the famous expat radio DJ, in his sixties, caught dating a teenage girl he was supposed to be mentoring, as well as the popular British pub owner, who took a friend's teenage son to a concert in Madrid, before making a move. Then there was the dodgy three-times imprisoned fraudster – a loud, ebullient character, who didn't miss a social event and even had a column in a rival newspaper. So many people talked about the retinue of young girls frequently seen arriving at his luxury villa, and we proved that a huge number of his friends and contacts were criminals.

In addition we carry frequent reports in the paper (at least one a fortnight) of an expat being arrested and extradited back to the UK, Germany or Scandinavia, say, to face trial for child abuse. It's so common, it mostly doesn't deserve more than a few paragraphs, particularly because the police in Spain and Portugal refuse to issue full names of those picked up, just their initials. It makes our jobs far more difficult, unless we get a call in from a reader or a relative. It's as if the police don't care.

Appendix 2

We Wish You Luck

During the course of this book I spoke a number of times to Clarence Mitchell, the long-time official spokesman for the McCann family. I also reached out to interview Gerry and Kate McCann about the new investigation towards the end of 2020, partly out of courtesy and partly as I believed they might have had some key extra insight into the investigation against Brueckner.

Clarence told me it would be 'extremely unlikely' and they only ever did any media interviews around the anniversary of their daughter's disappearance or "if the police specifically ask them".

'They've had such a tough time with it over the years, all the media scrutiny for years you can't really blame them. It was 24/7 and never stopped and we had continual enquiries from all round the world for years," he explained. "Even recently they spotted a photographer hiding in the bushes near their home in Rothley who had flown over from America. The police were called and he was swiftly removed thankfully."

Like me, a former local newspaper reporter from North London (later the BBC), we share a fair bit in common and have always had a good relationship. He also knows my views on the case and that I have never tried to sensationalise it. In particular he knows I have only ever been supportive of the McCanns. 'Unlike that electric ferret Sandra, as we call her, who is always changing her tune,' he recently joked.

While he is only now an 'unofficial spokesman', as he insists on being known, he said he would happily pass on a letter to the McCanns approaching them for an interview.

It was a full three weeks before he phoned me back with an answer. 'It is thanks, but no thanks,' he said. 'I'm sorry, but they do wish you luck with the book, they just don't feel they can get involved. They remember you and know they can't stop you investigating and have said if you wish to send on any specific information you come across they will happily consider it. The door is definitely open, so please keep us in the loop.'

He added that he had a 'very good feeling' about the suspect. 'Christian Brueckner is the most likely of all. I certainly haven't seen anyone with the same perfect modus operandi and background.

'The German police seem sure and I really hope they can catch him. It is the most excited I have been for 10 years'.

Bibliography

BOOKS

Kate McCann: Madeleine: Our Daughter's Disappearance and the Continuing Search for Her (Corgi, 2011)
Anthony Summers and Robbyn Swan: Looking for Madeleine (Headline, 2014)
Goncalo Amaral: Maddie: A Verdade de Mentira (Maddie: The Truth of the Lie) (Guerra & Paz, 2008)

BLOGS AND WEBSITES

entrelinhas.eu – the only interview with Paulo Pereira Cristovao and his detective agency
mccannpjfiles.co.uk – the official case files from Portugal's Policia Judiciaria
http://pjga.blogspot.com – Projecto Justica Goncalo Amaral, dedicated to the support of Goncalo Amaral
websleuths.com – excellent online crime portal

NEWSPAPERS AND MAGAZINES

Bild
Braunschweiger Zeitung
Daily Mirror, The
Diario de Noticias
Der Spiegel
De Telegraaf
Expresso
FOCUS
Frankfurter Allgemeine Zeitung
Guardian, The
Mail, The
MailOnline
Mail on Sunday, The
Mirror, The
Nova Gente
Olive Press, The
Portugal News
Portugal Resident
Publico
Sun, The
Sunday Mirror, The

Telegraph, The
Times, The
To Vima
Verdens Gang
Visao

DOCUMENTARIES

Disarming Films: (2006) Deliver Us From Evil
Netflix: (2019) The Disappearance of Madeleine McCann
Discovery Channel: (2021) Prime Suspect: The Madeleine McCann Case

TELEVISION PROGRAMMES AND NETWORKS

Aktenzeichen XY … Ungelost
BBC
Channel 5
ITV
RTL
RTP
Sexta as 9
SKY
Spiegel TV
ZDF

IMAGE CREDITS

1 to 5 Jon Clarke
6 Cordon Press
7 Jon Clarke
8 - 9 Cordon Press
10 Jon Clarke
11 - 12 Police photos
13 Jon Clarke
14 to 17 Police photos
18 to 27 Jon Clarke
28 to 29 Jon Clarke (*screengrabs from RTP*)
30 to 32 Jon Clarke
33 Facebook
34 Jon Clarke (*screengrab of Der Spiegel TV*)
35 to 50 Jon Clarke
51 Menkes family (*legacy.com*)
52 Twitter
53 Joana family
54 Jon Clarke (*pic of police file*)
55 to 56 Jon Clarke
57 to 59 Police photos

Printed in Great Britain
by Amazon